Contents

Introduction

I LEARNED TO FLY FLOATPLANES WHILE LIVING in Hawaii, and was perfectly happy until the day I wandered into a bookstore during my lunch hour and came across a little volume on floatplanes. I bought the book, titled *Flying with Floats* by Alan Hoffsommer, and read it that night. By the time I put it down, I knew that this was the kind of flying I wanted to do.

My resolve was further strengthened by the countless seaplanes I saw during my annual vacations in Alaska and the Yukon. Although I did not have the time or the money during those trips to obtain a seaplane rating, I took lots of pictures and spent many an evening back home in Honolulu with my slide projector, dreaming of the day I would finally step onto the pontoon of a floatplane for my first lesson. As it turned out, I had a long wait.

The only kind of seaplanes that stood a chance in the big swells of Hawaii were the Navy's Catalina, Mariner, Marlin, and Mars flying boats. Of course, they were only memories by the time I arrived on the scene, so the only seaplane I ever saw in Hawaii was a two-place, Thurston Teal amphibious flying boat owned by the flight school where I was a student. Occasionally, someone would try to keep the tradition alive by taking the tiny plane out for a few touch-and-goes on the gigantic seaplane runways the Navy had dredged out next to the airport for their Martin Mars flying boats, but the end of the seaplane era as I knew it came the day a student landed the Teal in the water with the wheels down. It was fished from the lagoon and shoved into a hanger, and while it may have been repaired since, I never saw it again.

There were no floatplanes in Hawaii. The water was far too rough for them, and there wasn't anyplace to go, anyway. I had to be content with my photographs until 1979, 6 years after my first trip to Alaska, when I moved to Seattle in the Pacific Northwest. There are several commercial floatplane operators in the Seattle area, and once I was settled in, I lost no time in obtaining my rating. The experience was everything I had dreamed it would be, and more. Floatplanes combine the best of two worlds: the exhilarating environment of flight and the quiet beauty of the waterfront. I have scarcely set foot in a landplane since.

Now a word about this book. As a motion picture and television producer, I always define the audience for each of my productions before doing anything else, and all my subsequent efforts are directed specifically toward satisfying the needs of that particular group of people. This book has been written primarily for people who know how to fly but have never flown a floatplane. My purpose is not to teach people to fly floats—no book can do that—but to try and expose you to as many aspects of floatplane flying as can be crammed between the covers. It's my hope that, having read what I have written, aspiring floatplane pilots will at least have a good idea of what is *supposed* to happen the first time they climb into a floatplane, and this knowledge will put them much closer to obtaining, and enjoying, a seaplane rating.

I could not have produced a book of this scope without the help of some very special people. Walter J. Boyne, director of the National Air and Space Museum at the Smithsonian Institution, graciously supplied some of the historical photographs I needed, as well as articles written by some of the people who worked on, and flew, the Supermarine S-series of Schneider Trophy racing floatplanes. Naval Historian and Author Captain Richard C. Knott provided valuable information about the designer and builder of the world's first seaplane, Henri Fabre.

This project would not have gotten off the ground had it not been for the generous help of Jay J. Frey, the EDO Corporation's vice president in charge of its Float Division. From the moment I first approached him about the possibility of obtaining a few photographs of different models of airplanes fitted with EDO floats, he went out of his way to supply the material I needed, and in fact, send me three times the number of pictures I requested. As a result, the chapter on floatplane history is much more complete and interesting than I ever imagined it could be, and the benefits of his assistance are apparent throughout the rest of the book, as well.

I would not even have had anything to write about were it not for Lana Kurtzer, owner of Kurtzer's Flying Service on Seattle's Lake Union. Mr. Kurtzer has been flying seaplanes since 1928, and 56 years later, he taught me to fly them, too.

I live in Renton, Washington, located at the south end of Seattle's Lake Washington. At the north end of the lake is one of the finest seaplane facilities in the United States, and it is to the staff and pilots of this facility, Kenmore Air Harbor, that I owe the greatest debt of gratitude. The word *Kenmore* has become synonymous with the words *de Havilland Beaver,* and Kenmore Beavers have earned a worldwide reputation as the Cadillac of bush planes. Pilot Neal Ratti taught me to fly the rugged workhorse, and he is at the controls of the Beaver pictured throughout this book and on the cover. His assistance in obtaining the wide variety of action shots I needed proved invaluable.

Alaska-born Kevin Nelsen spent several years flying amphibious floatplanes as a commercial fish-spotter, and I received the benefit of his experience during a thorough checkout in the Cessna 185 "amphib" pictured in Chapter 17. Finally, I would like to thank Gregg and Bob Munro, owners of Kenmore Air Harbor: Gregg, for making it possible for me to obtain the experience and photographs I needed to complete this book; and Bob, for tactfully looking the other way whenever I backfired the big radial on N-17598 during startup. (Neal finally managed to drum the correct starting technique into my head, but I'm sure there were times when Bob wished I would stick to the Cessnas.) Thanks to the efforts of the Munros and their talented staff of pilots, mechanics, and office personnel, Kenmore Air Harbor has remained a first-class, professional operation, and I am indeed grateful to all of them for providing such a pleasant and interesting place to fly.

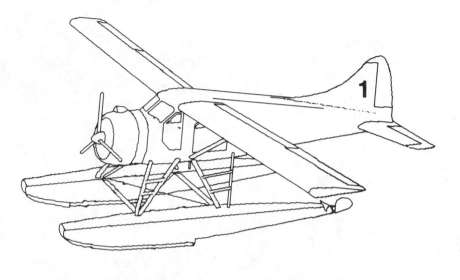

Flying Floats

"**Y**OU CAN FORGET ABOUT THE FLOATPLANE traffic after you get above 500 feet. Floatplanes don't go any higher. The words were shouted above the clatter of the old Cessna 150 I had rented on Merrill Field in Anchorage, Alaska. The checkout instructor was trying to explain the complexities of the Anchorage-area traffic. There were commercial and business jets out of the international airport; fighters, tankers, and transports from Elmendorf Air Force Base; seaplane traffic in and out of Lake Hood; and swarms of helicopters and general aviation aircraft from Merrill Field. Everywhere I looked I saw airplanes, and they were all flying directly at me.

For a private pilot whose flying experience was limited to the relatively uncongested skies over the Hawaiian Islands, the sight of all this traffic was a little unsettling. After cheerfully describing some of the near misses that apparently occurred hourly, the instructor attempted to calm my nerves by assuring me that, "Nobody actually gets hit, so just ignore all those other folks and they'll ignore you." Then came the bit about floatplanes never flying over 500 feet.

He was right about nobody getting hit, but I *did* see a couple of floatplanes above 500 feet that day. Most of them stayed low, however, skimming the trees, and I

remember thinking how frustrating it must be to be stuck down there, low and slow, dragging an ungainly set of floats around over the treetops. I felt sorry for the pilots. Maybe that's where you "paid your dues" before graduating to the real world of bush flying, with its Cessna 180s and 185s, Helio Couriers, Maules, Super Cubs, Otters, and Beavers. All mounted on big tundra tires or skis, of course.

As that first Alaskan vacation progressed, I began to notice that lakes, bays, and rivers outnumber runways up north by a considerable margin. If you want to get to the really neat places during the summer, a floatplane is a requirement (Fig. 1-1). I also found out that the floatplane drivers weren't flying low out of necessity, but by choice. It's beautiful down there.

In a world increasingly dominated by airways and area navigation, Terminal Radar Service, Positive Control, Microwave Landing Systems, and Category something-or-other Approaches, the floatplane offers an escape to a simpler, but more rewarding, flying experience.

The world looks pretty good from 500 feet. You begin to see things in a way that just isn't possible up at 7000, or 10,000, or 20,000 feet, surrounded by squawking radios

1

Fig. 1-1. Fishing access to remote lakes is just one of the activities a floatplane makes possible. (Courtesy of the EDO Corporation)

and blinking readouts. The floatplane opens a window—a very unique window—that provides a fascinating, detailed perspective on the scenery passing beneath its float keels.

Many pilots discuss past flights by describing the performance of their airplanes, the complexity of their navigation, or the accuracy of their approaches and landings. Most of the floatplane pilots I know speak of what they saw during their flight, and as you listen, you sense that their work means more to them than just guiding an airplane from point A to point B.

I recently talked with a young floatplane pilot who had been weathered in at Seward, Alaska. He had stayed up all night beside his airplane, sweeping the heavy, wet snow off the wings and tail surfaces so its weight wouldn't force the floats underwater. Later, he described flying from Cordova to Yakutat, 2 hours at 200 feet over a beach pounded by the swells rolling in from the Gulf of Alaska.

His talk was not of the potential danger of a forced landing or of his flying skill, but of the bear and moose he had seen along the beach, the beauty of the fog-shrouded mountains, and the interesting way the outside air temperature would drop below freezing every time he flew by a glacier. While he wryly admitted that the curves the weather always seemed to be throwing at him got a little frustrating, it was obvious that he wouldn't trade this kind of flying for anything else.

A UNIQUE EXPERIENCE

What makes flying a floatplane such a unique and rewarding experience? Certainly part of the answer lies in the opportunity to observe nature's never-ending panorama from a 500-foot-high ringside seat (Fig. 1-2).

Thin, curving lines of low-water sand stretch ahead

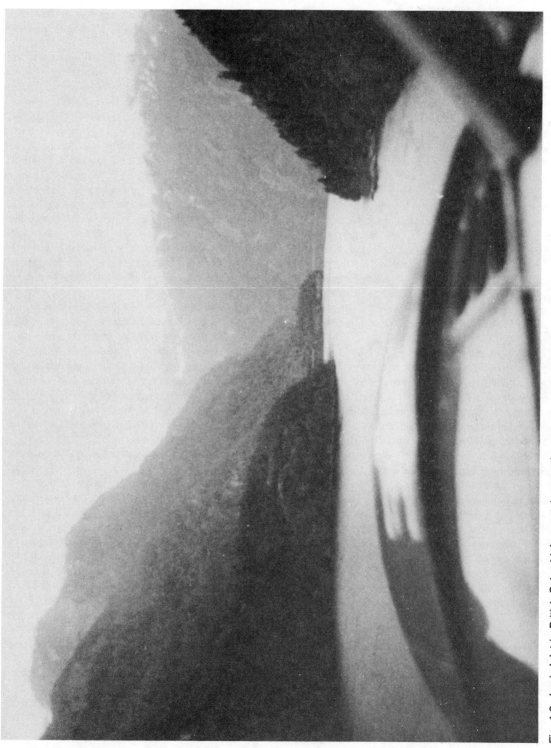

Fig. 1-2. Jervis Inlet in British Columbia's coastal mountains, as seen from the cockpit of a Beaver.

of you along the shores of a deep, narrow fjord, faced on one side by steep, sandy bluffs topped by dense stands of spruce and fir. The opposite shore rushes up out of the blue-green water to meet the near-vertical slopes of a glacier-draped mountain range.

The shoreline below the mountains is broken by countless streams and rivers whose headwaters lie in the snowfields and blue glacial ice 8000 feet above them. The sandbars are dotted with the gray, white, and black shapes of herons, gulls, and crows.

A sudden swirl of water a few yards offshore marks the presence of a harbor seal, and as the bubbles subside, you can see the seal's sleek form twisting gracefully beneath the surface in pursuit of a salmon. The seal had better keep a wary eye turned toward the deeper water of the sound, however, for Orca the killer whale, the seal's mortal enemy, is a frequent visitor. In fact, a mile or so up ahead, a feathery plume of spray and a 6-foot dorsal fin announce Orca's arrival. As you pass overhead, the powerful animal does a half-roll onto its side to keep an eye on you, revealing the telltale white markings on its streamlined black body. You hope the seal has seen the fin, too.

Another few miles up the sound you come to a large sawmill, with the little town that grew up around it neatly arranged on a hill overlooking the water. Even at 500 feet, the heady aroma of fresh-cut cedar is strong. Along one side of the inlet near the mill are rafts of logs that have been towed down from the logging areas up north. The rafts are dotted with the gray shapes of seals that have hauled out to sun themselves on the warm logs. Although they're safe from Orca, the seals keep a sleepy eye on the little round boom boat that's noisily butting logs into position to be pulled up into the saws.

A few miles more, another fjord comes in from the east. The resulting tide rips are popular with sport fishermen and, as you sweep past the motley collection of boats jockeying for position around the point, several fishermen look up from their tangle of lines and wave. One even holds up a good-sized fish, so at least somebody's catching something besides his neighbor's tackle.

Ahead, the sound takes on a pewter cast in the low afternoon light, and the silver sheet of water is dotted with the dark silhouettes of islands, the first of an unbroken chain stretching north for hundreds of miles (Fig. 1-3). Your destination lies somewhere among those islands. It may be a remote beach sheltered in a secluded bay, or perhaps a fishing resort nestled between the green mountain walls. Maybe you're headed for one of the coastal towns that promise adventure even in the sound of their names: Ketchikan, Sitka, Wrangell, Angoon, Skagway, or Yakutat.

The country that the floatplane calls home is invariably beautiful because it is invariably remote. Whether you're flying in the mystical myriad of islands and fjords of Southeast Alaska, the rugged interior of British Columbia or the Yukon Territory in Canada, the vast arctic distances of the far north, or the endless expanse of forests and lakes stretching from Minnesota to Hudson Bay, beauty and isolation go hand in hand.

And therein lies the challenge of flying floats. *You're on your own.* Even if you're landing in the crowded harbor at Vancouver, British Columbia, or on the East River in New York City, you're on your own. There's no marked runway, no glide slope, no localizer, no radar, and probably no wind sock. Only two seaplane bases in North America have formal control towers, and a few others have Unicom frequencies, but most of the time your radio will be silent.

Contrary to what you might think, however, one of the greatest satisfactions of flying floats is the fact that you *are* on your own. Seaplanes offer one of the last chances for a pilot to be truly independent. You determine the wind direction; you determine the safety of your landing site, you designate your runway; you plan your approach, and you figure out how to get the floatplane to the dock. After your floatplane is safely tied to that dock, you can take pride in what you've accomplished because you've done it by yourself.

Federal Aviation Regulation (FAR) 91.3 states that, "The pilot in command of an aircraft is directly responsible for, and is the final authority as to, the operation of that aircraft." I've talked to student pilots who believed the final authority governing the operation of their aircraft lay not with themselves, but with Air Traffic Control. The students were wrong, of course, but considering the ever-increasing amount of airspace regulation and control facing pilots today, I can understand why they felt their flying was being controlled from the ground.

There are, however, a few areas where FAR 91.3 is still considered aviation's first commandment. It's the primary insurance policy for the pilots of crop dusters, water bombers, aerobatic and experimental aircraft, bush planes, and seaplanes. No other type of flying offers pilots the same chance to so completely control their own fate.

To this opportunity to be your own master in the air, the seaplane adds the beauty of its environment. It's an unbeatable combination.

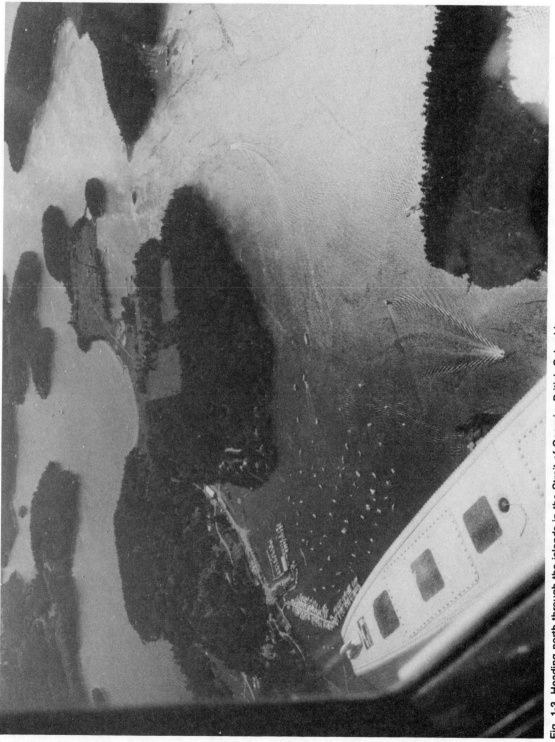

Fig. 1-3. Heading north through the islands in the Strait of Georgia, British Columbia.

THE WORLD OF SEAPLANES

So why isn't everyone out flying seaplanes, if they're so great? Before answering that question, I think we should run through some definitions. You may have noticed that all of a sudden I've started using the term *seaplanes* instead of *floatplanes*. While this book is about floatplanes, I don't want to suggest to any readers who might be flying boat pilots that they don't experience the same independence, freedom, and beauty enjoyed by those of us who fly floatplanes. They do, for these privileges are enjoyed by all water flyers.

The terms *seaplane, floatplane, flying boat,* and *amphibian,* all refer to airplanes that can operate on the water, and it's important that you understand the exact meaning of each to avoid confusion.

A seaplane is any airplane that can land on, and take off from, the water. Floatplanes, flying boats, and amphibians are all seaplanes. Seaplanes can be either single- or multi-engined, and the engines can be reciprocating, turboprop, turbojet, fanjet, or some future powerplant as yet undiscovered. The ratings added to a pilot's Private, Commercial, or ATP certificate are for this class of aircraft, i.e., "single-engine sea" and "multi-engine sea."

A floatplane is a seaplane that is supported on the water by one or more separate floats, or pontoons (Fig. 1-4).

A flying boat is a seaplane whose fuselage is also the "hull" that supports the airplane on the water. Unlike conventional airplanes, the bottom of a flying boat's fuselage is designed for maximum efficiency in the water, having a V-shaped keel, one or more planing "steps," spray rails, and so forth. Most flying boats also have small, pylon-mounted wing-tip floats to keep the plane on an even keel when it's on the water (Fig. 1-5).

An amphibian is any seaplane that can operate from both land and water. Amphibians can be flying boats or floatplanes. Amphibious flying boats have landing gear that retracts into the fuselage or wings, while the landing

Fig. 1-4. The two-place, tandem-seat Piper Super Cub is popular both as a trainer and as a bush plane. Equipped with a 150-horsepower engine, the Super Cub can lift heavy loads out of small lakes.

Fig. 1-5. This Grumman Widgeon is a typical flying boat that also happens to be an amphibian. Many Widgeons have been updated with modern, horizontally opposed engines, but this one still has its original, in-line Rangers.

Fig. 1-6. A huge floatplane to begin with, the de Havilland Otter becomes even bigger when fitted with amphibious floats.

Fig. 1-7. The Dornier DO-X, built in 1929, needed no less than twelve, 500-horsepower, Siemens Jupiter engines to get off the water. During flight, mechanics could crawl out to the engine pylons through tunnels in the massive wings and service the accessory groups at the rear of each engine. (Courtesy of National Air and Space Museum, Smithsonian Institution)

gear of an amphibious floatplane retracts into the floats (Fig. 1-6).

Back to my question. Why isn't everyone out flying seaplanes?

As we will see in the next chapter, the seaplane was a popular design during the early years of aviation because, while runways and airports were scarce, protected bodies of water were not. These *seadromes,* as they came to be called, were plentiful and free.

Many commercial transport designers consider landing gear the most critical element in the overall design of an airplane. Because seaplanes are supported by water, not wheels, they were not limited in size by the primitive landing gear technology of those early years. In fact, the problem was not supporting the big flying boats that were built in the 1920s and 1930s, but getting

the monsters to fly. The Dornier Do-X, built in 1929, needed no less than 12 engines to get off the water (Fig. 1-7).

Even as late as the 1940s and 50s, landing gear and runway technology was not capable of supporting such floating giants as the Hughes H-4 "Spruce Goose" (wingspan of 320 feet), the Martin JRM "Mars" (200 feet), or the Saunders Roe SR-45 "Princess" (219 feet). By contrast, the Boeing 747 has a wingspan of "only" 195 feet, 8 inches.

Unfortunately, seaplanes, and particularly flying boats, have several built-in disadvantages. Compared to landplanes, they are very expensive to build. The fuselage of a landplane can be relatively lightweight and simple in design, because its main function is to provide aerodynamic streamlining to the passengers, cargo, and pilots carried inside. The fuselage of a flying boat, on the other hand, must be strong enough to withstand the terrific pounding it will receive as it slams through the water during takeoffs and landings. The complex shape of the hull, with its watertight bulkheads and compartments, is costly to design and construct.

Two other factors that contributed to the demise of the large commercial seaplane were its inefficient aerodynamic shape and high maintenance costs.

Advances in landing gear technology allowed landplanes to grow in size, and retracting the gear made for higher speeds and longer ranges. World War II spurred the development of long-range, land-based bombers, and it was only natural that some of these designs evolved into passenger airplanes. The world's first, four-engined, pressurized airliner, the Boeing Model 307 Stratoliner, was derived from the B-17 Flying Fortress, and after the

war, the Boeing B-29 Superfortress acquired a double-deck fuselage and became the Model 377 Stratocruiser. The era of the big commercial seaplane was over.

There may be a future for medium to large seaplanes in island countries like Japan, where there is precious little land to spare for airports. For the most part, however, the seaplane has been pushed back by the advance of asphalt and concrete, until today its environment is limited to those places where landplanes dare not tread.

So to answer my question, the reasons for the seaplane's limited popularity today are its relatively remote environment and specialized design. Seaplanes are not for everyone.

In those parts of the world, however, where airports and roads are scarce, but lakes, rivers, and bays are plentiful, the words *survival* and *seaplane* are often synonymous. In addition to carrying the food, mail,

Fig. 1-8. A nice catch of silver salmon taken near Big Bay Resort, on Stewart Island, British Columbia. The only access to the island is by boat or seaplane.

medicine, machinery, and all the other things needed in a remote community, a seaplane is often required to assist in the preservation of life itself through mercy flights.

Seaplanes are used for mineral exploration, fish spotting, law enforcement, game management, forest fire protection, and the multitude of interesting, and sometimes strange, tasks that fall under the general heading of charter flying.

Seaplanes play an important recreational role, too, and it is here that we will probably see the greatest increase in seaplane popularity. The best fishing, camping, and hunting spots always seem to be a little farther away each year, and often a seaplane provides the only way to get to them (Fig. 1-8). Many fishing and hunting resorts now have their own seaplanes, and most of them provide docking facilities for city-dwelling guests who like to use their own airplanes to get away from it all for a few days.

The most popular and economical type of seaplane today is the floatplane. Modern floatplanes are production landplanes that have been modified to accept a pair of floats in place of the landing gear. This system has several advantages. The floats can be removed, and the wheels reinstalled if the owner wants to use the airplane

on land for awhile. Many northern operators use the same planes year-round by installing floats during the summer and changing back to wheels or skis for the winter.

Most floatplanes are high-wing airplanes. Unlike a flying boat, a floatplane does not require wing-tip floats; so it is easier to dock, since its high wing will clear many obstacles that would catch the wing-tip floats of a flying boat. High-wing floatplanes are generally easier to load and unload, too, thanks to their large side doors which extend down to the floor of the cabin. Heavy cargo can be slid directly into, or out of, the plane. The doors of flying boats are often too small for bulky cargo, and as a rule are mounted fairly high, since the cabin floor is usually below the waterline.

Floatplanes come in all sizes and shapes, from the tiny ultralights to the massive, single-engine de Havilland Otter. Some floatplanes have two engines, like the Beechcraft Model 18, or "Twin Beech," and the de Havilland Twin Otter (Fig. 1-9). Turboprop powerplants have their advantages, especially in underdeveloped countries where there is usually an abundance of cheap kerosene (Fig. 1-10). For those who love that turbine whine, there is the Pilatus Porter and the de Havilland

Fig. 1-9. A Beechcraft Model 18 "Twin Beech" on EDO floats. (Courtesy of the EDO Corporation)

Fig. 1-10. The turboprop de Havilland Twin Otter is the largest floatplane in production today. This one, operated by Air B.C., is taxiing in after landing in Vancouver harbor, British Columbia.

Fig. 1-11. Although most de Havilland Beavers are powered by 450-horsepower Pratt & Whitney radials, the factory made a few powered with Pratt & Whitney's PT6-A turboprop. This one is fitted with Wipline amphibious floats.

Turbo-Beaver, as well as conversion kits for Cessna's 185 and 206 and the radial-engined de Havilland Beaver and Otter (Fig. 1-11).

Before we tackle the techniques of flying a floatplane, however, let's take a brief look at its colorful history. It's the story of two men who were determined that flight from the water was possible. It's the story of a floatplane which launched a company that today is the world's leading manufacturer of jetliners. It's the story of a little racing floatplane, and how it was responsible for an en-

tire country's survival in a world war. It's a story of discovery, exploration, and adventure.

It's a story that deserves more than just one chapter in one book. In fact, it would take several books to properly document the floatplane's place in history, but for now, we'll examine some of the headlines in the chronicle of events that has resulted in this wonderful machine—a machine that carries us to the challenging, rewarding, and beautiful world of wings, water, and floats.

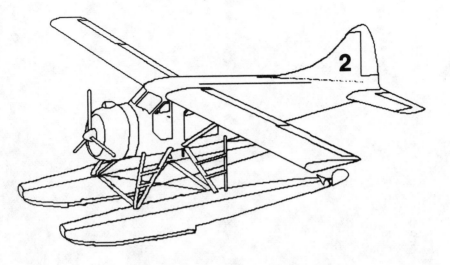

The Historical Floatplane

THE SEED OF THE FLOATPLANE FAMILY TREE WAS planted in 1906, when Henri Fabre, the son of a French shipowner, started work on what he hoped would be the world's first successful seaplane. Four years later, the seed pushed up an ungainly little sawhorse of an airplane called the *Hydravion* (seaplane).

It was a high-wing monoplane with a rear-mounted engine and a pusher propeller. The "fuselage" of the *Hydravion* consisted of two long beams running fore and aft, one about 5 feet above the other. The wing was mounted on the aft end of the upper beam, just ahead of the engine. The pilot sat in front of the wing, and the horizontal stabilizer was in front of him giving the skeletal machine a canard configuration (Fig. 2-1).

The elevator was a separate horizontal surface that sat several feet above the stabilizer. Twin vertical rudders were mounted on the elevator and moved with it. The pilot, who sat astride the upper beam in a sort of wicker tractor seat, gripped two tiller-bars that ran forward to control the elevator-rudder assembly.

The pilot's feet dangled down into a pair of pedals which were attached to the wing-warping mechanism. Like the Wright brothers before him, Fabre achieved roll control by wing warping; there were no ailerons.

The wing itself had a unique design. The single main spar also served as the leading edge, and consisted of a massive wooden truss that extended the entire length of the wing. The spar sat, fencelike, on top of the wing, and nobody seems to understand why this arrangement didn't act like a full-span spoiler and kill the wing's lift completely. One possible answer is that Fabre's wing developed most of its lift on the underside, like a kite. Gracefully curved ribs extended aft from the spar, and the wing itself was constructed of light canvas, which could be detached from the ribs and furled against the spar like a sail.

After experimenting with long, catamaran-style floats, Fabre decided to use short, wide flat-bottom floats instead. There were three of them, and their upper surfaces were curved to produce additional lift once the plane was airborne.

One float was mounted up forward, on the lower end of the same vertical strut that carried the stabilizer and elevator. The other two were mounted on storklike legs extending down from the main wing spar. The float arrangement was not unlike today's tricycle landing gear, complete with a steerable forward float which provided some degree of directional control on the water.

Fabre's previous seaplane design, built in 1909, used

Fig. 2-1. Henri Fabre's *Hydravion*. The plane is in its original configuration with the rudders mounted up forward. (Courtesy of Genevieve Fabre)

three, 12-horsepower Anzani engines linked together to drive a single propeller. This arrangement did not develop enough power to get the craft off the water; so Fabre went in search of a more powerful engine for the *Hydravion*.

He settled on the Gnome 7-cylinder rotary engine, which produced 50 horsepower at 1100 rpm, and swung an 8 1/2-foot propeller. One advantage of the rear-engine configuration became apparent the first time the Gnome was started up. Like all early aircraft engines, the little rotary threw oil all over the place, but Fabre was safely out of the line of fire in his wicker chair up forward.

On March 28, 1910, Fabre conducted some high-speed taxi tests of his floatplane off the town of La Mede, France near Marseilles. The *Hydravion* handled well, and Fabre, who had never flown an aircraft of any kind before, decided to attempt his first flight that afternoon. He later described the experience:

"I started at a great speed. For a long time, I continued this fast hydroplaning without opening entirely the throttle and, thus, risking a take-off. My machine had been built to be stabilized automatically. The weather was so calm, I knew I should be able to fly it without moving the controls.

"With my hand on the throttle, I let the airplane increase speed. One of the rear floats started to lift up; I slowed down and was able to equalize the wings by neutralizing the throttle. I accelerated again; this time, both rear floats lifted at the same moment. The hydroplane was balancing on the front float, which, in turn, began to rise above the water. I was airborne, totally stable, gliding over this glassy water, or buzzing a few meters above the surface. The feeling was the same.

"Pulling on the throttle, I soon saw the front float touching gently the surface of the water, leaving a thin trail like a diamond on glass. Again, I took off. My flights lasted longer and longer. I was making wide turns. Never a sudden move, never a hard landing. I had the greatest confidence in my hydroplane.

"When I returned, the spectators thought I had a great machine whose moves were so smooth that they shouldn't cause any anxiety."

And so the world of water flying was born. The following day, Fabre flew the *Hydravion* from La Mede to Martigues, a distance of about 4 miles, thus completing the world's first cross-country seaplane flight.

Fabre continued to make improvements to his machine. He moved the rudders aft, and also added little water rudders to the rear floats for better directional control on the surface (Fig. 2-2).

On May 18, 1910, Henri Fabre, the world's first pilot of the world's first seaplane, became the world's first victim of the phenomenon which has probably caused more seaplane accidents than any other: glassy water. While demonstrating the *Hydravion* to a prospective financial backer, Fabre misjudged his height above the water, and landed too fast and too hard. The machine broke apart, throwing Fabre into the water. The fact that he was not hurt led him to the immediate conclusion that seaplanes were safer than landplanes. As we will learn in a later chapter, he was right.

The *Hydravion* was repaired and exhibited later that year at the second *Salon de l'Aeronautique* in Paris. Among the visitors to the exhibition was the American aviation pioneer, Glenn H. Curtiss, who met with Fabre and discussed his experiences with the little seaplane. Curtiss had been experimenting with the concept of taking off and landing on water since 1909, but so far, he had been unsuccessful.

In March, 1911, Fabre hired pilot Jean Becue to demonstrate the *Hydravion* during a motorboat exhibition at Monaco. The first flight was successful, but after the second, the spindly floatplane got caught in the surf and was destroyed. Becue was unhurt, and the remains of the airplane were pulled from the water. Years later the airplane was rebuilt, and today Henri Fabre's *Hydravion* hangs in the *Musee de L'Air* in Chalais-Meudon, near Paris.

Fabre himself, having accomplished what he set out to do, did not build any more seaplanes, although he constructed floats for other seaplane manufacturers. He died on June 29, 1984, at an age of 101.

THE PRACTICAL FLOATPLANE

Meanwhile, on the other side of the Atlantic, Glenn Curtiss was still trying to get an airplane off the water. His biggest problem seemed to be one of float design. Curtiss' approach was to take an airplane that had successfully flown as a landplane and mount it on floats. His first attempt was made with the Aerial Experiment Association's "Loon," in 1908.

The Loon never had a chance. The engine only produced about 30 horsepower, and the bottoms of the long, twin floats were completely flat. While the Loon did man-

Fig. 2-2. Fabre's Hydravion in flight, after the rudders were moved aft. Note the small water rudders attached to the rear of the main floats. (Courtesy of Genevieve Fabre)

age to plane across the surface of Lake Keuka at Hammondsport, New York, the engine simply did not have the power to overcome the suction of the water on the flat float-bottoms, and the airplane refused to become airborne.

In his next attempt, Curtiss decided to stick with proven designs. He mounted a standard Curtiss Model D airplane on a canoe. This didn't work either, but it convinced Curtiss that a single-float design handled better on the water than a twin-float, or catamaran, design.

Finally, in 1911, Curtiss got it right. Again using a Model D, he replaced the main wheels of the tricycle-geared airplane with a single, large float similar in design to one of Fabre's floats. The nosewheel of the Model D was replaced with a small, scowlike float, and a hydrofoil was mounted in from of it to keep the forward float from digging in when power was applied. Curtiss successfully flew his float-equipped Model D from San Diego Bay on January 26, 1911 (Fig. 2-3).

He then replaced the rather complicated tandem float arrangement with a single long, narrow float. Three weeks after his first successful seaplane flight, Curtiss flew his plane across the bay to the *U.S.S. Pennsylvania*. After landing next to the cruiser, the Model D was hoisted aboard by one of the ship's cranes. An hour later, it was lowered back into the water for the return flight to North Island.

The Navy was intrigued, and in July 1911, it commissioned the airplane under the designation Curtiss Hydroaeroplane, Navy A-1. It was the first of the Navy's long line of shipboard scout planes.

Glenn Curtiss was responsible for at least two more innovations that have become standard design features of all seaplanes flying today. In May 1911, Curtiss was flying a single-float Model D from Lake Keuka, when the float sprung a leak. The weight of the water which entered the float did not prevent him from taking off, but when he pitched the plane down to begin his landing descent, the water rushed to the front of the float, causing the airplane to nosedive into the lake. Curtiss was not seriously injured, but the airplane was completely destroyed.

From then on, all floats contained bulkheads which divided the float into several watertight compartments. Not only did this prevent any water that might be present from running freely from one end of the float to the other, the results of which Curtiss had just experienced, but the water-tight compartments would ensure that the

Fig. 2-3. Glenn Curtiss' first practical floatplane, the Model D. (Courtesy of National Air and Space Museum, Smithsonian Institution)

floatplane would not sink if the float sprung a leak or was damaged while on the water. This design practice was later applied to flying boat hulls as well.

Curtiss is generally given credit for another important innovation in seaplane design. In the summer of 1911, he was testing his first true flying boat. The machine failed to get off the water for the same reason that his earlier floatplanes refused to become airborne: its long, flat bottom could not be pulled free of the water's suction. Curtiss came up with the idea of *wedging,* or stepping, the bottom at the airplane's center of gravity, so the seaplane could be rocked back and forth to break the suction.

This is usually considered to be the first appearance of the step-hydroplane bottom that has been used on every floatplane, flying boat and high-performance speedboat since. Henri Fabre, however, in his book about his aviation experiences, makes reference to a racing boat called the *Ricochet,* which was designed by a Monsieur Bonnemaison in 1905. The *Ricochet* had a step-hydroplane bottom, so perhaps Curtiss' real contribution was the first use of a hydrodynamic step on a seaplane.

Although the floats used by Curtiss and his contemporaries incorporated the hydrodynamic step, the bottom sections were still flat in cross section. This flat bottom allowed the floats to quickly assume a planing attitude after takeoff power was applied, but in anything other than absolutely calm water, the airplane was subjected to a terrific pounding. Rather than cut through the waves, the flat-bottom floats simply slammed into them, throwing spray in all directions and drenching the pilot, to say nothing of putting a tremendous strain on the airframe.

In an effort to solve these problems, float designers developed the wave-cutting, spray-deflecting, V-shaped bottom that is used on almost every float manufactured today.

THE FLOATPLANE THAT LAUNCHED A JETLINER

From Glenn Curtiss and sunny San Diego, we move up the coast to the rain-swept forests of the Pacific Northwest and a wealthy timber baron who thought it would be fun to build an airplane. His name was William E. Boeing.

Born to a family who had acquired vast holdings of timber and iron ore in Minnesota's rich Mesabi Range, William Boeing decided to strike out on his own when he was 22. The Pacific Northwest, with its apparently endless forests of spruce, hemlock, cedar, and fir, seemed to be a promising destination for a young man who was looking to make his fortune in the lumber business, and

Boeing eventually settled in Seattle, Washington.

In January 1910, the first international aeronautical tournament held in the United States took place near Los Angeles. There were balloons, dirigibles, and airplanes built by Bleriot, Farman, and Curtiss. The airplanes competed in endurance and cross-country events, and among the 25,000 spectators was 29-year-old William Boeing.

He was fascinated by the airplanes and tried to get a ride with the pilot of a Farman biplane. Although the pilot agreed, either an upcoming event or a local dignitary who wanted a ride always seemed to take priority over Boeing's request. He returned each day of the tournament and waited patiently for his turn to fly, but it never came.

At the end of the air meet, the Farman was disassembled, crated, and shipped away. Boeing returned to Seattle disappointed, but intrigued with the idea of air travel.

A few years later, Boeing met Conrad Westervelt, a naval officer and engineer who was assigned to the Moran Shipyard in Seattle. Back in 1910, 9 months after Boeing had attended the air show in Los Angeles, Westervelt had represented the Navy at a similar tournament held at Belmont Park, New York. Like Boeing before him, Westervelt came away with a tremendous enthusiasm for the airplane, and recommended in his report that the Navy pay close attention to the rapid advancements taking place in the field of aviation.

Westervelt and Boeing, who had studied engineering at Yale before moving west, shared a common interest in anything mechanical, and they soon became good friends. When a pilot named Terah Maroney arrived in Seattle with a Curtiss seaplane and began selling rides, it was only natural that Boeing and Westervelt were among his first customers. On the Fourth of July 1914, Boeing finally got his first airplane ride.

One day, after another ride in Maroney's Curtiss, Boeing remarked to Westervelt that they could probably build a better airplane than the flimsy pusher Maroney was flying. Westervelt, ever the engineer, obtained all the information he could about airplanes, their stability and control, the types of stresses to which they were subjected, what kinds of motors were available, and so forth. He did some strength calculations using his naval engineering tables and the dimensions of the structural members in Maroney's plane, and reached the startling conclusion that the strength of the parts in the Curtiss was just about equal to the load they supported in flight. There was no margin of safety, and Westervelt couldn't understand why Maroney's airplane hadn't fallen apart a long time ago.

Boeing became intrigued with the idea of building a sport airplane he could use himself. He also felt that the war raging in Europe would eventually envelop the United States, and he was concerned that the United States was falling behind in the field of aviation.

In 1915, Boeing and Westervelt organized a small group of craftsmen and set about building two airplanes, which would be given the name *"B & W"* for Boeing and Westervelt (Fig. 2-4). Before construction began, however, Boeing went to Los Angeles to learn to fly. When he returned, he brought with him a Martin seaplane, which the group used to determine some of the dimensions for their own airplanes.

Each B & W would be a floatplane, partly because the Martin was also a floatplane, and also because there weren't any airfields in the mudflats that lay at the base of Seattle's steep hills. There were plenty of lakes, however, and the protected bays and coves of Puget Sound offered countless landing sites.

The airplanes' components would be constructed at Boeing's shipyard, located in the maze of sloughs and tideflats south of the city. Upon completion, the components would be taken to a boathouse on Seattle's Lake Union and assembled.

Ed Heath, who ran the boatyard, was put in charge of building the twin floats for each airplane. They were beautifully crafted out of thin wood, and at one point, after being cautioned by Boeing for the hundredth time to keep the floats light, Heath reported that they were already so light he was afraid to open the door for fear that the floats would blow out.

Unlike the scowlike floats used by Glenn Curtiss on his early airplanes, Boeing's floats were similar in appearance to the floats used today. They utilized a step-hydroplane bottom, which had a shallow V-shape. The tops of the floats were gently curved to reduce drag. There were no water rudders; so the only directional control was from the airflow over the vertical rudder.

An interesting feature of the B & W was the small tail float that occupied the same position as the tail skid used on landplanes. Although this float did not help support the airplane while it was on the water, it may have

Fig. 2-4. This little biplane is the direct ancestor of the Boeing 747. Called the "B & W," the wood and fabric floatplane was the first airplane built by William E. Boeing. (Courtesy of the Boeing Company)

been installed to keep the tail surfaces from striking the water during takeoff and landing. It was not used on later Boeing floatplanes.

The B & W was a two-place airplane, with a wingspan of 52 feet, and a length of 27 feet, 6 inches. The plane had a gross weight of 2800 pounds, and was powered by a water-cooled, 125-horsepower Hall-Scott engine, giving it a top speed of 75 miles per hour, and a cruising speed of 67 miles per hour.

Conrad Westervelt was transferred back to an assignment on the East Coast before the first B & W was ready to fly, so on a June day in 1916, Boeing worked to get the airplane ready for its first flight. The pilot, Herb Munter, was late, so Boeing finally took the airplane out himself. After a taxi test, he lifted the B & W off the water for a short, straight flight before returning to the boathouse. For the next several days, Munter performed more taxi tests until making the B & W's first real flight from Lake Union to Lake Washington.

With his first airplane flying successfully, Boeing began to realize that, someday, the airplane would become an accepted means of transportation. He decided the future was bright for a commercial airplane company, and on July 15, 1916, he incorporated the Pacific Aero Products Company. The company's first order was from the Navy, for 50 Model C seaplanes. The Model C was a much-refined version of the B & W, and was used by the Navy as a trainer. The two B & Ws were sold to the New Zealand government, where they were used for many years as trainers.

On April 26, 1917, Pacific Aero Products became the Boeing Airplane Company I wonder if even William Boeing himself could conceive of what was to follow.

WOODEN FLOATS

When Boeing decided to build his own airplanes, he set about putting together a team of the best local craftsmen he could find. Seattle had become the busiest port city on Puget Sound; so it was only natural that he look to the shipyards for the experienced men he needed.

One of the greatest challenges facing the designers and builders of the early floatplanes was to reduce the weight and bulk of the floats themselves. Boeing decided to find someone who could design a lighter, stronger float than the ones used on the B & W.

His search took him to the University of Washington, where he was introduced to George Pocock. George, together with his brother, Dick, was building lightweight racing shells for the university's rowing team, and as Boe-

ing inspected the beautifully crafted eight-oared shells in Pocock's shop, he decided that this was how he wanted his floats made.

The Pocock brothers did not immediately accept Boeing's offer of employment. A short time later, however, the University of Washington ran out of funds to keep the Pococks busy building racing shells, so they decided to go to work for the newly formed Pacific Aero Products Company.

Their first assignment was to design and build a lighter, stronger float. After outlining the general specifications for the new float, Boeing's chief engineer asked George Pocock for a rough weight estimate.

"One hundred and fifteen pounds," was the immediate reply. The chief engineer was skeptical, and said he would buy Pocock a new hat if the float came in under 125 pounds. The two brothers went to work, and when the first float was finished, it weighed in at a fraction over 114 pounds. Presumably, George got his new hat.

The Model C was the first airplane to use the new floats, and after the first 2 floatplanes passed inspection at Pensacola, the Navy ordered 50 more. The Pocock floats were made entirely of wood and were built around a longitudinal keel. There were four watertight compartments (Fig. 2-5). Lightweight bulkhead and stringers supported the thin outer planking, which was applied diagonally for extra strength. Also, like the racing shells that came before them, Pocock's floats were beautifully streamlined (Fig. 2-6).

Despite the improvements, however, the wooden floats still had several drawbacks. For one thing, their elaborate construction made them expensive to manufacture (Fig. 2-7). In addition, the thin wooden skin, while strong enough for normal operations, was easily damaged upon hard contact with a dock or ramp.

After World War I, the increasing use of floatplanes for both military and civilian purposes created a demand for floats which were stronger, lighter, and cheaper. In 1925, a World War I veteran named Earl Dodge Osborn set out to design just such a float.

EDO'S ALL-ALUMINUM FLOAT

Osborn was interested in seaplanes, and he began building and testing both airframes and floats. In 1925, he used his initials to name his new firm, which became the EDO Aircraft Corporation. Shortly afterwards, the company introduced the first practical aluminum float, and it became an immediate success.

Fig. 2-5. The underside of one of George Pocock's wooden floats, showing the central keel and watertight bulkheads. (Courtesy of the Boeing Company)

The advantages of building in aluminum were many. It made for a lighter and less cumbersome float, and yet one that was stronger and more damage-resistant than the old wood floats. An aluminum float was easier to build and did not require a work force of skilled cabinetmakers to assemble. Aluminum is easier to shape than wood, and the EDO Company was able to develop a very efficient fluted bottom for its floats which develops maximum hydrodynamic lift while giving a smooth ride over the surface and minimizing spray.

The best thing about EDO's new aluminum floats was that they could be fitted to many of the popular landplanes of the period. The company offered the floats in several sizes, and they were attached in place of the plane's landing gear by a relatively simple system of aluminum struts. All sorts of airplanes began showing up on floats, including the boxy Ford Trimotor, the Army's Martin B-12 bomber, and even Beechcraft's sleek new Model 17, which quickly acquired the nickname "Staggerwing Beech" (Figs. 2-8 through 2-10).

Aerial exploration became popular during the 1920s and 1930s and many of the expeditions to the undeveloped

Fig. 2-6. Side view of a Boeing float, showing off its beautiful lines. (Courtesy of the Boeing Company)

Fig. 2-7. The interior of the Boeing float shop in 1918. Note the complex forming jig in the foreground. (Courtesy of the Boeing Company)

areas of the world required the use of a seaplane. All you had to do to get one was to purchase a proven landplane design, fit it with a set of EDO floats, and you were ready to go.

In the early 1930s, Admiral Richard E. Byrd explored the shores of Antarctica in a Curtiss Condor, a large, twin-engined biplane which had been fitted with EDO floats. In 1931, Colonel Charles Lindbergh and his wife, Anne, explored Alaska and the Aleutian Islands on the their way to Japan in a Lockheed Sirius, also mounted on EDO floats (Figs. 2-11 and 2-12). In 1935, the American polar explorer, Lincoln Ellsworth, and his Canadian pilot, Herbert Hollick-Kenyon, made a 2300-mile flight across Antarctica in a Northrop Gamma they named the *Polar Star*. The big Northrop was fitted with EDO floats, which enabled the plane to land on the snow-covered surface of the continent when necessary (Fig. 2-13).

Some aircraft manufacturers of the period saw a market in the export of airplanes that could be converted to military uses by overseas customers. Because arms-control laws forbade the export of aircraft that were actually fitted with armament, the planes were sold as "reconnaissance" models, but they were designed to be easily converted to fighters and bombers by the customer. In order to appeal to as many countries as possible, some of the manufacturers, like Bellanca and Curtiss, offered their customers a choice of either conventional landing gear or EDO floats (Fig. 2-14).

Osborn's aluminum float probably did more to spur the popularity of floatplanes that any other development, and for years the EDO Company enjoyed a monopoly in the manufacture of twin aluminum floats. EDO floats were available for the two-place Piper Cub, the 10-passenger "Twin Beech," and just about everything else in between (Fig. 2-15). The largest floatplane ever was created when EDO designed and built amphibious floats for the C-47, the military version of the famous Douglas DC-3. Each massive float had a displacement of 29,400 pounds, and the landing gear retracted into wheel wells complete with gear doors. The plane flew quite well, but the Army cancelled the order after only two had been built (Fig. 2-16).

EDO has some competition today, but it remains the world's foremost supplier of aluminum floats. Its current line of "straight" (no wheels) and amphibious floats are certified for many of today's popular landplanes, from the

Fig. 2-8. A Ford Trimotor on EDO Model 14060 floats. (Courtesy of the EDO Corporation)

Fig. 2-9. A Martin YB-12 bomber fitted with EDO MOdel 15750 floats for coastal defense. (Courtesy of the EDO Corporation).

Fig. 2-10. EDO's aluminum floats could even be installed on the beautiful Beechcraft Model 17, or "Staggerwing Beech." This one is resting on a special dolly so the plane can be moved around on the ground. (Courtesy of the EDO Corporation)

two-place Cessna 150 to the big de Havilland DHC-2 Beaver (Fig. 2-17).

THE FLOATPLANE THAT SAVED A NATION

Today's float-equipped de Havilland Beaver has a cruising speed of about 110 miles per hour, but back in September 1931, there was a floatplane zipping around in excess of 400 miles per hour. Its pilot, Flight Lieutenant George Stainforth of the British Royal Air Force, became the first man in history to break the 400 mile per hour limit. The world's fastest airplane was a floatplane.

It is unlikely that Hermann Göring, soon to be the head of German Chancellor Adolf Hitler's powerful Luftwaffe, gave much thought to the record-shattering speed runs being made by the little silver and blue floatplane across the channel in England in 1931. It's probably just as well he didn't, for the song thundering from the floatplane's exhaust stacks was destined to become the death knell for Germany's invincible air armada 9 years later.

How could a single airplane, and a floatplane at that, affect the outcome of a World War? In December, 1912,

Jacques Schneider, heir to some steel and munitions factories in France, announced he was offering a new international trophy race to promote the development of seaplanes. It would be a closed-course race, and any country winning the trophy three times within five consecutive contests would keep it, thus ending the competition. The trophy itself was a rather elaborate affair featuring a nude, winged woman flying over, and kissing, an ocean wave with the face of a man. It was officially called the *Coupe d'Aviation Maritime Jacques Schneider*. The English aviators who competed for it called it the "Flyin' Flirt," and the race itself became known simply as the Schneider Race.

One of the English entries in the 1925 Schneider Trophy race was the beautiful Supermarine S-4, designed by R. J. Mitchell. It represented quite an advancement over the other racing planes of its day, being a mid-wing monoplane with extremely clean lines (Fig. 2-18). In tests, it had broken every existing record, exceeding 226 miles per hour at only 3/4 throttle. Unfortunately, it crashed during a trial run just before the race. The pilot escaped with only a broken wrist, but the plane was destroyed.

The design of the S-4 set the stage, however, for the

Fig. 2-11. Admiral Richard E. Byrd's Curtiss Condor near a supply ship during his antarctic expedition. Powered by two, Wright Cyclone supercharged engines developing 725 horsepower each, the plane was fitted with EDO Model 16800 floats. (Courtesy of the EDO Corporation)

Fig. 2-12. Charles and Anne Lindbergh pose for photographers in front of their Lockheed Sirius, mounted on EDO Model 6235 floats. (Courtesy of the EDO Corporation)

Fig. 2-13. Lincoln Ellsworth's sleek Northrop Gamma, mounted on EDO Model 7080 floats. (Courtesy of the EDO Corporation)

Fig. 2-14. A Bellanca Model 77-140 export bomber mounted on EDO Model 15750 floats. The plane was powered by two, 715-horsepower Wright Cyclone radials. Note the gunner's position on the nose. (Courtesy of the EDO Corporation).

three planes that were to follow from Mitchell's drawing board. The S-5 won the 1927 race, the S-6 took the 1929 contest, and in 1931, Supermarine rolled out the magnificent S-6B, which permanently retired the "Flyin' Flirt" to England (Fig. 2-19).

The three airplanes were low-wing monoplanes, with a fuselage profile similar to the S-4. The S-4 had been constructed entirely of wood, with an aluminum engine cowling, while the S-5 combined wooden wings with an aluminum fuselage. The S-6 and S-6B were of all-aluminum construction.

Mitchell had used the 700-horsepower Napier "Lion" engine in the S-4, and a geared version developing 875 horsepower in the S-5. The "Lion" was unusual in that the 12 cylinders were arranged in 3 banks of 4 cylinders each. From the front, the engine looked like a broad arrowhead pointing down.

Although the S-5 had roared to victory in the 1927 Schneider Trophy race, it became obvious to Mitchell that he had gotten everything he could out of the Napier "Lion." The United States, France, and Italy were all determined to recapture the trophy, and in order to stay competitive, Mitchell needed a bigger engine.

It was provided by Sir Henry Royce, who guaranteed that his company, Rolls-Royce, would deliver an engine

developing 1500 horsepower. While Mitchell set about designing an airplane around the promised engine, the Rolls-Royce engineers set about designing the engine itself. It was called the Rolls-Royce "R" engine at first, and its development was surrounded by the utmost secrecy. Ten years later, however, a derivative of this big V-12 would become a household word. It would be called "Merlin." Sir Royce's engine delivered 1900 horsepower at 2900 rpm and weighed only 1530 pounds.

On Saturday, September 7, 1929, to the cheers of more than a million spectators, Flight Officer Waghorn's S-6 blasted across the finish line to give England her second consecutive win. Waghorn's course speed was 328.63 miles an hour (Fig.2-20).

After the 1929 race, the British Air Ministry decided not to underwrite the development and construction of any more Schneider Trophy airplanes, and R.A.F. personnel would not be allowed to fly in the race. If it were not for the generosity of a remarkable woman, Göring's Luftwaffe would have had an easier time of it in the skies over England in 1940.

Lady Houston was indignant over the government's decision to abandon the development of racing planes; so she offered to put up £100,000 to finance the British effort. The offer was accepted, and the government also

Fig. 2-15. The popular little Piper J-3 Cub, mounted on a pair of EDO floats. (Courtesy of the EDO Corporation).

Fig. 2-16. EDO designed and built special amphibious floats for the Douglas C-47 (DC-3) during World War II. Each float displaced a whopping 29,400 pounds to make this the largest floatplane in the world. Although the plane performed quite well, only two were ever built. (Courtesy of the EDO Corporation)

Fig. 2-17. Quite a contrast to the float-equipped C-47, the Cessna 150 can also be fitted with EDO floats, the Model 1650. This popular two-place airplane performs well on floats, but does not have quite enough power to make it a satisfactory floatplane trainer. (Courtesy of the EDO Corporation)

Fig. 2-18. R. J. Mitchell's revolutionary Supermarine S-4, designed and built for the 1925 Schneider Trophy race. (Courtesy of National Air and Space Museum, Smithsonian Institution)

Fig. 2-19. The Supermarine S-5, winner of the 1927 Schneider Trophy race. It was the last of designer Mitchell's racing planes to use the 12-cylinder, "broad-arrow," Napier Lion engine. (Courtesy of National Air and Space Museum, Smithsonian Institution)

Fig. 2-20. This is the Supermarine S-6 that won the Schneider Trophy for England in 1929. It was the first use of the Rolls-Royce "R" engine. (Courtesy of National Air and Space Museum, Smithsonian Institution)

rescinded its order banning R.A.F. personnel from flying in the Schneider race. Mitchell went back to his drawing board, and the Rolls-Royce engineers went back to theirs. The result was the magnificent S-6B (Fig. 2-21).

The S-6B was 28 feet, 10 inches long and had a 30-foot wingspan. The engine cowl was closely fitted around the V-12's two long cylinder heads, and the fuselage itself was no wider than the engine block. The 24-foot aluminum floats were joined to the fuselage by a pair of streamlined A-frames, which carried the full-length engine supports.

The engine was a Rolls-Royce "R-29." The original "R" engine had been boosted to an amazing 2350 horsepower by increasing the engine speed, the size of the air intake, and the supercharger gear ratio. The "R-29" delivered its maximum power at 3200 rpm, and the engine was designed to hold together at this speed just long enough to win the race. It turned a huge, two-bladed, fixed-pitch metal propeller.

One of the greatest challenges facing Mitchell was the problem of providing enough cooling to keep the engine running for the duration of the race. The wing skins were actually radiators, made by riveting together two thin sheets of aluminum separated by 1/16-inch spacers. The radiator panels were fastened directly to the wing spars and ribs, and formed the actual aerodynamic surfaces of the wings. Hot engine water was pumped to

the wings for cooling, and then returned to the engine.

This arrangement had worked quite well on the earlier S-6, but wing radiators alone were not sufficient to dissipate the tremendous amount of heat generated by the "R-29." Mitchell solved the problem by covering the entire upper halves of the floats with radiators as well. The floats did double duty by serving as the fuel tanks for the thirsty V-12. The starboard (right) float carried considerably more fuel than the port float in an attempt to balance out the tremendous torque developed by the engine.

The oil cooling system was ingenious. From the engine, the oil passed through cooling tubes faired into the sides of the fuselage and up to the top of the vertical tail. The hot oil was sprayed onto the tinned-stell inner skin of the tail, after which it ran down to a collection tank and filter. It was then pumped back to the engine via more cooling tubes under the fuselage. After much experimentation, it was found that by placing small vanes in the cooler oilways, the hot oil could be kept in constant contact with the outer surfaces, thus increasing the efficiency of the cooling system by 40 percent. Even so, the pure castor oil used by the Rolls-Royce engine disappeared at the rate of 14 gallons per hour.

The most important instruments in the cockpit were the engine temperature gauges, for these determined how far the pilot could open the throttle. The races were flown with the engine at its maximum temperature, a factor which undoubtably contributed to its short life.

Italy, France, and the United States had all built floatplanes to compete in the 1931 contest, but none of them were ready in time. At 2 minutes after 1 o'clock on Sunday, September 13th, a single Supermarine S-6B was launched from its barge on the Solent in England, and Flight Lieutenant John Boothman flew unopposed around the triangular course at an average speed of 340 miles per hour, winning the Schneider Trophy for England once and for all.

A few days later the airplane was prepared for a crack at the World Speed Record. Rolls-Royce had developed a special sprint version of the "R-29" engine, but it had an unnerving tendency to explode when full power was applied, so a reconditioned and slightly modified Schneider-race engine was used instead. It burned an exotic, foul-smelling, methanol-based fuel, and turned a special propeller designed specifically for the record attempt.

On September 29, 1931, Flight Lieutenant George Stainforth made his successful assault on the World Speed Record, raising it above 400 miles per hour for the first time in history. He made five runs over the 3-kilometer course, and his official average speed was 407.5 miles per hour.

The floatplane he did it in, Supermarine S-6B number S1595, is on display in the Science Museum in London. R. J. Mitchell went back to his drawing board, and an example of his next famous design sits near the record-breaking floatplane in the museum. Though a landplane, its racing-floatplane heritage is obvious in the sleek lines of its fuselage, the gracefully rounded wingtips, and the powerful V-12 nestled in its nose.

Mitchell's new plane was also designed to win races, but they were races with death. The dark clouds of war were starting to gather over Europe, and the excitement of the Schneider races would soon be forgotten as England struggled for her very life. Her survival would come to depend on a little airplane conceived in the thunderous exhaust of England's racing floatplanes, for Mitchell's new plane was the Spitfire.

THE ULTIMATE FLOATPLANE

The Italians had hoped to wrest the Schneider Trophy away from the British in 1931 with a truly awesome

Fig. 2-21. The magnificent S-6B, which won the 1931 Schneider race, and permanently retired the trophy to England. Note the oil cooler running the length of the fuselage and the massive, fixed-pitch propeller. (Courtesy of National Air and Space Museum, Smithsonian Institution)

Fig. 2-22. On June 2, 1933, Warrant Officer Francesco Agello drove this Macchi-Castoldi MC-72 to a new World Speed Record of 440.67 miles per hour. Note the radiators mounted on the floats and the counter-rotating propellers. (Courtesy of National Air and Space Museum, Smithsonian Institution)

floatplane. Called the Macchi-Castoldi MC-72, the bright red plane might well have won the race, but it was not ready in time. Italy asked for a postponement, but it was refused since a similar request by England had been turned down by the Italians only a few months earlier.

The MC-72's powerplant consisted of two Fiat V-12 engines in tandem which drove concentric, counter-rotating propellers. The 24 cylinder engine developed a staggering 3100 horsepower (Fig. 2-22).

Having lost out on their bid to recapture the Schneider Trophy, the Italians set their sights on Lt. Stainforth's speed record, and on June 2, 1933, Warrant Officer Francesco Agello piloted the MC-72 floatplane to a new World Speed Record of 440.67 miles per hour.

The racing landplanes of that same year were over 100 miles per hour slower. Although this speed record was soon broken by the fast fighters that were being developed as a result of World War II, Agello's record has never been equalled by another seaplane.

WORLD WAR II AND BEYOND

We have seen how the development of the long-range, land-based bomber during World War II rendered the large flying boat obsolete, but the Navy hung onto its floatplanes for a while longer.

Ever since Glenn Curtiss' flight across San Diego Bay to the *U.S.S. Pennsylvania* in 1911, the Navy saw the potential of using airplanes as aerial observation platforms

Fig. 2-23. A formation of Vought OS2U Kingfishers, one of the most popular catapult-launched observation planes used by the United States Navy during World War II. The large rear-cockpit canopy was designed to afford the observer maximum visibility. (Official U.S. Navy Photograph. Courtesy of U.S. Navy)

Fig. 2-24. EDO built this handsome floatplane, the XOSE-1, during the closing days of World War II. Designed to be launched from shipboard catapults, the airplane was intended to use the new, inverted, V-12 Ranger engine. (Courtesy of the EDO Corporation)

for its surface ships. The recently perfected catapult would allow the planes to be launched from amidships, off the stern, or even from the tops of the gun turrets.

Launching an airplane was one thing; getting back again was something else. One of the Navy's first retrieval schemes called for the pilot to simply crash his airplane in the water, climb out, and wait for a lifeboat to come fetch him back to his ship. While easy enough to execute, this method proved to be rather expensive, since a new airplane had to be purchased after each flight. The obvious solution was to use a seaplane of some sort, and do what Glenn Curtiss had done. After landing on the water next to the ship, the airplane could be hoisted back aboard with a crane and used again. After much experimentation, this method proved successful, and catapult-launched floatplanes became standard equipment on all the Navy's large surface ships until the close of World War II.

The retrieval of the floatplane was an interesting process. Prior to the airplane's arrival, a landing mat would be rigged from a long pole extended out from the ship's side and parallel to the water. The ship would then make a sweeping turn to an upwind heading, which flattened out the waves and created a stretch of smooth water for the pilot to land on. After touchdown, the floatplane was taxied up over the landing mat and the power cut. This caused the airplane to settle onto the mat, which was constructed in such a way as to snag the float keel at the step. The plane was then pulled along by the landing mat at the same speed as the ship, and the hook on the ship's crane could be attached to the lifting fixture on the floatplane.

Lifting the plane aboard was not always an easy task, especially if the ship was rolling in a heavy swell. Most of the battleships and cruisers designed during World War II had their catapults mounted on the stern, so when the planes returned, they simply landed in the ship's wake and taxied up under the fantail, were an aft-mounted crane picked them up.

Almost all of the floatplanes used by the U.S. Navy were of the single float design, and they had to be extremely rugged to withstand the tremendous pounding received during open-ocean operations. One of the most popular of the ship-launched floatplanes was the Vought OS2U Kingfisher (Fig. 2-23). This versatile reconnaissance plane earned the affection of many a downed airman who was plucked from the ocean by the two-man crew of one of these sturdy seaplanes.

One of the best-looking catapult-launched floatplanes ever designed came from the drawing boards at EDO during the closing days of World War II. The airplane, called the XOSE-1, used the new air-cooled, inverted V-12 Ranger V-770 engine. Only the prototype of this single-float scout-observation plane was built, and the project was cancelled at the end of the war (Fig. 2-24A).

The Japanese produced a handsome floatplane version of the famous Mitsubishi A6M "zero-sen," called the Nakajima A6M2-N. Codenamed "Rufe" by the Allies, the single-float airplane was designed to defend remote island outposts that didn't have landing strips.

As the United States carried the war deeper into the Western Pacific, the Navy decided it needed a similar float-equipped fighter. Plans were made to fit 100 Grumman F4F Wildcat fighters with twin EDO floats, but the program was cancelled when it was found that the Navy's Sea Bee construction crews could build airstrips as fast as the Marines could secure a beachhead. Only two of the planes, nicknamed "Wild Catfish," were ever built.

We've looked at just a few of the historical highlights of the floatplane's development. There's much more to the story, and some of the books on the subject that I've found particularly interesting are listed in the Appendix. The modern floatplane has a rich and colorful heritage, and as you taxi away from the dock, listen carefully. You can almost hear the clatter of Henri Fabre's little rotary engine, the echoing thunder of a Schneider racer, or the hissing boom of a steam catapult as it flings a rugged, single-float observation plane into the sky.

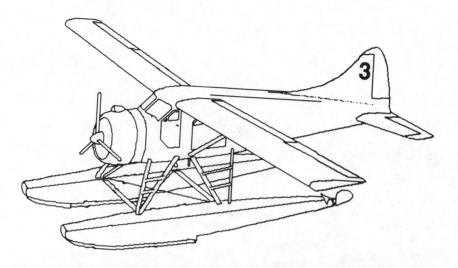

The Modern Floatplane

T HE VOUGHT KINGFISHER AND THE CURTISS SEA-
hawk of World War II marked the end of an era.
They were the last catapult-launched floatplanes to be
produced for the U.S. Navy, and they were the last production airplanes to be designed exclusively as
floatplanes. Since the close of World War II, virtually all
floatplanes have been landplane designs adapted for use
on floats.

One exception was the Noorduyn Norseman,
nicknamed the "Thunderchicken" by the pilots who flew
it (Fig. 3-1). Originally designed in 1935 to meet the rugged demands of Canadian bush flying, its production was
continued after the war by Canadian Car and Foundry.
The Norseman was designed primarily for use on floats
or skis, but wheels were necessary to bridge the period
between winter's solid ice and the open water of summer. The landing gear designed for the "Thunderchicken" had the look of an afterthought about it, and
the massive, single-engined plane looked rather comical,
squatting on its tiny wheels.

CURRENT FLOATPLANE MODELS

Today's floatplane is generally a high-wing, single-engine
landplane fitted with twin floats. The single-float configuration favored by the U.S. Navy has virtually disappeared. Landplanes that have become popular as
floatplane conversions include the Cessna 150, 172, 180,
185, and 206; the Champion Citabria and Scout; the de
Havilland Beaver, Otter, and Twin Otter; the Helio
Courier; the Maule M-5, 6, and 7; the Pilatus Porter; the
Piper Super Cub; and the Taylorcraft.

Some of the higher-powered models in the Piper Cherokee line of low-wing airplanes are certified for floats,
but their popularity is limited because of the difficulties
imposed by the low wing when docking and loading the
airplane (Fig. 3-2). In addition to the turboprop de
Havilland Twin Otter, twin-engined landplanes occasionally found on floats include the venerable Beechcraft
Model 18 "Twin Beech,", and a modified Piper Aztec
called the "Nomad" (Fig. 3-3).

ULTRALIGHTS

At the other end of the scale, floats are available for many
of the ultralight airplanes which are becoming so popular
today (Fig. 3-4). Ultralights offer a relatively inexpensive
way to get into the air, and while a pilot's license is cur-

Fig. 3-1. A rare shot of a Noorduyn Norseman "Thunderchicken" in United States military markings. (Courtesy of the EDO Corporation)

Fig. 3-2. Some low-wing airplanes can be mounted on floats, like this Piper Cherokee Six, but the low wing makes for difficult docking and loading. The plane pictured here has been fitted with EDO Model 3430 floats. (Courtesy of the EDO Corporation)

Fig. 3-3. A Piper Aztec is modified by Huntsville Air Service, mounted on a pair of EDO Model 4930 floats. (Courtesy of the EDO Corporation)

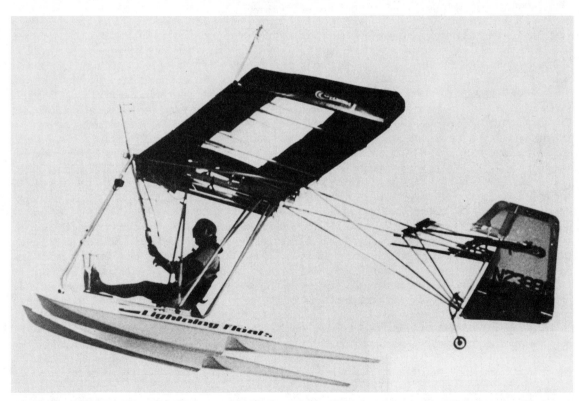

Fig. 3-4. One of the many ultralights that can be mounted on floats. While its behavior on floats is similar to conventional airplanes, the ultralight's small size and light weight restrict it to use on relatively calm water and in light winds. (Courtesy of Lightning Floats)

rently not required, the FAA has set some basic design parameters for the little planes. Part 103 of the Federal Aviation Regulations limits the empty weight of an ultralight to no more than 254 pounds. Top speed is limited to 55 knots, and no more than 5 gallons of fuel may be carried on board. A set of ultralight floats may not weight more than 60 pounds—or 30 pounds per float—bringing the maximum allowable empty weight of an ultralight floatplane to 314 pounds.

Ultralight floats are available in both aluminum and fiberglass, and as their popularity increases, we may see a trend toward the new, lightweight composite materials like graphite and Kevlar.

The flying characteristics of an ultralight are considerably different from those of a conventional airplane, and since each ultralight model is unique, I don't want to go into a long discussion about individual handling and control quirks. Suffice it to say that most of them have a completely different "feel" in comparison to general aviation airplanes, and no one, including experienced pilots, should attempt to fly an ultralight without receiving some instruction first. There are similarities, however, between the operation of a float-equipped ultralight and a conventional floatplane; so most of the techniques and procedures described in this book apply equally to both types of airplanes.

Size is an ultralight floatplane's greatest limitation. Water conditions that would merely bounce a Piper Super Cub around a little bit could easily overstress an ultralight. Ultralight floats are, however, surprisingly strong for their size, and many of them are filled with foam, making them virtually unsinkable. With a gross weight of only 500 pounds or so, the airplane is very susceptible to wind, and while it may be able to survive the rough water conditions brought on by a strong breeze, a sudden gust could quickly put an ultralight on its back. If you're planning to fly a float-equipped ultralight, pay special attention to the sections of this book that describe the wind's effects on a floatplane and how to deal with them. If you should encounter strong winds and rough water while flying an ultralight, it is essential that you follow the proper procedures to avoid flipping the plane.

If operations are restricted to relatively calm water in light or no-wind conditions, float-equipped ultralights are a lot of fun. In many ways they capture the true feeling of water flying far better than the closed-cockpit, multi-instrumented floatplanes most of us are used to. Sitting exposed to the elements, it's easy to imagine yourself as Henri Fabre or Glenn Curtiss taxiing a prototype floatplane out for its first flight.

FLOAT INSTALLATION

Converting a landplane to floats is a little more involved than simply removing one undercarriage and bolting on another. Before the floats can be installed, there are several modifications that must be made to the airplane itself. The number and type of modifications required varies among models.

Some airplanes are designed from the outset to accommodate floats. The de Havilland Beaver, for example, was designed and built to be used on wheels, floats, or skis, and most of the mounting hardware required by these systems was built into each airplane on the assembly line. A Cessna 206, on the other hand, may or may not spend part of its life on floats, and if the airplane is to be used on wheels only, there's no point in wasting fuel and useful load by dragging around a bunch of unused attachment hardware.

There is also the matter of expense. The modifications required to provide attach points for the floats, add strength to the fuselage, and protect the airplane from corrosion are collectively referred to as *float kits* by most manufacturers, and *float kits* are not cheap. Today's airplanes are expensive enough as it is, so why spend money for equipment that's not going to be used?

Actually, there are occasions when it might be wise to add the expense of a float kit to a new airplane, even though the owner may never intend to install floats. If the landplane being ordered is also popular as a floatplane, a factory-installed float kit will considerably increase the airplane's resale value. The Cessna 185, for example, is very popular among commercial floatplane operators; so it's not uncommon to find used 185s with factory-installed float kits which have never been attached to a pair of floats.

A good example of the modifications required to prepare a landplane for a life on the water is the float kit offered by Cessna for the Model 206 Stationair (Fig. 3-5).

First, additional fuselage hardware is added to provide attach points for the float struts. This attachment hardware must be strong enough, and mounted securely enough, to transmit the entire weight of the airplane to the float structure.

A V-brace is installed inside the cabin, between the upper corners of the windshield and the cowl deck, adding torsional stiffness to the fuselage.

Because the nosewheel will not be needed, removable panels are installed over the nosegear opening. The stall sensor is relocated so it will not be affected by turbulent air coming off the floats, and the left-hand forward-fuselage static source is deleted to ensure proper airspeed

Fig. 3-5. The Cessna 206 is a popular workhorse, and it is made even more versatile when mounted on floats. Both straight and amphibious floats are available for the 206, and the spacious cabin has room for six adults or a lot of bulky freight. This one has been fitted with EDO Model 3430 floats. (Courtesy of the EDO Corporation)

system calibration.

To improve directional stability, the standard vertical tail is replaced by one which has been redesigned to accommodate a larger rudder, and a ventral fin is installed below the tailcone. The new tail necessitates the use of a different tail "stinger," as well as a redesigned flashing beacon installation. The position of the ventral fin requires replacement of the single tail tie-down ring with a dual ring assembly.

A new nose cap with revised engine baffling is fitted, and special cowl flaps, cowl flap side extensions and cowl flap controls are installed to provide proper engine cooling.

Hoisting rings are attached to the top of the wing center section, and the wing flap limit switch is adjusted to restrict the maximum flap extension to 30 degrees. The flaps on the 206 normally have a maximum extension of 40 degrees.

The elevator trim tab rigging is changed to increase the maximum down-travel, and the rudder-trim bungee is replaced by a bungee with a lighter spring. The airframe receives a lot of additional corrosion protection, especially on the inner surface of the fuselage, and stainless steel control cables are used throughout the plane. Finally, to aid in fueling the floatplane, steps and assist handles are mounted on the forward fuselage, and steps are mounted on the wing struts.

Floatplanes are subjected to a lot of pounding, and on some models, the float kit includes additional strengthening of the engine mount attach points.

Many float kits, particularly those for planes that use fixed-pitch propellers, include a special seaplane prop. In order to overcome the tremendous drag created by moving a float through, and over, the water, a floatplane needs every bit of horsepower it can get. Horsepower is a function of rpm; so these special "water props" are longer and flatter-pitched to let the engine spool up to its maximum allowable rpm, thus developing maximum horsepower during the takeoff run. This is why a floatplane makes so much noise when it takes off: it's not the engine you're hearing, but the howl of that long, flat prop as the blade tips approach the speed of sound. Although it allows the engine to develop maximum horsepower, a fixed-pitch seaplane propeller does not take as big a "bite" of air in cruise as does a cruise prop; so for a given power setting, a seaplane prop won't pull an airplane along as fast, or as far, as a cruise prop.

A good example of the effect a propeller can have on a floatplane's performance is the experience the British had in 1931 with their entry in that year's Schneider Tro-

phy race. The airplane was the Supermarine S-6B which, as we learned in the previous chapter, was a further refinement of the 1929 race winner, the Supermarine S-6. The S-6 had been fitted with a Rolls-Royce V-12 engine which developed 1900 horsepower and swung a 9 1/2-foot propeller. For the 1931 race, Rolls-Royce managed to get 2350 horsepower out of its big V-12, and it was fitted with a new, shorter, coarser-pitched propeller, making the airplane potentially capable of over 400 miles per hour. When Wing Commander A.H. Orlebar took the S-6B out for its first test flight, however, the plane wouldn't lift off the water, but instead went plowing around in circles. The engine ran beautifully, but the airplane simply refused to take off. During the frantic testing which followed, someone suggested they try fitting the S-6B with one of the old, longer propellers from an S-6. This was done, and the S-6Bs takeoff and water-handling problems disappeared.

Despite the engine's 2350 horsepower, the new, short, coarse-pitched "cruise" prop couldn't develop enough power to overcome the water's drag on the floats. The propeller would have worked beautifully once the floatplane was in the air, but it wasn't flat enough to power the plane off the water. The Schneider Trophy racers all used fixed-pitch propellers, and a constant-speed, or at least a variable-pitched, propeller would have solved a lot of problems, as they do today.

A plane manufactured without a float kit can have the necessary modifications installed at a later date, but since the airplane must be partially disassembled before the work can be done, the cost will probably exceed that of a factory-installed kit. If there's a chance the airplane will be used on floats sometime in the future, or if the installation of a float kit will enhance the plane's resale value, it's probably worth having the manufacturer install the kit on the assembly line.

THE FLOAT SYSTEM

The float kit prepares an airplane to receive a float system, which is composed of two basic groups: the attachment hardware, and the floats themselves (Fig. 3-6).

The Attachment Hardware

Each float is positioned properly underneath the airplane with forward and aft vertical struts which connect the float to the fuselage. A diagonal strut, installed between the top of one vertical strut and the bottom of the other one, provides fore and aft stiffness. The de Havilland Beaver uses twin V-struts to attach each float to the fuse-

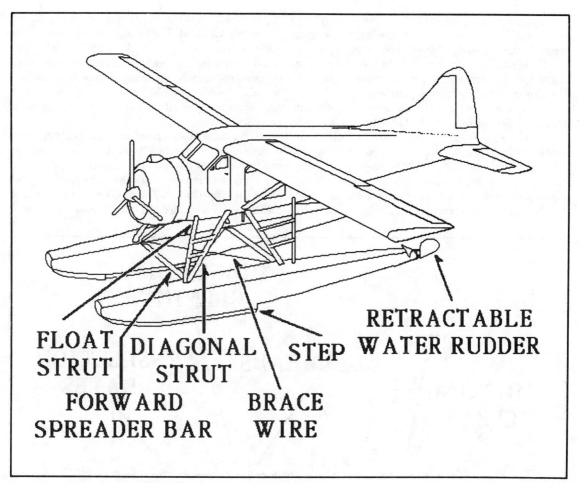

FLOAT STRUT   DIAGONAL STRUT   STEP   RETRACTABLE WATER RUDDER

FORWARD SPREADER BAR   BRACE WIRE

Fig. 3-6. A typical floatplane and the components of its float system.

lage. There are other strut arrangements as well, but in each case the purpose is the same; proper positioning of the float, and fore and aft stiffness.

The floats are held the correct distance from each other by the front and rear spreader bars. Both the struts and the spreader bars are streamlined in cross section, and one manufacturer even gains a little lift by giving its spreader bars an airfoil shape.

Additional stiffness is provided by the bracing wires, which may run diagonally between the left and right vertical struts or the front and rear spreader bars. Although they are called *wires,* they are usually streamlined, stainless steel rods with tension adjustments at each end. Their purpose is to further stiffen the float system and distribute the stress encountered during water operations among the various attachment components.

The Floats

The other major components of a float system are, of course, the floats themselves (Fig. 3-7). There are several companies manufacturing them today, and they are available in both aluminum and fiberglass. The model number of a float usually indicates its water displacement in pounds. Float sizes range from the 16-foot Capre Model 1500 for the Piper J-3 Cub, to the Canadian Aircraft Products Model 12000, a 31-foot, 6-inch monster for the de Havilland DHC-6 Twin Otter.

The de Havilland Beaver pictured throughout this book is mounted on EDO 4930 floats, each one of which displaces 4930 pounds of water. The two floats together have a total displacement of 9860 pounds, which seems a little like overkill when you consider that the gross weight of a Beaver is only 5090 pounds. However, the floats are required by law to have a combined buoyancy of at least 180 percent of the airplane's gross weight, which in the case of the Beaver comes to 9162 pounds.

Each individual float is required to have at least four watertight compartments and must continue to support the airplane with any two compartments flooded.

Most floats have a V-shaped bottom to help cut through the waves, soften the impact of landing, and provide some degree of spray control. An exception to this configuration is the inverted V-bottom used on the fiberglass floats manufactured by the Fiberfloat Corporation. The theory behind the reverse-V shape is that the air being scooped into the "tunnel" underneath each float will help lift the plane onto the step faster, assisted by the upward force of the spray deflected into the tunnel.

Spray Control. Float designers try very hard to minimize the amount of spray thrown off by their floats. Besides impairing the pilot's vision and thoroughly soaking down the airplane, spray can be very damaging to a propeller. Its effect on a high-revving prop is very much like shot-peening, and it can cause serious pitting on the propeller's leading edge.

Spray is not really a problem when the floatplane is either moving very slowly through the water or very rapidly over it. At low speeds in smooth water there isn't any spray, and at high speeds the spray is thrown well aft of the propeller arc. The problem occurs just after takeoff power is applied. As the floatplane accelerates,

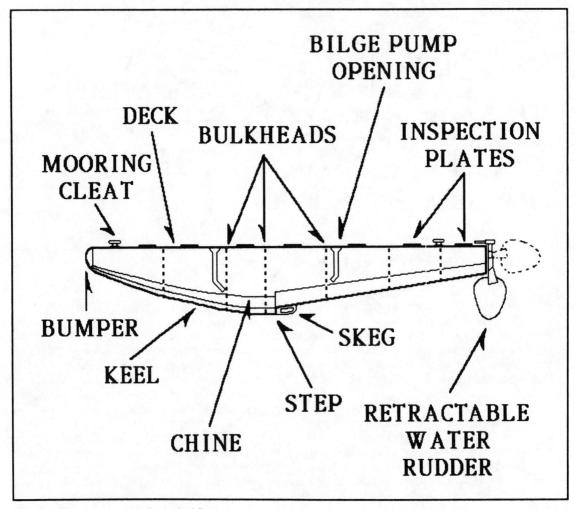

Fig. 3-7. The components of a typical float.

the floats begin to mush through the water prior to achieving a planing attitude. A lot of spray is generated at this point, and because of the floatplane's low forward speed, the spray remains in the general vicinity of the propeller.

There are several ways to control this spray. One is to contour the bottom of the float in such a way as to deflect the spray out to the side. This is accomplished by designing the float with a flared V-bottom and hard chines where the bottom meets the sides of the float. An alternative is the inverted-V bottom used by Fiberfloat, which deflects much of the spray into the tunnel under the float.

Another spray control device is the spray rail, attached to the forward section of the float chines (Fig. 3-8). These metal strips act as extensions of the chines, and deflect the spray out and down. The disadvantage of spray rails is that, like any additional surface, they create aerodynamic drag. For this reason, and to prevent them from snagging and bending on docks, most operators install spray rails on the inboard sides of the floats only, where they are quite effective in keeping spray away from the propeller.

The Water Rudders. At the aft end of each float is a water rudder which is used to steer the floatplane at low speeds on the surface. The water rudders are linked by cables to the floatplane's vertical air rudder and are controlled by the rudder pedals in the cockpit. Before takeoff, and while sailing or beaching the floatplane, the water rudders must be pulled up, so an additional set of cables connects each rudder to a retraction handle on the floor of the cockpit (Fig. 3-9). The water rudders are held down by their own weight, and in the case of larger floatplanes like the Beaver, a healthy tub on the retraction handle is necessary to lift the heavy rudders clear of the water.

Unlike conventional landing gear, the water rudders do not lock down when they are lowered. Because the only thing keeping them down is their own weight, the rudders are free to "kick up," like an outboard motor, if they hit the bottom or an underwater obstacle (Fig. 3-10).

It is very important that the water rudders be retracted before takeoff. Water rudders that are left down

Fig. 3-8. A spray rail as fitted to an EDO Model 4930 float on a de Havilland Beaver.

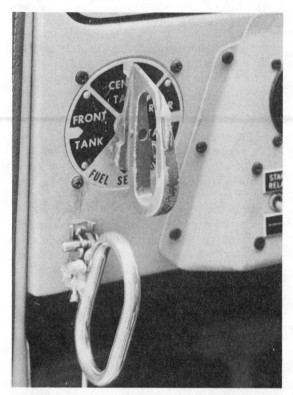

Fig. 3-9. The water rudder retraction handle on a de Havilland Beaver. The handle is attached to the water rudders by the line shown extending toward the floor of the cabin. When the handle is in its bracket, as shown here, the water rudders are up. Lifting the handle out of its bracket and lowering it to the floor lowers the rudders.

during takeoff could cause the airplane to veer off to one side and possibly overturn. Because the rudders don't lock down, they will begin to bang up and down as the floatplane's speed across the water increases. This banging can damage the rudders and weaken the stern of the float, causing the seams to open up and leaks to develop.

Getting the Water Out. Even though a float is divided into four or more watertight compartments, this does not ensure that it will remain dry on the inside. There are many ways that water can leak into the float compartments. Rainwater and spray can seep in around the access and inspection plates; the seams in the float can begin to work open with use, and moist air can condense on the inside of the float.

The resulting water trapped in the float must be removed before each flight, and the float manufacturers have provided a couple of ways to accomplish this. The deck covering each watertight compartment contains one

or more access hatches. The covers over these hatches can be removed, allowing any water present to be swabbed out with a large sponge. This method works best on small floats; there is difficulty in reaching the bottom of a large float through the access hatches.

The most efficient way to remove water from the compartments of larger floats is with a bilge pump. These lightweight hand pumps can be inserted through an open access hatch or applied to the deck openings of special bilge pump down-tubes. The down-tubes extend from the deck to the bilge of each watertight compartment, and act as bilge pump extensions. The end of the pump is inserted into the recessed down-tube fitting in the deck of the float. When the pump is activated, any water present in that compartment is sucked up the down-tube into the pump and thrown overboard (Fig. 3-11).

Float Accessories. The bow of each float is usually in the form of a rubber bumper to absorb shock if the airplane contacts a dock nose-first. Mooring cleats are mounted fore and aft on the deck of each float, and many floats have provisions for carrying a paddle on the inboard side (Fig. 3-12). A nonskid surface is often applied to the float decks for better footing.

Some manufacturers use the center watertight compartment for additional baggage space and offer large, hinged hatch covers for easy loading and unloading. EDO even offers a 6-gallon gas can that fits into the center compartment of some of its float models.

These float compartments can come in very handy. During the production of a marketing film for the Boeing Company, I was faced with the necessity of shooting both underwater and aerial sequences, with very little time to do either.

The solution to my problem came in the form of a de Havilland Beaver. The bulky scuba tank, along with wetsuits, flippers, masks, and towels fit nicely in the port float compartment, leaving the cabin free for cameras, accessory cases, and the film crew. We flew to our first location in Puget Sound's San Juan Islands, tied a diving flag to the propeller, and shot the underwater sequence, using the Beaver as a diving barge. We then stowed all the scuba equipment back in the float compartment, removed one of the main doors, stashed it in the back of the cabin, and proceeded to film the aerial sequences. A 2-day job was reduced to 4 hours using the floatplane.

Most floatplanes have mooring lines permanently attached to each float. They are usually 6 to 8 feet long, and in flight they lie quietly on top of the floats; there's no tendency for them to wave about in the breeze. Many operators also fasten 3-or 4-foot long grab-lines to the end

Fig. 3-10. The water rudder on an EDO Model 4930 float shown in the retracted position (top), and the lowered position (bottom). The cable attached to the top of the rudder blade on each float goes to a yoke under the fuselage from which a single line runs to the retraction handle in the cockpit.

Fig. 3-11. Pumping the floats on a Beaver. The most efficient way to remove water from the float compartments is with a manual bilge pump. The water is discharged on the up-stroke of the pump. Make sure you aim the opening at the top of the pump away from yourself and your passengers.

of each wing. These lines are used to pull the floatplane up to a dock, or as handholds while turning the airplane around. In flight, they stream back against the lower side of the wing.

HOW FLOATS WORK

The floats support the airplane while it's on the water. This is obvious enough, but actually this support is rendered in two ways: water displacement and hydrodynamic pressure.

When the floatplane is at rest on the water or moving slowly through it, the floats act like two boats, and support the airplane's weight by displacing an equal weight of water. Put another way, if the amount of water displaced by the two floats could be weighed, it would be found to weigh exactly as much as the airplane. As weight is put into the plane in the form of passengers or

50

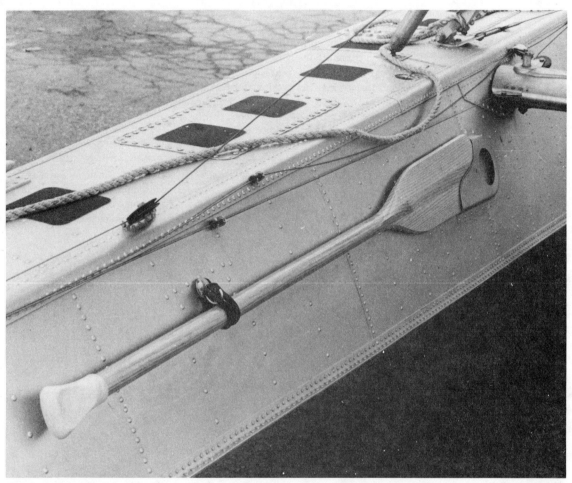

Fig. 3-12. A paddle can come in very handy, and it should be easy to reach in a hurry. Many floats are equipped with exterior paddle brackets like this one, which is mounted on an EDO Model 4930 float.

cargo, the floats will sink lower into the water because they have to displace an additional pound of water for every pound of weight added to the airplane.

Support by water displacement works fine up to a point. The problem occurs when you try to accelerate the floats to a higher speed through the water. The water exerts a tremendous amount of drag on the partly submerged floats, and it's simply not possible to accelerate beyond a certain speed, called *hull speed*. Because the hull speed of an aircraft float is much slower than the speed required for flight, a method had to be found of reducing the hydrodynamic drag on the floats while still allowing them to support the airplane on the water until the plane could become airborne.

The answer was to design the floats to plane, or skim,

across the surface of the water when a certain speed was achieved. Once the floats were riding on *top* of the water instead of driving *through* it, the hydrodynamic drag would be considerably reduced, and the airplane could accelerate to liftoff speed.

When the plane is at rest or is taxiing slowly, the entire length of each float is used to support the airplane by water displacement. As power is added and the floatplane accelerates, however, the hydrodynamic pressure on the bottom of the floats increases, lifting them up until they are planing across the surface of the water.

As we saw in the last chapter, some of the early floats built by Glenn Curtiss refused to lift from the water, even though they were driven fast enough to achieve a planing attitude. Their long, flat bottoms, necessary to support the floatplane at rest, were unable to break free of the water's suction. The solution to this problem was the single-step hydroplane bottom, which is the configuration used on all floats today. The step, or break, in the bottom of each float allows air to flow in under the afterbody, eliminating the suction problem that so plagued Curtiss. As the speed across the water increases, the hydrodynamic pressure on the bottom of each float also increases, forcing them to ride higher and higher. Eventually, the only wetted surface of each float is that portion of the bottom just ahead of the step. This small surface is all that's necessary to support the weight of the floatplane, and hydrodynamic drag is drastically reduced.

Also, don't forget that the wing starts developing lift as the airplane accelerates. As far as the floats are concerned, the plane weighs less and less as the takeoff run progresses, and requires less and less support from the floats. Eventually the wing's lift is equal to the weight of the floatplane, and there is nothing left for the floats to support. At this point, the airplane can be taken off the water completely.

This sequence of weight transfer occurs in reverse order when the floatplane lands. The plane first touches down and runs along on the step for a short distance before settling back into the displacement mode of support.

Before we discuss the specific techniques for takeoffs, landings, and everything else in between, however, let's set the stage by examining the most important floatplane technique you'll ever practice: the technique of floatplane safety.

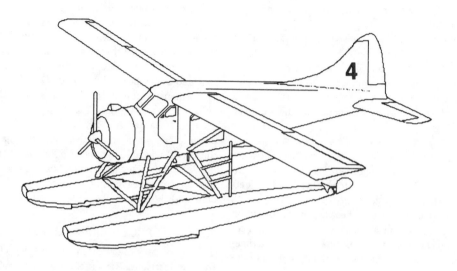

Floatplane Safety

T HE PILOT OF THE SIX-PLACE FLOATPLANE WAS tired after his long cross-country flight and was in a hurry to land. He was behind a larger floatplane as he began his final approach toward shore. Witnesses said later he appeared to be following the first airplane too closely and was caught by wake turbulence just before he touched down. Others thought the pilot felt he was going to overshoot the landing area and tried to force the plane onto the water too soon. Still others thought he may have hit a boat wake. Whatever the cause, the result was disastrous. Digging one float into the water, the plane tipped up on one wing and cartwheeled over onto its back. Thanks to the quick action of nearby boaters, the occupants were saved from drowning as the overturned plane settled into the mud at the bottom of the lake. There were no injuries.

The pilot of the four-place floatplane began his pretakeoff engine runup while taxiing crosswind in gusty conditions. With the airplane mushing through the choppy water under partial power in an unstable, nose-high attitude, a sudden gust lifted the upwind wing and tipped the plane onto its side. There were no injuries.

The pilot of the small, two-place floatplane was taxiing downwind on a blustery day prior to taking off. When the strong tailwind started to weathercock the plane around, the pilot attempted to "catch it" with a burst of power and opposite rudder. The added power dug in the downwind float, and the plane turned over. There were no injuries.

These three accidents had two things in common. In each case, there were no injuries, which says something about the safety of floatplanes, and, in each case, poor judgment on the part of the pilot was the direct cause of the accident.

RULE ONE: EXERCISE PROPER JUDGMENT

Poor judgment is probably the single greatest cause of aviation accidents. Whether on the part of a pilot, an air traffic controller, or a mechanic, the results of poor judgment are often irreversible. Floatplanes are not dangerous. In fact, in many ways they are much safer than their wheeled counterparts, but because of their unique and constantly changing environment, proper judgment is absolutely essential to floatplane safety.

As I noted earlier, the pilot of a floatplane is pretty much of his own. At least landplane pilots have their landing sites defined for them. Not only do floatplane

53

pilots have to choose their own landing sites for each landing, but they also have to determine if they're safe. Are there any floating logs or deadheads lurking just beneath the surface? Is the water too shallow? Too rough? What about boat traffic?

Then there's the wind. Which way is it blowing? How hard? Is it gusty? Will you be able to taxi to the dock, or will you have to sail the plane in backwards?

If all this sounds too complicated to master, relax. The techniques for obtaining the answers to all these questions are easily learned. The important thing is what you do with the information once you've obtained it. If you think the water looks too shallow, should you attempt a landing anyway? The obvious answer is no, but what if that's where your passengers are paying you to take them? Or maybe the weather is deteriorating, or it's getting dark. What do you do then?

All you can do is use your best judgment, based on the pertinent facts of the situation, your own experience, and what you have been taught. If this sounds like a time-consuming procedure, it can be—which brings us to the next floatplane safety rule.

RULE TWO: DON'T ALLOW YOURSELF TO BE RUSHED INTO MAKING A DECISION

There's nothing wrong with overflying a landing site several times until you're sure you can land safely. There are a lot of things to look for, especially if you're unfamiliar with the area. You don't want to be in such a hurry that you overlook a power line, or a floating log, or some rocks just below the surface. Take your time. At least you won't have a tower controller constantly squawking orders at you on the radio.

RULE THREE: THINK THROUGH THE CONSEQUENCES OF EACH ACTION

This is a good rule to follow for any type of flying, but it is particularly applicable to flying floats. For example, while floatplanes come to a stop quickly, they can take a long time to become airborne. If you find a small lake you'd like to visit, make sure you will be able to take off again *before* you land. You don't want to end up having your plane lifted off the lake by a helicopter. In Chapter 19, we'll look at a method of determining the length of a lake while flying over it.

If you operate a floatplane in coastal waters, don't forget the tide (Fig. 4-1). I know of at least one pilot who beached his airplane and left it, only to find several hundred yards of mud between the plane and the nearest wa-

ter when he returned. The tide had gone out, and my friend was faced with a 6-hour wait for its return. At least he still had his airplane, which he probably wouldn't have had if he had beached it during low tide.

Even the simplest of maneuvers can have dire consequences if you aren't alert. I once tied a Cessna 172 floatplane to a dock that was several feet higher than the docks I normally used. When it was time to leave, I followed the standard procedure of turning the airplane out 90 degrees from the dock. Just as I was about to step onto the rear of the left float and walk forward to the cockpit, I realized that my weight would force the tail of the plane down and slam it onto the planking. Fortunately, I was able to move the floatplane to the end of the dock and depart from there, but had I not anticipated the consequences of my original plan, I could have damaged the tail.

RULE FOUR: PLAN AHEAD

This is probably the most important rule to follow when flying a floatplane. Remember, you're driving a machine that has no brakes, no reverse, and somewhat vague steering. As soon as you untie it, it's at the mercy of the wind. You won't get into trouble, however, if you plan each course of action well in advance.

I have a friend who spends a lot of his time flying floatplanes up and down the Inside Passage along the coasts of British Columbia and Alaska. While describing the constantly changing weather and water conditions with which he has to contend during each trip, he remarked that no matter what the forecast was, he always prepared for the worst. "That way," he said, "I'm never surprised."

RULE FIVE: WHEN IN DOUBT, DON'T

If you *think* you saw a log under the surface, don't land there. If the water *might* be a little too shallow, stay out of it. If it *looks* like the beach could be too rocky, stay off of it. If you *think* that sailboat might tack back across your path, stay away from it. If you're *not sure* that the water is smooth enough for your floatplane, land somewhere else. If you have *doubts* about the weather, don't go.

RULE SIX: KNOW YOUR OWN LIMITATIONS

It's vitally important that you be constantly aware of your own limitations. Don't take on anything you're not sure you can handle. For example, floatplanes are regularly landed on snow and ice by experienced pilots. They know

Fig. 4-1. A Cessna 172 tailed into a beach on the Hood Canal in Washington's Puget Sound. While this scene looks innocent enough, the tide was ebbing rapidly, and the plane had to be moved every 15 minutes to keep it from becoming stranded.

their airplanes' performance and are experts at picking just the right surface conditions that will safely allow such operations. The slightest miscalculation can destroy the floatplane, to say nothing of endangering the lives of the occupants, yet the procedure looks surprisingly easy. Actually, it is. The hard part is deciding when and where to make the landing, and deciding in your own mind whether or not the risks are too great. These are decisions that can only be based on experience—a lot of experience—and it cannot be acquired from a book or a few "hangar flying" sessions.

Another good example is docking a floatplane. It always looks so easy. You just slide up alongside the dock, step gracefully out, and gently pull the airplane to a stop. You'll soon find out there's much more to it than that. A smoothly executed docking is a combination of good planning, good timing, and good judgment, all of which take some time to acquire. My initial floatplane instruc-

tion took place in airplanes that were operated from a ramp. Docking was simple. You just hit the ramp head on, slid up it a short ways, and stopped. When I started flying at a facility that used docks instead of ramps, it took a couple of sessions with an instructor before I felt competent enough to try docking the floatplane myself, and even then I had some nervous moments. I still do.

If you already know how to fly, you know enough not to take on weather conditions that are beyond your abilities. The aviation publications are full of stories every month about people who tried unsuccessfully to push the weather. Floatplanes, like cars, bicycles, skis, scuba equipment, and landplanes, can get you into trouble only if you take on something you can't handle. Build your experience gradually and safely. Above all, don't fall into the trap of thinking that flying with an instructor after you've obtained your rating is demeaning, or shows incompetence on your part. I, for one, would not want to

55

take on the potential dangers of landing on rivers or small, high, mountain lakes without the benefit of some instruction from a pilot experienced in these advanced techniques.

In summary, floatplane safety is really just another term for plain, ordinary, common sense. While it may seem that the constantly changing wind and water conditions throw an almost insurmountable bunch of variables at you, the challenge of successfully coping with these variables is what makes flying floats so rewarding. To prepare you to meet this challenge safely, a thorough course of flight instruction is absolutely essential.

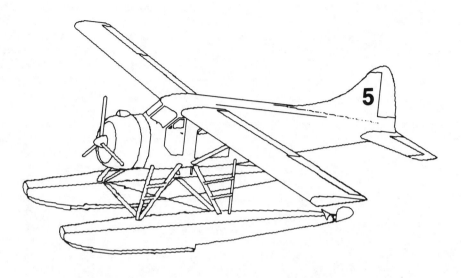

Floatplane Instruction

L ET'S ASSUME YOU'VE DECIDED TO GIVE FLOAT FLY- ing a try. Great! Now, how do you go about doing it? Obviously, you'll have to get some flight instruction, and the question that immediately comes to mind is, "How much flight instruction?"

There is no minimum-hour requirement specified by the FAA if you are simply adding a seaplane rating to your existing pilot's certificate. If, however, you plan to receive your primary flight instruction in a floatplane, you'll have to meet the same requirements the FAA has defined for all student pilots, including a written exam and a flight test. A written exam is not required if you are merely adding a seaplane rating to your existing pilot's certificate, but you will have to pass a flight test designed to demonstrate your floatplane proficiency.

On the average, it should take 10 to 12 hours of in- struction to receive a single-engine sea rating at a good flight school. Some places claim to be able to qualify pilots for the rating in less than half that time, but I would ques- tion the quality of their instruction, even though it represents a considerable monetary savings. Ten to 12 hours is little enough time as it is, and you have a lot to learn.

A thorough floatplane course should cover the follow- ing procedures and techniques:

☐ Preflight Inspection. While the basic preflight in- spection techniques are the same for both land- planes and floatplanes, floatplanes have additional systems that must be checked and some specialized equipment that must be on board to ensure the safety of each flight.

☐ Boarding and Starting. As soon as a floatplane is untied from its dock, it's at the mercy of the wind and the current. It's important that you learn the quickest way to get in and get going so your plane won't drift into trouble.

☐ Low-Speed Taxiing. Directional control is by means of the water rudders, and you will begin to develop the judgment necessary to maneuver your plane in tight quarters around docks and boats.

☐ Engine Runup and Systems Checks. Like the pre- flight inspection, these procedures are basically the same for both landplanes and floatplanes, but since you'll be moving while you do them, you'll have to learn to keep an eye on where you're going.

- ☐ Takeoff. You'll learn to control a floatplane during the three phases of a takeoff run; the displacement phase, the plowing, or "hump" phase, and the planing phase. The planing phase is also known as being *on the step*.
- ☐ Airwork. You'll get used to your floatplane's slower climbing and cruise speeds, and you'll learn that you need to pay a little more attention to your turn coordination when you're flying a floatplane.
- ☐ Landing. There are techniques for determining wind direction, judging water conditions, and choosing a landing site, which you'll learn as you practice landings.
- ☐ The Step Taxi. The step taxi is an efficient way to cover distance quickly while on the water, but it takes practice to develop the correct "feel" for this manuever.
- ☐ The Step Turn. You'll learn how to do this odd-feeling maneuver, and also when, and when not, to do it.
- ☐ Sailing. This is how you'll dock or beach your floatplane when the water rudders aren't powerful enough to overcome the plane's weathercocking tendency in a strong wind. You'll learn to use the air rudder, ailerons, flaps, engine, and even the cabin doors to control your direction and speed as you drift backwards toward the dock or beach.
- ☐ Docking. It takes practice to be able to judge the best approach to a dock, and you'll learn the specific techniques for stopping a floatplane alongside a dock and mooring it securely.
- ☐ Rough Water Takeoffs and Landings. Rough water can subject your floatplane to a pounding severe enough to over-stress or break the float-system components. You will learn to get your plane off the water as soon as possible during takeoff, and how to make the touchdown and run-out as gentle as possible during landing.
- ☐ Glassy-Water Landings. Landing on glassy water is potentially the most dangerous condition you'll face as a floatplane pilot. The problem is not the water's effect on your airplane, but its effect on your ability to judge altitude. There are specific procedures for making safe, glassy-water landings, and your instructor should make sure you get plenty of opportunities to practice them.

LEARNING TO FLY: WHEELS OR FLOATS?

There's nothing that says a person has to learn to fly in a landplane, and each year many people receive their Private Pilot certificates in floatplanes. I've had several friends who were interested in learning to fly ask me which I thought made the better primary trainer: a wheelplane or a floatplane. Unfortunately, there's no easy answer, and each class of airplane has its advantages and disadvantages. let's examine the advantages first.

Landplanes are more numerous and are generally less expensive to rent than floatplanes. Ground handling is easy to master in a landplane, and as a student, you won't have to contend with currents, winds, tides, boat wakes, and docking techniques. Probably one of the biggest advantages of learning to fly in a landplane is that you will become proficient with the radio. Most airports of any size require you to communicate with Ground Control and the Tower, and often with Approach and Departure Control as well. Some airports may even want you to contact Clearance Delivery before each flight. Talking on, and listening to, the radio will soon become second nature to you, and you'll also learn to scan constantly for other aircraft, a good habit to get into regardless of the type of airplane you may be flying.

If you learn to fly at a busy airport, you'll also get used to being around many different sizes and shapes of aircraft, all of which are traveling at different speeds. I learned to fly at Honolulu International Airport, and many times I would find myself landing wingtip to wingtip with a Boeing 747 which was touching down on the parallel runway. I'll never forget how important I felt when one busy day the tower barked out, "United heavy, follow the Cessna 150 to the ramp." All I could see in the 150's little rearview mirror was a huge nosewheel strut.

The point I'm trying to make is that as you become used to flying in congested airspace, you'll be able to concentrate on flying safely, and you won't let all the traffic flying in your vicinity intimidate you into making a mistake.

Learning to fly in a floatplane has its advantages, too, however. The fact that you do have to contend with currents, winds, tides, boat wakes, and docking techniques makes learning to fly all that much more interesting and challenging. You also won't spend a lot of your valuable flight time waiting in line to take off, or chasing vectors around the sky as the tower controller lands the six planes that are in front of you. In fact, one of the best things about learning to fly in a floatplane is the absence of control from the ground. You'll learn to think for yourself, and the success and safety of each flight will depend primarily on your good judgment. For this reason, floatplane pilots tend to be more self-sufficient than their landplane counterparts.

The flying characteristics of landplanes and floatplanes are very similar; so there's no real advantage of one over the other as far as your airwork will be concerned. They both turn, climb, descend, cruise, and stall for the same reasons and with the same flight controls. As we noted earlier, an airplane on floats doesn't have the climb and cruise performance enjoyed by the same plane on wheels, but this won't make much difference to a student pilot.

The decision as to whether or not you should receive your primary training in a floatplane is really dependent upon what you hope to get out of the flying experience. If you want to make use of the air traffic control system and fly on instruments, take long, fast cross-country trips, or get into aerobatics, you're better off receiving your initial flight instruction in a landplane. You can always add a seaplane rating to your pilot certificate later.

If, on the other hand, your idea of flying is to head for a remote lake for a weekend of camping, hiking, fishing, or hunting, surrounded by spectacular, unspoiled scenery, or perhaps to spend a day digging for clams on a distant, deserted beach, you should think about using a floatplane for your primary instruction.

THE INSURANCE PROBLEM

There is another difference between landplanes and floatplanes you should be aware of—insurance. Let's say you receive your Private certificate at a land-based flight school. After filling out and signing a form which says that you understand and will comply with the school's insurance requirements, you are free to rent its airplanes for your own use, be it a short, local flight or a 3-day cross-country trip. Any damage that may occur to the airplane will be covered, less the deductible amount you're responsible for, by the flight school's insurance policy. The insurance on an airplane itself is called *hull insurance,* and a hull insurance policy for a landplane is fairly reasonable in cost. Since the flight school can afford to insure its aircraft, it is willing to let you rent them for an extended period of time and take them on cross-country flights.

Unfortunately, this is not the case with floatplanes. Most flight schools carry *liability insurance,* which covers the occupants of their planes, but hull insurance is incredibly expensive, and many operators simply can't afford it. Consequently, their floatplanes are uninsured, which means they, the owners, have to pay the cost of repairing any damage, regardless of the cause of that damage. So while a floatplane flight school will teach you to fly, or give you the instruction necessary to obtain a sea-

plane rating, many of them will not rent you a floatplane for your own use after you obtain your certificate or rating because of the risk involved. Those flight schools that do rent out their floatplanes generally have restrictions on where you can take their planes and the length of time you can keep them. You may also have to sign an agreement stating that, for the time you are renting one of their floatplanes, you will be responsible for it. In other words, you damage it, you pay for it.

Each flight school handles the insurance problem differently. The *Water Flying Annual,* published by the Seaplane Pilots Association, lists every seaplane flight school in the United States and Canada and indicates which schools have solo rates on their planes. A copy of the *Water Flying Annual* can be obtained directly from the Seaplane Pilots Association at 421 Aviation Way, Frederick, MD 21701.

According to the insurance companies, the reason for the extremely high hull insurance rates on floatplanes is simple. If a landplane is damaged, it doesn't go anywhere, and unless it's completely wrecked, it can generally be repaired. The insurance companies claim that, unlike a landplane, a floatplane can become a total loss as a result of what is actually very minor damage. They have decided that a damaged floatplane usually sinks, thus adding salvage and water damage costs to the cost of repairing the original damage, however slight it may have been. The actual floatplane accident statistics do not necessarily support the insurance companies' theory, but insurance rates remain high, nevertheless, and the debate between the floatplane operators and the insurance companies goes on.

CHOOSING A FLIGHT SCHOOL

The ideal flight school would be both big enough to offer all the facilities and services you'll need, and small enough to give you the personal attention you should have (Fig. 5-1). Of the two, the latter is more important. There's nothing more valuable than good, personalized flight instruction, and this can often make up for a lack of fancy facilities.

It's also important that the flight instruction staff, even if it's only one person, actually has the time to give instruction. Many floatplane schools also do charter work, and there's nothing more frustrating than arriving at the lake just in time to be told that the airplane you were going to use is off on another assignment, or that your instructor had to make a last-minute charter flight.

I ran into this a lot while I was working toward my seaplane rating, but I was lucky in that the owner of the

Fig. 5-1. Instructor and Charter Pilot Neal Ratti explains the purpose of the stabilizing fin on this de Havilland Beaver to a new student.

flight school, who was also my instructor, would often let me go with him on those spur-of-the-moment charters. He would even let me fly after he dropped off his paying passengers, enabling me to add several hours of free flying time to my log book. So there can be advantages to having a lesson cancelled in favor of a charter flight, but most of the time it's just a frustrating inconvenience. Make sure your instructor will be able to give you the kind of attention you should have, and will be paying for.

Look over the flight school's airplanes. Their age is not as important as their condition. I would rather fly an immaculate, 1946 Taylorcraft than a run-down, abused, 1983 Cessna 172. Are the interiors of the airplanes in good shape? Are the exteriors kept clean and waxed? Are the aileron, flap, elevator, and rudder hinges well greased? This is very important on a floatplane, especially if it's operated on salt water. Check for corrosion, or bubbles in the paint, especially on the tail surfaces. The presence of a lot of corrosion indicates poor maintenance. Do the

floats, attachment hardware, and water rudder cables look like they're in good shape? I realize that, at this point, you probably aren't very familiar with floatplane hardware, but a frayed cable is a frayed cable! The condition of the airplanes, and the facility in general, will tell you a great deal about the quality of the instruction you're likely to receive at that school.

Fine, you say, but how do I go about *finding* a flight school that offers floatplane instruction? Again, the *Water Flying Annual* is your best bet. The flight school directory includes the types of floatplanes used at each school, the hourly rates, and the average length of time required to obtain a seaplane rating at each facility. The schools are listed by state: so it's a simple matter to find the facility nearest you.

DOCKS VS. RAMPS

Some flight schools operate their floatplanes from docks, and some from ramps. Which is better?

Ramps are certainly easier to operate from, since the floatplane is simply run up onto the ramp nose-first. Also, because the manuever is done under power, wind direction and strength are rarely critical factors. Prior to departure, the floatplane is pushed into the water, turned around, and pulled tail-first back up onto the ramp. The pilot can then take all the time he wants getting in, adjusting the seat, and starting the engine. There's no need to hurry since the plane will not leave the ramp until power is applied.

Operating a floatplane from a dock, on the other hand, requires considerably more skill on the part of the pilot. The moment it's untied, the airplane is at the mercy of the winds and currents, and in a good breeze, things can get pretty lively while you clamber in and get the engine started (Fig. 5-2). When you return, you're often faced with the challenge of trying to slip the plane into the last open spot on the dock, which is inevitably sandwiched between two other floatplanes.

Don't be intimidated, though. Personally, I think a dock makes the best learning environment. If you plan to do any cross-country floatplane flying after you get your rating, you'll find that docks are far more common than ramps. Many of the most interesting places to go in a floatplane only have boat facilities, so the more docking practice you can get, the better. If, however, the floatplane school in your area uses a ramp, don't despair. Just make sure its course of instruction includes plenty of docking experience using boat docks in the area for practice.

FLOATPLANE TRAINERS

Another question commonly asked is, "What's the best kind of floatplane to learn in?" Unfortunately, there's no easy answer, since just about anything from an ultralight to a de Havilland Twin Otter can be mounted on floats. The final decision is usually based on economics, but there are some other factors to consider as well.

Many people consider the Piper J-3 Cub and the venerable Cessna 150 to be the best primary trainers ever made. Both airplanes can be mounted on floats, but there are a couple of reasons why I don't think either one of them makes as good a trainer on water as it does on land. Both airplanes are underpowered when fitted with floats, and the floats themselves are rather small. The combination of small floats and low horsepower make both these airplanes unsuitable for use in anything other than relatively calm water.

I don't mean to imply that the Cub and the 150 are not good floatplanes. They are, but considering their limitations, I don't believe they are suited for dual instruction. In fact, two good-sized adults and a load of fuel could easily exceed either floatplane's gross weight.

Floatplanes need more horsepower than their wheeled counterparts to overcome the additional weight and drag of the floats and to pull the floatplane free of the water's suction and onto the step. The most popular floatplane trainers are the Cessna 172, especially the newer models with the 160-horsepower engine, and the Piper PA-18 Super Cub, which has a 150-horsepower engine (Fig. 5-3). The 150-horsepower Citabria is also used for instruction. Both the Super Cub and the Citabria, with their high horsepower-to-weight ratios and load-carrying capabilities, are also used as working floatplanes by commercial operators. In fact, the Super Cub may well qualify as the most popular all-around bush plane in northern Canada and Alaska.

The Cessna 172, on the other hand, has some definite limitations as a floatplane. As a landplane, the 172 is a nice, economical, four-place airplane, with a useful load of 993 pounds. The floatplane version of the 172 has a useful load of only 634 pounds, 359 pounds less than the landplane. Three of the FAA's theoretical, 170-pound adults weigh a total of 510 pounds, leaving 124 pounds of useful load for fuel, or about 20 gallons. That's assuming the three people aren't taking anything heavier than a wallet with them, of course. Any baggage carried will reduce the fuel load even more.

Four 170-pound passengers weigh a total of 680 pounds, or 46 pounds more than the floatplane's useful load; so the only time you'll ever get four adults into a float-equipped 172 is while it's sitting on the showroom floor. With only two people on board and just enough fuel for a lesson plus some reserve, however, the 172 makes a nice, economical floatplane trainer with adequate performance, and the floats are big enough to allow the student to safely get some rough water experience.

In my opinion, the 230-horsepower Cessna 180, or its 300-horsepower look-alike, the Cessna 185, are the ideal floatplane trainers. They are probably the most widely used commercial floatplanes, and their powerful engines, constant-speed propellers, and large floats enable them to take on all kinds of wind and water conditions. Unfortunately, they are quite expensive to rent, especially when you add in the cost of an instructor.

Of course, if money is no object, and you really want to go first class, you could get your seaplane rating in a de Havilland Beaver. With its 450-horsepower Pratt & Whitney radial engine, eight-place cabin, and 22-foot-long

Fig. 5-2. Departing a dock crowded with floatplanes can be tricky. Fortunately, the wind was light the day this picture was taken at Kenmore Air Harbor's facility at the north end of Seattle's Lake Washington.

Fig. 5-3. The Piper PA-18 Super Cub is one of the most popular floatplane trainers around. (Courtesy of the EDO Corporation)

floats, you would be getting your rating in one of the best commercial floatplanes ever made. In reality,though, the flight school in your area will probably use a Cessna 172, a Piper Super Cub, or a Citabria for flight instruction, any one of which makes an excellent trainer that's also a lot of fun to fly.

FLOATPLANE FLIGHT INSTRUCTORS DEFINED

There is really no difference between a good landplane instructor and a good floatplane instructor. The basic elements are the same. A good instructor should have a thorough knowledge of what he is trying to teach and a way of passing that knowledge on to you that is both understandable and interesting. A good instructor should be genuinely interested in teaching, and not just trying to "build hours" toward that hoped-for airline job.

A good instructor knows just when to take over the controls. Too soon or too often, and the student's confidence can be seriously eroded. Too late, and an acci-

dent may be the result. It's a fine line, and probably one of the hardest decisions an instructor has to make. Patience is important too, because something that is almost second nature to an instructor may be frustratingly difficult for a student to grasp.

There's no way an instructor, however dedicated, is going to prepare you for every situation you may encounter. The floatplane environment encompasses a lot of variables. Every takeoff, every landing, every docking will be different, even if you take off, land, and dock at the same places every day. Wind and water conditions are constantly changing, and the dock that's empty today may be crowded tomorrow. Add to this the need to be constantly alert for boat wakes, currents, floating debris, and other surprises, and you can see how complex the world of float flying can get. The best your instructor can do is see that you thoroughly understand the basics so you can safely begin adding to your floatplane skills through your own experience (Fig. 5-4).

Earlier, I mentioned that many of the same companies

Fig. 5-4. Neal Ratti explains the cold-start procedure for the Pratt & Whitney R-985 radial engine used on the de Havilland Beaver. His student will have to pump the engine primer another 10 to 12 strokes before she can hit the start switch.

that offer floatplane instruction also specialize in charter work, and that you should make sure your instruction won't suffer because of it. There is a definite advantage, however, to having a working charter pilot for an instructor. Charter pilots run into just about every situation imaginable, and they will often pass techniques and "tricks of the trade" on to their students, along with examples of things *not* to do. When a high-time charter pilot tells you about the time he sat for 6 hours on a mudflat in a Beaver full of irate passengers because the tide went out faster than he did, you'll probably make a mental note to always carry a current tide chart with you and use it.

You can't put a price on experience. I learned many of the techniques described in this book from a bunch of charter pilots who fly de Havilland Beavers and Cessna 180s along the coasts of Washington, British Columbia, and Alaska, fighting fog, rain, snow, and 10-foot tides. Occasionally they have a nice day. If you hang around people like this long enough, you're bound to pick up some valuable information; so pay attention if your instructor starts telling you about the time he flew a creaking, old, overloaded Norseman into a high mountain lake that was so small, the only way he could take off again was to... and so on. His story might get you out of a tight spot some day.

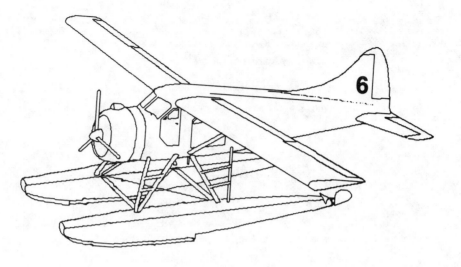

Launching the Floatplane

BEFORE WE DO ANYTHING WITH A FLOAT-
plane, we have to put it in the water. Most
floatplane operators sleep a lot better at night if their
planes are pulled out of the water when they aren't being used. For one thing, all floats, with the possible exception of new ones, leak a little, and if a plane is left
in the water for any length of time, the floats could conceivably fill up and pull the airplane under. Wakes from
passing boats can slam the floats against the dock, and
the constant motion of the plane could eventually chafe
through the mooring lines. High winds can be a threat
if the wings aren't tied down, and heavy snowfalls have
been known to sink unattended floatplanes.

As you will see in later chapters, there are techniques for preventing all of these disasters if you find
yourself forced to leave your airplane on the water, but
the best safeguard is to get the plane out of the water
completely. There are basically two ways to do so. The
first, and easiest, is to run it up on a wooden ramp after
each flight, using just enough power to pull the floats clear
of the water before the plane comes to a stop. This is the
method used most often by private floatplane owners who
keep their planes on their own property, and by the
smaller commercial operators whose waterfront space is

limited (Fig. 6-1). Although simple, there is a proper procedure for ramping a floatplane, which we'll examine in
detail in Chapter 13.

The second form of dry storage is a little more complicated, and is used primarily by large commercial
operators. The floatplane is positioned over a submerged
platform, usually a railcar or elevator. The platform lifts
the plane out of the water, and a modified forklift is used
to pick up the plane and move it to a tie-down area. Most
operators prefer to rest the floats on a couple of boards
instead of setting the plane directly on the pavement. The
wings can then be tied down to rings set in the pavement,
concrete-filled oil drums or some other form of heavy
weights.

A variation of the forklift method involves the use
of a small dolly which fits under the airplane's's floats.
An empty dolly is fastened to the elevator, and goes down
with it. The floatplane is positioned over the submerged
dolly, and when the elevator is raised, the dolly comes
up under the floats. The elevator stops level with the dock
or parking area; the dolly is unfastened and the plane is
wheeled by hand to a parking place. This procedure is
reversed when it's time to put the plane back in the water.

If the floatplane you're going to fly is still in its tie-

Fig. 6-1. The owner of this Piper Tri-pacer is able to keep his plane at home, thanks to this backyard ramp.

down position, you'll have to get someone on the line crew to put it in the water for you. Driving a forklift with an expensive floatplane balanced on the forks is a real art, and not something you should undertake yourself. The specially designed forks are very long, and are surfaced with wood, carpet, or rubber to avoid marring the airplane. In addition to the usual lifting and tilting movements common to all forklifts, some of them have been modified so the width between the forks can be adjusted from the cab. The forklift is positioned facing the nose of the plane and driven forward until the forks are under both spreader bars between the floats. The operator then adjusts the width of the forks so they will contact the spreader bars as close to the floats as possible. If the forks are set too close to the center of the spreader bars, the bars could be overstressed or even bent when the plane is lifted.

The driver then gently brings the forks up under the spreader bars and lifts the airplane. In a crowded parking area, the plane will have to be lifted quite high so its wings will clear the tails of the airplanes around it, and it's quite a sight to see a big de Havilland Beaver perched 10 feet in the air, rocking and swaying on its trip to the railcar (Fig. 6-2).

Once the floatplane is set on the railcar or elevator, the operator will lower it into the water until the plane is floating on its own, at which point it can be pulled down the dock and tied up. The line crew may have more planes to put in the water after yours; so if you are the one

responsible for mooring your plane to the dock after it's been put in the water, make sure you leave enough space for the other floatplanes as they come off the lift.

If your floatplane is on a ramp, the launching procedure is somewhat different. Actually, you're not so much launching it as turning it around so you can pull it back up the ramp tail-first. The next chapter will cover the proper preflight inspection procedures for a floatplane, but since it's easier to preflight a ramped floatplane before it's turned around, we'll assume you've already performed your inspection. Make sure the water rudders are retracted (up) before sliding the floatplane backwards down the ramp. If they're down, they could dig into the wood and be severely damaged.

The floats will slide easier on the wooden ramp if it's wet, so throw a couple of bucketfuls of water under and behind the floats to soak down the boards. Before you untie the floatplane and get ready to push it backwards into the water, fasten one end of a long line to the stern cleat on one of the floats, and *hold on to the other end.* Once the plane is in the water, this line is the only way you're going to get it back, so hang on to it.

Although you wouldn't think so, there is a trick to pushing a floatplane backwards down a ramp. Don't lift up on the bows of the floats as you push. If you do, all the weight of the plane will be put on the rear edges of the float steps, and they'll dig into the wood, making it very difficult to slide the plane backwards. Many floats have little rounded keel extensions designed to protect the sharp trailing edges of the steps, but these extensions will dig into the wood too, if you lift up on the floats. The idea is to push straight back, which keeps the weight of the plane distributed along the length of the forebody keel of each float. True, there is more float surface in contact with the ramp, and theoretically there should be more friction, but the weight at any given spot along the keel is less, and the plane slides easier. I don't really understand the physics involved, but I do know that the plane slides easier, so push straight back. Once the plane starts to slide, make sure you give it enough of a push so it will drift well clear of the ramp.

Once the plane is floating free, you need to turn it around and pull it back up on the ramp tail-first so you can get in and start the engine. The reason you couldn't do so before is obvious: with the plane pointed up the ramp, you could get in, but you couldn't go anywhere.

Now you can see the reason why the line you are hopefully still hanging onto is fastened to a stern cleat. When you pull on it, the floatplane turns around (Fig. 6-3). If you had fastened the line to one of the bow cleats, the plane would come back to the ramp nose-first, and you'd

be back where you started.

You don't need to pull the floatplane very far up the ramp this time. In fact, most of each float will remain doing just that; floating. All you want to do is keep the plane from sliding forward into the water before you're ready. As you pull the plane in toward you, the tail will extend back over the ramp. To securely "park" the floatplane after the rear of the floats have contacted the ramp, position yourself in front of and facing the leading edge of the horizontal stabilizer. Put your hands under the stabilizer close to where it joins the fuselage and preferably under one of the spars or stiffeners. Lift up and back to raise the rear of the floats and set them farther up the ramp. Again, make sure the water rudders are up before you do this step. Depending on the steepness of the ramp and the weight of the floatplane, you may have to repeat this lifting maneuver a couple of times before the plane is securely resting on the wood. Now you and your instructor or passengers can get in, and you can begin going through your prestart checklist (Fig. 6-4).

A word of caution about ramps. They get wet a lot

Fig. 6-2. A de Havilland Beaver on its way to the railcar. The forklift has been equipped with special forks that can be adjusted from the cab to exactly match the width between the floats. The forks are also surfaced with wood so they will not mar the undersides of the spreader bars.

Fig. 6-3. Before pushing this Beaver backwards off the ramp, Neal attached a long line to one of the stern cleats. With the plane now floating free, he is using this line to turn the plane around prior to tailing it back up onto the ramp. Note the water rudders in their retracted position.

Fig. 6-4. The Beaver has been turned around and is tailed up onto the ramp, ready for loading.

and they're usually slippery, especially at the water's edge. This can be a real advantage when you're driving a floatplane up the ramp or sliding it off, but when you're working around the plane, be very careful of your footing. Once you start to slide, it's hard to stop. One ramp was so slick and mossy a passenger who slid into the water couldn't pull herself back up until someone threw her a line. Ducks and geese are particularly fond of seaplane ramps because the ramps make it easier for them to get in and out of the water, too, and the droppings they leave in gratitude don't do much to improve the situation.

Those of you operating from ramps have already done your preflight inspections, but the rest of you are still standing on the dock next to your airplanes, waiting, so let's take a look at what goes into a good, thorough preflight inspection of a typical floatplane.

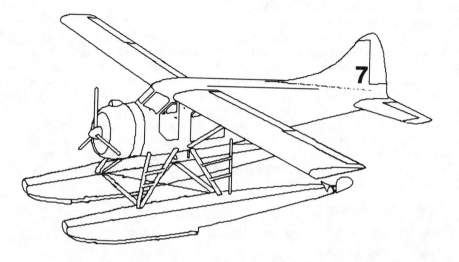

The Preflight Inspection

O NE OF THE BEST WAYS TO GUARANTEE A SAFE and enjoyable flight in any airplane is to perform a thorough preflight inspection. It's better to be on the ground when you discover a problem than to be in the air. A proper preflight inspection is certainly important when you're flying a landplane, but it's absolutely vital if you're flying a floatplane. Everything is riding, literally, on the floats, and you must make certain that they are still watertight, and that their attachment hardware is strong and secure. Although the preflight checks of the fuel, oil, pitot-static, and flight control systems are essentially identical to those you would perform on a landplane, there are a couple of things to keep in mind when you're checking these items on a floatplane.

First of all, try not to fall in the water. I've seen at least one person step off a dock in an attempt to get a closer look at the outboard aileron hinge. Unless you're preflighting a ramped floatplane, the water is never more than a couple of steps away. As we saw in the last chapter, ramps have their little problems, too, so be careful.

If you get lucky and the floatplane you're about to fly hasn't been put in the water yet, you may be able to talk the line crew into letting you perform your preflight inspection before they launch the plane. Now you can give the plane a good going over without the worry of stepping off the dock or slipping on the ramp. For now, however, I'll assume the airplane is already in the water and securely moored alongside one of the flight school's docks.

There are probably as many different ways to perform a preflight inspection as there are pilots, but the order in which things are inspected is not nearly as important as the fact that they are inspected. Your instructor will undoubtably have a favorite way to perform the preflight and, in time, you'll probably come up with your own system. In the meantime, let me describe how I was taught to do it as a way of introducing you to the items you will need to inspect.

THE COCKPIT

The first thing you should do when you open the door to the cockpit is reach across and open the other door. In order to inspect the other side of the airplane, you're going to have to turn it around, and there's nothing more annoying than turning the airplane around only to find the other door locked.

Remove the control locks and make sure the magnetos are off. Next, turn on the master switch to check the amount of fuel in the tanks. Some airplanes, like the Beaver, have a separate switch for the engine instruments, so don't forget to turn that on, also. While the master switch is still on, lower the flaps if they are electric. If the flaps are manual, as in the Cessna 180/185 series of airplanes, or manual/hydraulic, like those in the Beaver, turn off the master switch and lower the flaps with the appropriate lever. Make sure the water rudders are down, and lower them if they're not. Finally, get the bilge pump out of the cabin and set it on the dock.

On some radial-engined airplanes, like the Beaver, the oil filler pipe, with its cap and dipstick, protrudes through the firewall and into the cabin. While you're up in the cockpit, check the oil level, and make sure you put the oil cap back on securely. After you start the engine, the pressure in the oil tank will increase, and if the cap is not fastened tightly it will blow off, covering the front seat occupants with engine oil.

THE PROPELLER

I like to preflight each side of a floatplane in two stages: first the airframe and engine, then the float system. Starting at the front, check the prop spinner, and make sure it's fastened securely. Next, carefully inspect the propeller for erosion (Fig. 7-1). The effect of spray on a metal propeller is almost like shot peening, and if the tiny pits are not dressed out, they will deepen until the metal actually begins to split. If this is allowed to continue, the propeller will not only become less efficient, but a crack could develop which could weaken the blade and lead to eventual failure.

Fig. 7-1. Checking the propeller of a de Havilland Beaver for spray erosion.

Incidentally, rain drops can also erode propellers, and some pilots reduce engine rpm if they have to fly through rain for any length of time. Unfortunately, floatplane propellers are subjected to the greatest amount of spray while they are turning at maximum rpm during takeoff, and since the water drops found in spray are much larger than rain drops, propeller erosion is virtually unvoidable.

The pitting which results can be dressed out by honing the leading edge of the prop with a smooth steel bar to even out the rough surface without removing any metal. If the initial dimpling of the propeller is allowed to develop into deeper pits, the leading edge will have to be filed smooth, a process which does remove metal. Care must be taken to file each blade equally. If one blade has more metal removed than any of the others, the propeller could become slightly unbalanced and begin to vibrate.

As you're checking the propeller blades, it's a good idea to pull the prop through backwards. If for some reason there is still fuel in the manifold, and if one of the magnetos is "hot," the engine could fire if the propeller is pulled through in the normal direction. You'll eliminate the possibility of an accident completely if you make it a practice to assume the engine will start whenever you touch the prop.

If you're flying an ultralight on floats, be aware that water erodes the leading edges of wooden propellers extremely fast. In fact, your propeller could lose a noticeable amount of efficiency after only one or two exposures to spray. Several manufacturers of ultralight propellers have come up with solutions to the erosion problem; so if you have attached floats to your ultralight or are thinking of doing do, you would do well to consider replacing the standard wooden propeller with a prop specifically designed to resist spray erosion.

One manufacturer inlays a "steel composite" leading edge into its scimitar-shaped wooden propellers, and another builds the entire propeller out of composite materials. In each case, the problem of spray erosion is dramatically reduced.

THE ENGINE

While you're up front checking the prop, take a look at the engine, too. If you're preflighting an airplane with a closely cowled, horizontally opposed engine, you won't be able to see very much of it, but what you're looking for are signs of corrosion or rust that could indicate poor maintenance and possible engine problems. It's not uncommon to see a little bit of surface rust, especially on the cooling fins, but be careful if the engine is heavily encrusted with rust or corrosion.

You should be able to see the spark plug wires going to the first cylinder in each bank; so make sure they appear to be in good condition. Insulation that's cracked or split is a good indication of a worn-out wiring harness and possible ignition problems.

On larger floatplanes like the Beaver, make sure the oil cooler and carburetor air scoops are unobstructed. If the airplane has cowl flaps, check the operating linkages for signs of damage or wear. Wiggle the exhaust stack or stacks back and forth. If they feel loose, they probably are and should be checked by a mechanic. You don't need carbon monoxide leaking into the cabin during your flight.

If the floatplane you're preflighting has a radial engine, it's easy to get a good look at its general condition since it's all sitting right there in front of you. The magnetos, fuel pump, carburetor, oil tanks, and other engine accessories, however, are all mounted on the rear of the engine; so you won't be able to get a look at them unless you remove the cowls completely, a time-consuming and tedious process. Radial engine cowls come off easily enough, but they're a real pain to put back on, and they never seem to fit right.

There is an additional preflight duty to be performed on a radial if it hasn't been run for some time, and this is to drain the oil out of the lower cylinders. Any oil left in the engine after shutdown will eventually drain down into the lower cylinders and collect there. Given time, some of it will work its way past the piston rings and into the combustion chambers. If this oil isn't removed, a hydraulic lock could occur when the engine is turned over by the starter, and the resulting pressures could send some of the cylinder heads to the bottom of the lake. To remove any oil that may have accumulated in the lower combustion chambers, remove one spark plug from each of the lower cylinders, and turn the engine over by hand. If there is any oil present, it will drain out the spark plug hole.

If the oil dipstick is on the side of the engine closest to the dock, check the oil level. If it's on the other side, you'll have to wait until you turn the floatplane around to check it. If the airplane is equipped with a fuel sump drain, this is a good time to make sure the fuel in the line is uncontaminated. If possible, try to catch the fuel in a container of some sort so you won't be dumping raw gas into the water. You can throw it out later on the dock where it will evaporate, or if the fuel is clean and you're really budget-conscious, you can put it back into the tank.

THE FUEL SYSTEM

If your floatplane has fuel tanks in the wings, climb up

on the fueling steps and visually check the fuel level. While you're up there, check for any damage to the wings. Be on the lookout for dents and dings in the leading edge that may have been caused by scraping or hitting the tall pilings found in many boat harbors. Obviously, you'll have to wait until you turn the airplane around before checking the fuel tanks on the other side.

Not all floatplanes have their fuel tanks in the wings. The Beaver, for example, has three fuel tanks in the belly, and the filler necks and fuel caps are located behind a hinged panel aft of the pilot's door. Because of the plumbing layout, it's impossible to visually check the amount of fuel in the tanks; so you'll have to trust the gauges in the cockpit. All you can do during your pre-flight inspection is make sure the filler caps are fastened securely.

Next, drain some fuel from the tank, or tanks, into the sample cup, and make sure it's free of dirt, rust, and water. This step is especially important if the plane has been fueled with gas from drums or 5-gallon cans. The marine environment is not all that clean, and even large fuel storage tanks and transfer pipes can become contaminated with water and rust, particularly if they are near salt water. The fuel in your tanks should be free of any contaminants, especially if your floatplane has a fuel-injected engine. A tiny piece of dirt or rust can cause a very big problem if it manages to plug an injector.

THE PITOT-STATIC SYSTEM

Check the pitot tube for blockage and make sure it hasn't been damaged or loosened by striking a piling or other obstruction. Remember also to check the static port. This often overlooked item is very important, because if it should become plugged with wax or dirt, all your pressure instruments will read erroneously. Static port locations vary, and you may have to refer to the owner's manual to find the exact location of the port on your particular airplane. Incidentally, don't be alarmed if the airspeed indicator jerks erratically when you fly through a rainstorm. The jerks are caused by rainwater momentarily blocking the static port.

THE CONTROL SURFACES

Check the flap tracks and extending mechanism. They should be well-greased, and the adjustment and lock nuts on the control rod should be tight. The ailerons, if you can reach them, should move freely without binding. Some floatplanes, like the Cessna 172, have spring-loaded interconnects between the ailerons and the rudder; so you may feel some resistance as you move the ailerons, but there should be no obvious binding. The aileron control rod should be free of any longitudinal play, and the adjustment and lock nuts should be tight. If you can see the aileron hinges, make sure the cotter pins that keep the hinge pins from falling out are in place, and that the hinges themselves are thoroughly greased. Finally, check the trailing edge of the wing for damage. Careless pilots sometimes run the wing backwards into an object while they're sailing or turning the plane around.

As long as you're checking control surfaces, walk back and take a look at the horizontal tail. (If you're preflighting an Otter, you'll need a 12-foot step ladder for this part.) The elevator should travel between full up and full down without binding. Make sure the trim lab is working properly. As with the ailerons, the elevator and trim tab hinge points should be well greased.

The horizontal tail is often completely enveloped in spray during takeoffs and landings, and it's not just the outside skin that gets soaked. The water will find its way to the inner surfaces as well, and if the plane is operated on salt water, severe corrosion could be the result. To combat this corrosion, the floatplane must be thoroughly hosed off with fresh water after the last flight of the day, with particular attention given to the tail. If a floatplane has been poorly maintained, corrosion may actually start to pit the outer surfaces of the horizontal and vertical tails, and the paint will start to blister and flake off. Usually, however, corrosion forms where it's difficult to see—in the nooks and crannies around the spars, stringers, and other structural members of the airplane. One place to check for corrosion is in the gap between the stabilizer and the elevator. Depending on the construction of the airplane, you may be able to see some of the inner structure and check it for evidence of corrosion.

Don't feel you have to include a magnifying glass in your flight bag, though. Most floatplanes used for flight instruction get a lot of attention, and any potentially serious corrosion is usually discovered and eliminated long before it becomes a problem. The main thing to look for is corrosion evidence on the outer skin surfaces, as it may be warning you of a much more dangerous situation inside the plane.

The warmer and more humid the climate, the faster corrosion will develop and spread; so if you're flying in Florida, the Gulf of Mexico, or the Caribbean, you'll need to be more wary of corrosion than if you were flying in Canada or Alaska.

THE FLOAT SYSTEM

After you've finished checking the first side of the airframe, go back to the nose where you will now begin to inspect the hardware that makes it all possible: the float system. As we learned earlier, the float system is made up of the floats themselves, the spreader bars, float struts, bracing wires, and water rudders, with their steering and retraction cables, brackets, and pulleys. Each component should be inspected carefully before flight, because the safety of the airplane is dependent upon their integrity.

Pump Out the Floats

Starting at the bow of the float, check each compartment for water using the bilge pump, which should be kept in the floatplane at all times. If the float is equipped with built-in bilge pump down-tubes, operate the pump in the manner described in Chapter 3. The recessed opening at the top of each down-tube is kept plugged with a soft rubber ball. The ball keeps spray, rain, and waves which break over the deck from running down the tubes into the float compartments. To prevent the rubber balls from being lost overboard, they are fastened to the float decks with short lengths of string. A word of caution: the balls do not float, and if the string is broken, it's all too easy to pop a ball out of its tube only to watch it bounce overboard and sink out of sight. Pull them out carefully, and make sure they are securely tied to the float before laying them down on the deck.

If the floats on the airplane you're flying don't have built-in bilge pump down-tubes, you'll have to remove an inspection cover from the top of each compartment and insert the pump directly into the float to remove any accumulated water. If the airplane doesn't have a bilge pump on board, the access hatches in the floats are large enough to permit you to scoop out the water with a small bucket, or to swab it out with a sponge (Fig. 7-2).

Water in the Floats

Floats always seem to have a little water in them; so don't

Fig. 7-2. Some floats don't have built-in bilge pump down tubes; so you'll have to check for water by removing the access hatches in the float deck.

worry if the pump brings up a cup or two of water out of each compartment. Water can enter a float in one of several ways. It can leak in around the rubber balls plugging the down-tubes (the balls don't fit perfectly). It can also seep in around the access hatch covers in the float deck. Another source of water is the condensation of moist air on the cold metal inside the float. And finally, water can enter through float seams that have worked open.

Even under ideal conditions, floats receive quite a pounding as they skim over the water at speeds of up to 70 and 80 miles an hour, and eventually some of the seams in aluminum floats will begin to work open. This situation is not as bad as it sounds, for while a little water may begin to seep in through an unsealed seam, the strength of the seam is not at all compromised. It just isn't quite as watertight as it used to be.

Because a floatplane travels fastest while riding on the step, that is the part of the float which is subjected to the greatest pounding, and the seams will generally begin to leak there first. Floatplanes that are used for training spend much of their time taking off, landing, and step-taxiing, so don't be surprised if you discover a fair amount of water in the float compartment directly above the step. If you do pump a lot of water out of one of the float compartments, you don't necessarily have to cancel the flight, but the fact that one of the compartments contained a lot of water should be reported to the flight school personnel. They may already be aware of the problem, but since resealing a float is an expensive and time-consuming process, they may be trying to make it through the season before pulling the plane out of service for repairs. There's nothing wrong with this; just make sure you remember to pump out the floats before each flight.

The rear float compartment is also susceptible to water accumulation. The movement of the water rudders tends to put pressure on the seams around the stern of each float, and they could eventually open up slightly, allowing water to seep in. Leaving the water rudders down accidentally during a takeoff or while step-taxiing can also cause the float seams to work open. The floatplane's rapid forward motion through the water will cause the rudders to slam violently up and down against their stops, stressing the rear bulkhead seams.

Why is it so important that all the water be removed from the floats? Well, for one thing, any water trapped in the floats will reduce their buoyancy, and as the compartments fill up, the floatplane will ride lower and lower in the water. While the floats must continue to support the airplane with any two compartments flooded per float,

a badly leaking float could eventually fill completely and drag the airplane under.

Water weighs approximately 7 pounds per gallon. Any water trapped in the floats is weight the airplane is being asked to carry, and the plane's useful load will be reduced accordingly. If you neglect to pump out the floats, you obviously won't know how much water, and weight, is in them. If you then load your airplane with passengers, baggage, and fuel, you can see how the floatplane's gross weight could be exceeded without your knowing it. Almost every hangar flying session includes at least one story about someone plowing madly around a lake unable to take off because the airplane's floats were so full of water. These stories all end in one of two ways. The pilot either returns to the dock and sheepishly pumps out the water, or the plane ends up in the rocks, logs, bushes, or trees at the end of the lake. Neither situation is desirable, so pump out the floats before you cast off.

While the image of a waterlogged floatplane frantically dashing back and forth as it tries to take off is rather comical, there is another, more dangerous condition that can be brought about by a flooded float compartment. If water has accumulated in any of the rear compartments, its weight could conceivably move the airplane's center of gravity aft of its certified envelope. This condition would be most likely to occur in floatplanes with long, spacious cabins like the Cessna 206 and the de Havilland Beaver and Otter. These planes are often loaded to the extreme aft limit of their center of gravity envelopes to begin with, and any extra weight back in the tails of the floats could create a serious out-of-balance condition. Since the heavily loaded airplane will already be riding low in the water, the pilot may not notice that the tails of the floats are a little lower than they should be. Too often, a center-of-gravity problem does not become apparent until the airplane is airborne, at which time it may be too late. Make sure you check all the float compartments for water, not just the ones that are easily accessible.

THE ATTACHMENT HARDWARE

As you pump your way aft along the float, check the spreader bars and float struts as you come to them. You're primarily looking for cracks in the fittings that attach these components to the floats and the airframe. If you spot a crack, report it immediately. It may turn out to be just a scratch or crack in the paint, but don't let that stop you from reporting anything that looks suspicious. Most floatplane operators would rather send a mechanic out to investigate a paint scratch than send a salvage boat out to recover a capsized airplane.

If the floatplane you're flying is equipped with brace wires, check their attachment fittings too, and make sure the wires themselves are tight. A loose brace wire will allow the float system to flex and vibrate, possibly causing one or more of the strut or spreader bar attachment fittings to fail.

Make sure all the attachment bolts and lock nuts are tight and in place, and that none of them are badly rusted. Most float struts are fitted with boarding steps to the cabin, and they should be checked for cracks, too.

You may notice that many of the floatplane's fittings are covered with a kind of yellow or brown varnish. This is *paralketone*, and it's applied as a liquid over exposed parts to prevent rust and corrosion. When it dries, it forms a protective barrier to keep water from contacting the metal. Moving parts, like the rudder cable pulleys and pulley bracket hinges, are usually coated with grease.

THE WATER RUDDERS

As we saw earlier, the water rudders are operated by cables that are either attached to the floatplane's air rudder or directly to the rudder pedals in the cockpit. A separate set of cables retracts the rudders. The steering and retraction cables are guided around corners by brackets and pulleys attached to the exterior of the floats and airframe, and it's important that these pulleys rotate smoothly. As you work your way down the float, check the pulleys for freedom of movement, and make sure their mounting brackets are securely fastened to the float, strut, or airframe.

Inspect the cables, too. Look for signs of wear near the pulleys, and check the cable ends for fraying. The crimp fittings used to fasten the cables together should show no signs of slipping.

After you've pumped out the last compartment, inspect the water rudder itself. Make sure the steering cables are securely attached to the steering bar at the top of the rudder post, and that the retraction cable is firmly fastened to the rudder. Pull the water rudder up and check for damage. The rudder should hinge up and down smoothly, and the blade should not be bent or cracked.

It's important to check for weeds or branches that may be caught in the water rudders. I once rented a floatplane which had just been taxied through a weed bed on its way back to the dock. I checked all the cables, but I didn't bother to pull up and inspect the rudders themselves, so I never saw the long streamers of water milfoil hooked on each blade. As I taxied away from the dock, I pushed down on the right rudder pedal to begin a turn toward the main part of the lake. Nothing happened. I had the pedal all the way down, but the plane kept plowing straight ahead. I opened the door and looked back at the water rudder on my side of the airplane. Even though I was holding the right pedal clear to the floor, the rudder was pointing straight back. I frantically seesawed the pedals back and forth, but the water rudder wouldn't budge. Finally, I saw the long streamers of weeds trailing behind the airplane. They were just under the surface, and their weight was holding the spring-loaded water rudders centered. The only thing I could do was shut off the engine, walk back to the tail of each float in turn, and remove the weeds. Fortunately, there was no wind, so I was in no danger of drifting into anything expensive. The only casualties were my shoes, which got soaked as the tail of first one float and then the other was forced underwater by my 200-plus pounds as I removed the weeds.

This situation could have been much more serious had it occurred in a crowded harbor where the inability to steer might have resulted in a collision with a boat, a dock, or another seaplane. Remember, a floatplane has no brakes, so all your defensive driving must be done with the water rudders.

As long as we're on the subject of weeds, you may be wondering what to do if you pick up weeds or branches with the water rudders after you leave the dock. Raising and lowering the rudders several times in quick succession will often knock the debris clear. If this doesn't work, and if you have plenty of room, add power until your floatplane is on the step. The increased speed through the water might tear the weeds loose. Remember to raise the water rudders before you do this, however, so they won't be damaged. If all else fails, you can always shut down the engine, climb out onto the floats, and manually remove the debris from the water rudders. This procedure works very nicely, but you'll probably get your feet wet.

TURNING THE PLANE AROUND

After you've finished preflighting one side of the floatplane, you'll have to turn it around to inspect the other side. It may not be practical, or possible, to turn a large floatplane like a de Havilland Beaver or Otter around, so you'll have to climb through the cabin to the outboard float. You can't get a good look at the wing and tail assemblies from there, but at least you can pump out the float and check its attachment hardware, water rudder, and related cables. If you're flying a smaller floatplane, however, get in the habit of turning it around to ensure a thorough preflight inspection.

Before you untie the plane, determine the direction and strength of the wind. The plane will drift a little with the wind as it's turning, and you want to make sure the wings and tail will clear any pilings, boat, or other floatplanes that may be nearby. After making sure the plane will clear all the obstacles present, untie the lines and push the nose of the plane out from the dock. Always push the nose out, as this will bring the tail back over the dock and give you something to hold onto as the plane turns (Fig. 7-3). Also, as the tail swings over the dock, you'll get a chance to inspect the rudder and vertical fin—items you couldn't get close to before. Don't let the water rudders hit the dock as the plane turns. If they get caught between the tires or in the planking, they could be bent, or the steering mechanism could be damaged.

As the plane continues to turn, walk forward, take hold of the wing-tip grab line as it comes in over the dock, and pull the plane in sideways toward the dock. When the float is against the dock, fasten the mooring lines on the float struts to the dock cleats and begin your inspection of this side of the airplane.

If the floatplane you're flying doesn't have grab lines hanging from the wing tips, of if it's windy, you may want to tie a long line to one of the float cleats and hold on to it, just to make sure the airplane doesn't get away from you. The important thing is to hold on to some part of the airplane at all times. There's nothing more embarassing than watching your floatplane drift gently out into the middle of the harbor while you helplessly jump up and down on the dock and wave your arms. The plane will not come back when you do this, so it's best not to let it get away from you in the first place.

One of the dumbest things I've done so far with a floatplane is to try and turn one around at a dock by pushing the tail out instead of the nose. The Cessna 172 I was preflighting was tied up between a Beaver and another Cessna, and I barely had enough room to turn my plane around. All three planes were moored with their tails to the 10-knot wind that was blowing off the lake, and I was afraid that in the time it took me to turn my plane around, it would be blown forward into the floatplane in front of me. After pondering the situation (not long enough, as it turned out), I came up with this great scheme of fastening a line to the bow cleat of the outboard float, untying the plane and pushing the tail out from the dock. In theory, the wind would push the tail of the plane around as I pulled on the line attached to the outboard float, and the plane would pivot neatly around without drifting anywhere. It was a good theory, but it didn't work. Oh, the plane pivoted around all right, but between my pulling on the rope, and the 10-knot wind pushing on the tail, the plane spun around at an alarming rate of speed. On top of that, it still drifted downwind, and only blind luck kept the downwind wing tip of my plane from slamming into the tail of the plane in front. Unfortunately, after letting my wing tip escape unscathed, blind luck went home, and the tails of the two airplanes collided. Only the quick action of a nearby instructor kept the situation from getting totally out of hand, and thanks to his intervention, no damage was done to either floatplane.

I include this little episode because I learned two important things from it. First, never turn a floatplane around at the dock by pushing the tail out, especially if the tail is pointing into the wind. Even if there had been no floatplane tied up in front of me, my plane would have pivoted into the dock with considerable force, possibly damaging the floats or their attachment hardware.

Second, I learned (again) that things can get out of control very fast, and the importance of thinking through your actions and their consequences cannot be overemphasized. If I had thought through this situation a little more thoroughly, I would have realized that the thing to do was to first give myself more room at the dock by untying the floatplane in front of me and moving it forward (there was plenty of room in front of it), and then get someone to assist me while I turned my plane around using the correct method. At least I was smart enough not to try and depart the dock by myself that day, but instead got someone to hold the tail of my plane while I climbed aboard and started the engine.

SPECIAL EQUIPMENT

Mooring lines, paddles, bumpers, anchors, life jackets, and life rafts: this sounds more like a check list for the family boat than for an airplane, but all this equipment can come in handy on a floatplane, and some of it should be carried at all times.

Every floatplane should have at least two long lines on board, and preferably more. The lines should be at least 50 feet long, and it's helpful if one end of each line is spliced into an eye, or loop. If you plan to do any cross-country flying, chances are you'll run into some pretty strange docking situations, and what had seemed like too much line can easily become just barely enough. The lines can be carried in the baggage compartment, but keep one up near the pilot's seat where you can grab it in a hurry. The preflight inspection is a good time to make sure the lines are coiled neatly and are free of tangles.

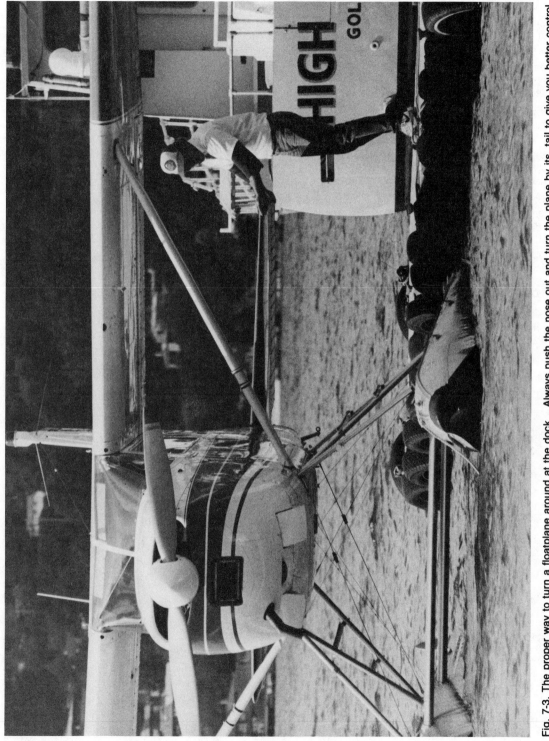

Fig. 7-3. The proper way to turn a floatplane around at the dock. Always push the nose out and turn the plane by its tail to give you better control of the plane, especially if there's a wind blowing.

Shortly after I received my seaplane rating, I misjudged my taxi speed and stopped a floatplane too far from the dock. An instructor happened to be nearby, and he offered to pull me in if I would throw him a line. Since I was slowly drifting toward another airplane, I thought this was an excellent idea, so I grabbed the line I had remembered to place on the floor behind my seat. Unfortunately, I hadn't remembered to coil it neatly, and when you're in a hurry, things tend to get snarled up even more. By the time I had untangled enough line to throw to the instructor, I was 5 feet from the other plane. Everything worked out fine in the end, but I learned a valuable lesson. Always check the lines before each flight.

Make sure there is a paddle on board the floatplane. This is your emergency engine, and while it isn't much use if the wind is blowing, it can be invaluable on a calm day if you have to inch the plane into that last open spot on the dock or slowly and carefully approach a rocky beach. In the unlikely event you have an engine failure, the paddle may be your only way to get the plane to shore.

If your floatplane doesn't have a paddle mounted on one of the floats, it will have to be carried inside the cabin, but don't put it in the baggage compartment. You may need it in a hurry sometime, and you don't want to have to climb over a couple of seats and wrestle it out from under all the other stuff that's back there. If you're flying a Cessna 172, a good place to keep the paddle is on the cabin floor with the handle between the front seats and the blade under the rear seat. It's easy to reach, and it doesn't obstruct the seat tracks or inconvenience the backseat passenger. In a later chapter, we'll look at what I've found to be the best way to maneuver a floatplane with a paddle, but for right now, just make sure there's one in the plane, and that it's positioned where you can reach it in a hurry if necessary.

Not all docks have tires or rubber strips around them, and it's a good idea to carry bumpers for those times you have to tie up to a bare wood, metal, or concrete dock. Two bumpers are generally sufficient, and while the heavy-duty, air-filled, rubber boat bumpers are best, they take up a lot of room in the plane. One alternative is to make some bumpers using an old automobile tire (Fig. 7-4). Cut some pieces of rubber 2 feet long and the width of the tread out of the tire. Punch a hole in one end of

Fig. 7-4. An easy-to-make bumper using a section of automobile tire and a short length of line. It's light, and several of them can be nested together and kept in the baggage compartment where they won't take up much room.

each piece, tie on some lengths of light line, and you have a handy set of bumpers that won't take up much room in the baggage compartment.

Unlike mooring lines, paddles, and bumpers, anchors are an option. Some pilots like them; some pilots don't. If you want to land on a lake and fish from the airplane, an anchor will keep you from drifting away from your selected spot. If a mooring buoy isn't available, you can anchor your floatplane off a beach in tidal waters so you won't get left high and dry when the tide goes out.

The main disadvantage of an anchor is that in order for it to be effective, it must be heavy. Many pilots don't like the idea of having a sharp, heavy piece of iron on board that could tear loose and fly around the cabin in heavy turbulence or during a forced landing. The anchor, together with its long line, also takes up space, and in a smaller floatplane, this could be a problem. If you do decide to carry an anchor, remember to include it in your weight and balance calculations. Don't rely on an anchor for overnight moorage except in an emergency. Unlike the large, heavy anchors used to position mooring buoys, floatplane anchors must be small enough to fit in the plane, and light enough to be pulled up by hand. These relatively small anchors can begin to drag if the current or wind is strong, and your floatplane will be damaged or destroyed if it ends up on the rocks.

While anchors are optional, life vests are not, and the plane should be equipped with enough vests for everyone on board. Make sure the vests are in good condition, and that the CO_2 bottles used to inflate them are still sealed and charged.

In the northern United States, Canada, and Alaska, the temperature of the water becomes the greatest danger if a floatplane capsizes or sinks. The survival time of the human body is measured in minutes in these frigid northern waters, and some pilots in the region now carry the same survival suits used by commercial fishermen. Although bulky and quite expensive, these suits offer the only protection against hypothermia in the event a person is forced into the water. Many of them are equipped with strobe lights for night use, and some even come with a built-in emergency locator transmitter (ELT).

Another survival item found in some floatplanes is an inflatable raft. The raft should be big enough to hold all the people that can be carried in the plane. In other words, a four-place plane should have a four-man raft, a six-place plane should have a six-man raft, and so on. Like the survival suits, rafts are fairly expensive, but if you plan on flying over large bodies of water in unpopulated areas, it could prove to be a good investment.

It is extremely unlikely that your floatplane trainer will be equipped with survival suits or a raft, but it should definitely have life vests in pouches on or under the seats. Make sure they are there.

After you've completed the preflight inspection, turn the bilge-pump upside down to drain the water out of it, and put it back in the plane. It's time to cast off from the dock and head for open water.

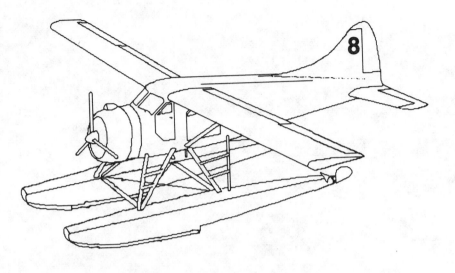

Starting Out

DEPARTING A DOCK IN A POWERBOAT IS PRETTY easy. You simply start the engine, untie the mooring lines, push the boat slightly away from the dock, turn the wheel hard over, shift from neutral to forward, and leave. Getting a floatplane underway is a little more difficult. For one thing, you'll begin to move forward as soon as you start the engine. Unless you're flying a fancy turboprop with a feathering or reversing propeller, you won't have the luxury of a neutral or reverse gear.

On top of that, a boat can make much sharper turns than a floatplane. A boat's rudder is usually placed behind the propeller, or propellers; so the propwash provides a turning force as soon as the helm is put over, even if the boat is standing still. This is why a powerful ski boat, for example, can be "kicked" around, or pivoted, almost within its own length from a dead stop. The water rudders on a floatplane, however, don't work unless the plane is already moving forward, and at low-power settings the propwash is too weak and the air rudder is too small to provide much pivoting action. If enough power is applied to make the air rudder effective, the floatplane will begin to move through the water so fast that the turn will be very wide.

Boats and floatplanes do have one steering trait in common, however, because of the aft location of their rudders. Let's say you want to make a turn to the left. If you're driving a boat, you turn the wheel left; if you're piloting a floatplane, you push down on the left rudder pedal. In both cases, the rudders are pivoted to the left. Boats and floats do not turn to the left because their bows are pulled to the left, however, but because their sterns are pushed to the right. Therefore, if your right side is up against a dock, the application of left rudder will not turn the front of a boat, or a floatplane, away from the dock, but will instead push its rear end into it. Rather than pulling away from the dock, you will merely slide down it.

What all this means to you as a floatplane pilot is that even with the rudder pedal pushed clear to the floor, your plane will tend to move forward down the dock when the engine is started rather than turn away from it. This isn't a problem if you're at the end of the dock, since you will quickly move into open water, but if you are behind another floatplane, or if a piling or some other obstruction is up ahead, you won't be able to turn away to avoid it (Fig. 8-1). So how can you get your floatplane out from between two other floatplanes or away from those pilings that are supporting the dock?

Fig. 8-1. This is one of the easiest departure situations you can find. The pilot of this Cessna 172 simply has to untie the plane, step onto the left float, and shove off. This shot was taken near Friday Harbor in the San Juan Islands, Washington.

THE 90-DEGREE DEPARTURE

Most floatplane pilots turn their planes out 90 degrees from the dock before getting in and starting the engine. The advantage of doing so is that as soon as the engine fires, the floatplane will begin to move away from the dock, and the risks of tangling with other floatplanes or boats moored nearby are minimized.

The procedure is quite simple. After completing your preflight inspection of the floatplane, load your passengers or cargo and get the engine ready to start. Remember, as soon as you untie the airplane and let go of it, it will be free to drift with the current or wind; so you want to minimize the time it takes you to get in and get the engine going. Before you untie your plane, reach into the cockpit and move the mixture control to full rich and, if necessary, prime the engine. If you're flying a floatplane with a radial engine, build up the fuel pressure with the wobble pump if that's part of the starting procedure. If the airplane has a key start, make sure the key is in the ignition, but leave the magnetos off. Some pilots like to turn the master switch on before untieing the plane. If your floatplane has

cowl flaps, make sure they are open, and if the wing flaps are still down from your preflight inspection, raise them. This last item is very important.

Before you untie the plane, take a moment to determine the best path to follow to open water. Once you start, you're committed, so check for any floatplane or boat traffic that may get in the way, and make sure you'll be able to clear any pilings, docks, or other obstacles in the area.

When you're satisfied the course is clear, untie the plane and push the nose away from the dock. Grab the tail as it swings around toward you and back the floats up to the edge of the dock, taking care not to damage the water rudders. Step onto the tail of the left float, walk quickly forward to the pilot's door, get in, and start the engine (Fig. 8-2). If you're flying a two-place, tandem floatplane like a Citabria or a Super Cub, you'll obviously step onto the right float, since the pilot's door is on that side.

Now you see why it's so important to raise the flaps before you board the airplane. When the flaps are extended, their trailing edges hang quite low, and in your

86

haste to get forward and start the engine you might not notice them. At best, you will suffer a painful blow if you run into a flap, and the shock of slamming full tilt into the sharp trailing edge could even pitch you overboard.

One other word of caution. If you're heavy, as I am, and you're flying a small floatplane like a Cessna 172 or a Super Cub, the stern of the float will probably submerge as you step onto it. The challenge here is to step forward on the float before the water has a chance to wash over the stern and soak your shoes. I make it about 50 percent of the time.

In my experience, the hardest plane to board when it's turned out from the dock is the Cessna 180. Its floats extend back almost to the tail, and when it's backed straight up to the dock, there isn't any room to get around in front of the stabilizer and step onto the float. If you turn a 180 out from the dock at an angle, it's easier to squeeze by the leading edge of the stabilizer and jump onto the float.

STARTING OUT FROM A RAMP

If your floatplane is tailed up on a ramp, getting under-

way is quite easy. After you've loaded your passengers or cargo, climb in yourself and get ready to start the engine. There's no hurry because the floatplane won't go anywhere until the engine starts and pulls it off the ramp. Once you're in the water, however, there's no backing up; so make sure you know where you're going before you hit the start switch. Take a moment to check for traffic and obstacles, and pick the safest path to open water.

If you've tailed the floatplane up on the ramp yourself, the floats will be just barely out of the water, and the plane will slide off the ramp the moment the engine fires. If for some reason the floatplane is sitting solidly on the ramp and clear of the water, you'll need to use a fair amount of power to start it moving down the ramp. The airplane will slide easier if there is some form of lubrication between the floats and the ramp; so before you get in and start the engine, wet the ramp down thoroughly with water.

As soon as the floatplane leaves the ramp, lower the water rudders. Some pilots like to lower the rudders before they start the engine. Their reasoning is that the rudders will drop into position as soon as the floats clear the ramp, making one less thing for the pilot to worry

Fig. 8-2. Once you've turned your floatplane out from the dock, you've got to get aboard quickly and start the engine before you drift into something that could damage your plane.

about if things get busy. I'm sure this works most the time, but the water rudders could be damaged if they catch on a board or if they hit the edge of the ramp as the plane settles into the water. It's best to play it safe and leave them up until the plane has cleared the ramp.

WHEN THE WIND BLOWS

So far, we've been assuming that your flight is taking place on a nice, calm, no-wind day. I've heard that such days exist but that they go into hiding whenever they see someone preparing to launch a floatplane. While this statement doesn't sound very scientific, it certainly seems to be based on fact, and the chances are good that there will be at least some wind on the day that you decide to go up.

Wind is the floatplane pilot's greatest concern. It affects every aspect of float flying, and it's often the determining factor when you're trying to decide whether to fly or not. As far as the wind is concerned, a floatplane is just a big weather vane, and it will always point its nose into the wind. A weather vane, however, remains in one place, rotating around the top of its stationary pole; not so a floatplane, which is free to drift wherever the wind wishes to take it.

To do battle with the evil forces arrayed against them by the wind, floatplane pilots have mooring lines, water rudders, an air rudder, an engine, and a propeller. As we've already seen, however, the water rudders are ineffective until the floatplane is moving forward, and the air rudder isn't worth much until the floatplane is moving forward fast. Between the time the mooring lines are released and the engine is started, the wind is in command.

Although there's nothing you can do about the wind, you at least have the advantage of knowing what it will do to your floatplane, and you can plan your moves accordingly. For instance, you know your plane will start to pivot into the wind as soon as you let go of it; so make sure the wings and tail will swing clear of any nearby obstacles. You also know the airplane will drift with the wind as you're scrambling aboard; so give yourself some extra time by moving the plane upwind as far as possible from any obstacles on the dock.

There is, however, no getting around the fact that no matter how weak or strong the wind is, your floatplane will begin to drift, generally the wrong way, as soon as you let go of it and start to climb on board. In the time it takes you to get on, get in, and get going, the airplane could be blown into a boat, a piling, or another floatplane, or pivoted so you'll taxi forward into something expensive as soon as you start the engine.

This probably sounds very intimidating, but there is an easy solution. If you get someone to hold the tail of your plane after you turn it out, your problems will go away. With someone on the dock holding the tail, the plane can't drift or start pivoting into the wind the moment you step aboard. It's not an admission of incompetence to ask someone to hold the tail for you on a windy day while you get aboard and start the engine. On the contrary, it's a sign of an experienced, conscientious floatplane pilot. It makes no sense to run the risk of damaging one or more expensive floatplanes by trying to prove you can beat the wind. Eventually you'll lose, and the consequences are irreversible.

Large floatplanes like the de Havilland Beaver and Otter are easily shoved around by the wind thanks to their large vertical surfaces, and on blustery days they can quickly become too much for one person to handle. In fact, the massive Otter is almost too much for one person on a calm day, let alone a windy one, so it would be advisable to have several people on the dock to help keep the monster under control. Regardless of your floatplane's size, though, make it a practice to get someone to hold the tail for you when the wind kicks up. It's good insurance.

If the wind is quite strong and your floatplane is on the downwind, or *lee*, side of the dock, it may be easier to get in and simply let the wind push you out into open water before starting the engine, instead of fighting the plane's weathercocking tendency at the dock. If you do decide to drift, or sail, away from the dock, remember that your nose will point into the wind and back toward the dock, so wait until there's enough distance between you and the dock that you can safely turn away from it before you start the engine.

This is actually your first introduction to the fine art of sailing, and a later chapter will be devoted specifically to sailing techniques. There is, however, one rule you need to know now. Whenever you drift a floatplane backwards, the water rudders should be up. When the rudders are up, the floatplane is free to point directly into the wind, and it will travel backwards in a straight line. Once you're well clear of the dock, you can start the engine, lower the water rudders, and turn toward the takeoff area.

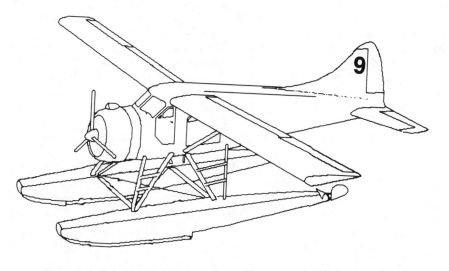

Taxiing the Floatplane

F LOATPLANES HAVE THREE FORWARD TAXI SPEEDS on the water. The slowest is called the *displacement taxi*, second gear is the nose-high, *plowing taxi*, and high gear is called the *step taxi*. Since the steering on a floatplane is somewhat vague and the brakes nonexistent, it's important that the plane's speed be kept well under control when maneuvering on the water. For this reason, you'll spend most of your time on the water taxiing in the displacement mode. You'll use the displacement taxi when you approach or depart a dock, ramp, or beach; when you maneuver through a crowded harbor; and when you have to taxi across rough water. In the displacement mode, the floatplane is being supported solely by the flotation properties of the floats, and all steering is done with the water rudders.

THE DISPLACEMENT TAXI

As a general rule, a floatplane's maximum displacement taxi speed is one at which there is only a slight increase in nose-up pitch over the plane's at-rest attitude on the water (Fig. 9-1). Most floatplanes seem to reach their maximum displacement speed at an engine speed of approximately 1000 rpm, but most of the time you will be taxi-

ing with the engine turning over only slightly faster than idle rpm. At this speed, the propeller won't pick up any spray, and the engine won't overheat.

When you're entering or leaving a dock or ramp area or maneuvering carefully in a crowded harbor, you'll want your plane to move at the slowest speed possible. The slower the propeller turns, the slower you will taxi, so many floatplanes have their idle rpms adjusted until their engines are just barely ticking over. In fact, if the engine in your plane starts easily and runs smoothly, but has a tendency to die when the throttle is pulled all the way back, it probably means the idle speed is set too low and needs to be adjusted by a mechanic. Another technique you can use to slow the engine down while taxiing is to switch off one magneto and pull the carburetor heat on. This will reduce the engine's rpm, but if you operate too long in this configuration, you could foul the spark plugs.

STEERING

In calm or light wind conditions, the floatplane will be quite responsive to the water rudders, and you'll easily be able to turn to crosswind or downwind headings. You may notice that the plane turns to the left faster than it turns to the right; this is due to *P-factor*. It's the same force that requires you to hold right rudder in any single-engine airplane when you take off, climb, or fly in a nose-high attitude while carrying power. The fancy engineering term for it is *asymmetrical disk loading*, and it means that the propeller blades going down generate more thrust than the ones going up. On calm days you can give yourself an interesting demonstration of this force by pulling up the water rudders while the engine is at idle. With no rudders to help maintain directional control, the floatplane will start turning to the left, pulled around by the P-factor, and it will keep on turning until you either run out of gas or lower the water rudders again.

In anything other than an extremely light breeze, the plane will *weathercock*, or point its nose into the wind, when you pull the water rudders up because the force of the wind moving past the tail is greater than the left-turning P-factor from the propeller. That P-factor is always there, however, so don't forget about it. It will come in handy later when you are trying make turns in stronger winds.

As mentioned earlier, the water rudders are spring-loaded. In other words, stiff springs are inserted into the steering cable system. These springs may be attached between the steering cables and the rudder bar in the cockpit, the steering bar on top of each rudder post, or the rudder bar in the air rudder assembly in the tail. The springs are there to protect the water rudders from damage if they strike an obstacle, and are responsible for the somewhat "mushy" feeling you'll experience when you are maneuvering on the water.

In fact, there may even be a time when the floatplane will refuse to turn, even though you have the rudder pedal clear to the floor. While debris may be the culprit, there are times when the rudders are kept from going over by water pressure alone. If you're taxiing in a crosswind or at right angles to the waves, your plane may be forced slightly sideways through the water, and the resulting side pressure may be enough to hold the rudders centered against their springs. You are most likely to encounter this problem in small floatplanes like the Cessna 172, which doesn't have much rudder travel to begin with.

The solution is to relax the pressure on the rudder pedals, pull up the water rudders, apply and hold full left or right rudder, and lower the rudders again. The water rudders on most floatplanes respond to pedal inputs in both the raised and lowered positions; so by pulling them up, you can turn them in the desired direction free of the water's influence. They should stay that way when you lower them again, and the floatplane will begin to turn

in the direction you want to go.

The larger the floatplane, the more positive the steering. A de Havilland Beaver is much more responsive on the water than a Cessna 172 because, compared to the Cessna, the Beaver has huge water rudders, very stiff steering-cable springs, and a lot of travel in the rudder system. The Cessna, on the other hand, has relatively small water rudders; the rudder springs are easily overridden; and the amount of rudder travel is quite limited.

It's a good idea to keep "testing" the water rudders as you taxi. By making slight turns from side to side to check your plane's steering response, you'll know what to expect if you have to make a sudden turn to avoid an obstacle or maneuver through a crowded harbor on your way to or from the dock. By knowing in advance how your plane will respond, you can plan ahead, and your first indication that you can't make a sharp enough turn to the dock won't be the sound of your wing tip slamming into another airplane.

KEEP THE FLOAT TIPS UP

It's important that the control wheel or stick be held full back while taxiing at slow speeds. The propwash, together with whatever wind is present, will push the tail down and raise the nose. This slightly nose-high attitude is desirable for several reasons.

First of all, raising the nose gets the propeller that much farther above the water and any spray that may be kicked up by the floats. This is especially important if the water is choppy because the floats will kick up a fair amount of spray as they butt their way through the waves. Raising the nose will also submerge more of the water rudders, and the floatplane will handle better.

Finally, keeping the nose up will prevent the bows of the floats from digging into the water. This is extremely important, because if the float tips should submerge, the forward speed of the airplane could drive them even deeper, caused the propeller to strike the water. Besides damaging the propeller itself, the sudden load could conceivably overstress the engine mounts, to say nothing of its effect on the engine's internal components.

There is another danger, as well. The floatplane may veer off to one side when the bows of the floats are driven beneath the surface, and if this causes a wing tip to contact the water, the plane will probably capsize.

The best way to avoid these expensive problems is to remember to keep the float tips up by holding full back pressure on the control column whenever you are taxiing in the displacement mode. The only exception to this rule is if you are taxiing downwind in a stiff breeze. You

Fig. 9-1. The displacement taxi. Note the lowered water rudders and up-elevator.

still want to keep the nose up, but since the wind is now coming from astern, you should hold the elevator in the full *down* position by moving the control column all the way forward. The wind will strike the trailing edge of the elevator and push down on the tail, thus raising the float tips.

USE THE AILERONS PROPERLY

It's very important that you use your floatplane's ailerons properly while taxiing. While you're on the water, the ailerons will help you keep the wind from getting under, and lifting, the upwind wing. If the upwind wing should start to lift, the downwind float will be forced deep into the water, and the added drag could cause the plane to capsize, especially if the downwind wing tip contacts the surface.

The proper aileron procedures are the same for both floatplanes and landplanes (Fig. 9-2). On any heading from directly upwind to directly crosswind, the yoke or stick should be held into the wind. In other words, the upwind aileron should be *up*, and the downwind aileron should be *down*. On any heading from crosswind to downwind, the yoke or stick should be held *away* from the wind. The upwind aileron will now be *down*; so the wind striking it from the rear will push the wing down, and the downwind aileron will be *up*. The ailerons should be neutral when taxiing either directly upwind or downwind. Always use the ailerons properly, even if the wind is light. If you aren't prepared, a sudden gust could ruin your whole day.

If you aren't sure which way the wind is blowing, there is an easy way to find out. Once you are well clear of the dock and any nearby obstructions, pull the power back to idle and raise the water rudders. If there is any breeze at all, the floatplane with weathercock into it.

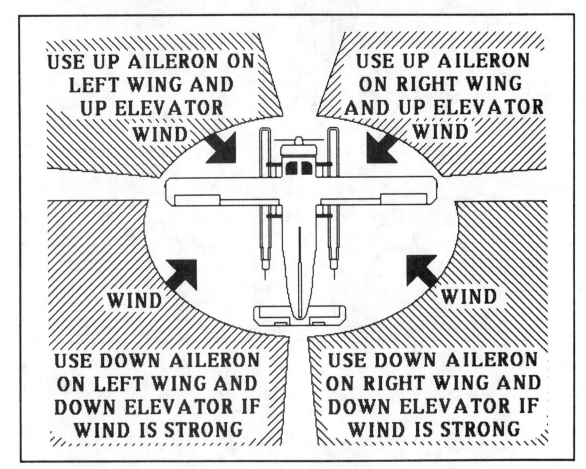

Fig. 9-2. The proper aileron and elevator positions for taxiing in the wind.

THE WEATHERCOCKING TENDENCY

As we have seen, taxiing a floatplane in light- or no-wind conditions is not much different than taxiing a landplane. The water rudders are more than sufficient to overcome whatever weathercocking tendency exists, and turns can be made to any point of the compass without difficulty. The picture changes, however, when the wind starts picking up.

As the wind gets stronger, so will the weathercocking tendency, and it will get harder and harder to turn the plane to a crosswind or downwind heading. Eventually, the application of full left or right rudder will only swing the nose a few degrees off the wind before the weathercocking force stops the turn in its tracks. This isn't a problem if your destination lies directly upwind, but what if you need to taxi in a crosswind or downwind direction?

In order to understand how to taxi a floatplane across or down the wind, you should first understand why the plane is so determined to weathercock into it.

Every airplane has an axis about which it pivots, or yaws, appropriately called the *yaw*, or vertical, *axis*. Most airplanes are designed with quite a bit more vertical surface behind the yaw axis than in front of it. This additional surface behind the yaw axis is the vertical tail, which, like the feathers on an arrow, keeps the airplane headed in the direction it's pointed, and prevents if from yawing around all over the sky making everyone sick.

When a floatplane is taxied across the water in its normal displacement attitude, a crosswind will strike all parts of the airplane with equal force, but because there's more vertical surface to "catch" the wind behind the plane's yaw axis than ahead of it, the plane will swing its nose, or weathercock, into the wind. The stronger the wind, the faster the plane will pivot.

We don't have any control over the factors which are responsible for the weathercocking tendency, but we do have some control over the forces which tend to amplify this tendency. By using the flight controls and the engine, we can reduce these amplifying forces, and make it possible to make crosswind and downwind turns which would otherwise be impossible.

When viewed from the side, the deepest part of a float is forward of the step. Aft of the step, the float tapers up to a very shallow stern. Somewhere along the length of the float, there is a point at which any sideways, or *lateral*, force will move the float sideways through the water. This point is called the *center of resistance to lateral motion*. If you push sideways on the float anywhere forward or aft of this point, the float will pivot in the direc-

tion you push, rather than move straight sideways. Because a float has a deep forward section and a relatively shallow after section, the center of resistance to lateral motion is not located exactly halfway down the length of the float, but is somewhere forward of the step. It's important to note that when a floatplane weathercocks, it pivots around its floats' centers of resistance to lateral motion, not its own yaw axis.

Now things start getting a little complicated. There is a point on the top of a float where, if a downward force, or weight, is applied, the float will settle deeper into the water, but will maintain the same level attitude, or fore-and-aft trim. This point is called the *center of buoyancy*. For a bunch of exotic mathmatical reasons, a float's center of buoyancy is *aft* of its center of resistance to lateral motion.

A floatplane is joined to its floats by the float struts, which, in effect, connect the airplane's center of gravity, or weight, to the floats' center of buoyancy to ensure that the plane will float on the water in the correct attitude. Since the center of buoyancy is located aft of the center of resistance to lateral motion, the wind's sideways force on the airframe is transmitted to the floats behind their pivot points, amplifying the weathercocking tendency and causing the floatplane to swing around into the wind even faster (Fig. 9-3).

Perhaps the easiest way to visualize this weathercocking business is to think of the floatplane's silhouette as a huge weather vane. Instead of mounting our weather vane at what would be the airplane's normal yaw axis, however, we have moved the mounting point even farther forward, to the float's center of resistance to lateral motion. With that much more of the weather vane's body aft of the pivot point, it's that much easier for the wind to swing it into a streamlined position.

As the wind gets stronger, so will the weathercocking tendency, until eventually the water rudders will no longer be able to overpower the wind. At this point, it will become impossible to turn out of the wind unless some means of reducing the weathercocking tendency is found. Fortunately, there is such a means.

THE PLOWING TURN

When the floatplane is in its normal displacement attitude on the water, the shallow keel area aft of its center of resistance to lateral motion makes it easy for the tail to skid sideways and weathercock. If enough power is added to make the floatplane lift it nose and drive the rear of the floats deeply into the water, the floatplane's centers of buoyancy and resistance to lateral motion will move aft, and there will be less wetted keel area ahead of these

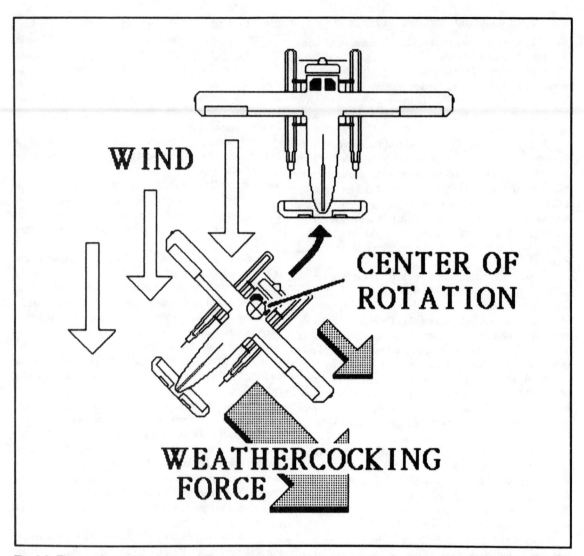

WIND

CENTER OF
ROTATION

WEATHERCOCKING
FORCE

Fig. 9-3. The weathercocking tendency. The plane will pivot around its center of rotation and point into the wind. The water rudders will help counter this tendency, but when the wind reaches a certain velocity, even the water rudders will be unable to keep the plane from pivoting into the wind.

two points than behind them (Fig. 9-4). With the pivot point of the plane moved so far aft, the plane may now even weathercock downwind but in any case, turns to crosswind or downwind headings will be much easier to make.

This nose-high, partial-power turn is called a *plowing turn,* so named because the floatplane is *mushing,* or plowing, through the water. It should only be used to turn the plane downwind in windy conditions. To put your floatplane into a plowing attitude, add power and hold

the yoke or stick all the way back. The force of the propwash striking the elevator will drive the sterns of the floats down and raise the bows out of the water. The added power will also make your floatplane taxi faster, and as the water "piles up" in front of the floats, the increased hydrodynamic pressure will force the bows of the floats even higher. Besides moving your floatplane's pivot point farther aft, this nose-high attitude has another advantage. As the sterns of the floats are driven down into the water, the water rudders will become more effective and exert more turning force on the plane.

In addition to driving the tail down, the blast of air from the propeller will also make the air rudder more effective, which will also help you turn downwind. And don't forget the P-factor mentioned earlier. Take advantage of your airplane's left-turning tendency, and make your plowing turns in that direction whenever possible. Having the P-factor working for you may make the difference between completing a downwind turn and getting "stuck" part way through it.

If the wind is strong enough, the weathercocking force may stop even a plowing turn shortly after you begin it. To avoid this problem, start your turn to the left by initially turning to the right while remaining in the displacement attitude. As soon as the plane is turned to the right, apply full left rudder. Aided by its weathercocking tendency, the airplane will begin a rapid swing to the

left. As it passes through its original upwind heading, apply just enough power to raise the nose and shift the centers of buoyancy and resistance to lateral motion aft. Continue to hold full left rudder until the plane approaches the downwind heading. Stop the turn when you are headed directly downwind, pull the power back to idle, and resume taxiing in the displacement attitude (Fig. 9-5).

Seen from above, your turn will look like a giant question mark. By first turning the floatplane to the right, you will take advantage of the wind's weathercocking force to accelerate the plane into the left turn, and this added momentum will help swing the plane through to the downwind heading.

TAXIING DOWNWIND

Once the turn to a downwind heading has been made, the power should be reduced to idle, and the floatplane tax-

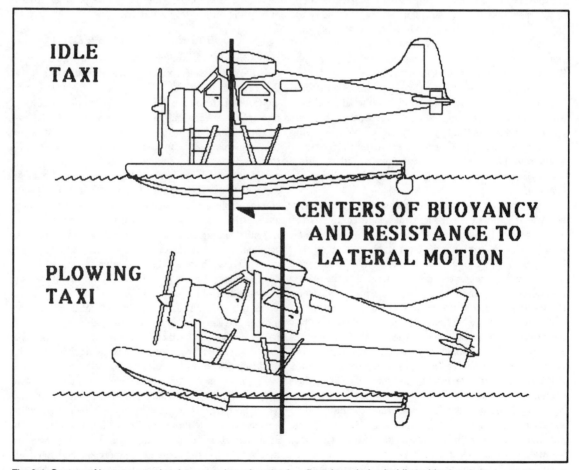

Fig. 9-4. Centers of buoyancy and resistance to lateral motion in a floatplane during its idle taxi (top) and plowing taxi (bottom).

ied downwind in the displacement attitude. Great care must be exercised while taxiing downwind, however, because if the plane should begin to turn even slightly off course, the wind will catch the side of the plane, and it will weathercock around with considerable force. Be alert for the first signs of weathercocking, and correct them immediately with the water rudders.

If the plane should begin to weathercock and using the opposite rudder doesn't stop it, you have to make a quick decision. You can either raise the water rudders and let the plane swing around into the wind, or you can try to force the plane back to its downwind heading. The course of action you take depends primarily on the strength of the wind and the handling and stability characteristics of your floatplane.

Generally, the *safest* thing to do is pull the water rudders up and let the floatplane pivot around into the wind. Raising the water rudders reduces the floats' resistance to weathercocking, and your plane will be less likely to capsize if the wind is strong. Once turned around and headed safely into the wind, you can decide whether you want to chance another downwind turn, or sail the floatplane backwards (see Chapter 15).

Your other alternative is to stop the plane from weathercocking and return it to its downwind heading. As soon as the plane begins to weathercock, apply power, opposite rudder, and full up elevator. These actions will raise the nose to the plowing attitude, and the sudden blast of air from the propeller will bring the air rudder to life, making it easier to turn the plane back to its downwind heading.

Don't try this method if the wind is strong, however, because if it doesn't work and the plane continues to weathercock, the plane may capsize as it swings around into the wind. Floatplanes are least stable when they are in a plowing attitude, and when this instability is combined with the high inertial forces generated as the plane weathercocks around under power, the plane will lean toward the outside of the turn. The wind can now get under that upwind wing and lift it, and the plane may be on its back before you even realize what's happening.

If the wind is moderately strong, the problem of weathercocking can be reduced by keeping the floatplane in the plowing attitude as you taxi downwind. With the centers of buoyancy and resistance to lateral motion moved aft, the plane will be much easier to control. As noted earlier, it may even weathercock downwind. There may, however, be a limit to the length of time you can maintain a plowing attitude.

First of all, the engine may overheat. Because you're developing power, the engine will be generating a lot of heat, but because you aren't moving very fast, the flow of air over the cylinders may not be sufficient to cool them properly. Keep a close eye on the oil and cylinder head temperature gauges if you decide to keep the airplane plowing through the water for any length of time, and be prepared to reduce the power to idle and swing around into the wind if the engine gets too hot. Radial-engined floatplanes like the Beaver are especially susceptible to overheating while plowing. The big radials develop a lot of heat, and at slow taxi speeds, the flow of cooling air over the cylinders is rather poor.

In addition, your forward visibility may be restricted by the floatplane's nose-high attitude while plowing, and it may be difficult to see and avoid other boat or floatplane traffic in the area. If, however, the distance you have to cover is relatively short, and if the wind is strong, it may be a good idea to keep the plane in a plowing attitude during the entire downwind taxi.

JUDGING THE WIND SPEED

If the wind is light and you are taxiing downwind faster than the wind itself is moving, hold the yoke or stick all the way back to keep the float tips up. If the wind is moving faster than you are, hold the yoke or stick all the way forward. As we saw earlier, the wind will strike the down elevator from the rear, pushing the tail down and raising the float tips. How can you tell, though, if the wind is moving faster than you are?

Most floatplanes have grablines hanging down from the wing tips or the upper ends of the wing struts. Besides coming in handy while maneuvering the airplane around a dock, the grablines make great wind speed indicators. If you're taxiing downwind and the lines are streaming aft, you're moving faster than the wind. As long as you keep moving, there will be no tendency for the plane to weathercock around if you should deviate from your downwind heading.

If the grablines are hanging straight down, you are moving the same speed as the wind. Although there will be some tendency for the plane to weathercock when you turn away from your direct downwind heading, this tendency will be easily overpowered by the water rudders.

If, however, the lines are streaming out ahead of the wing, beware, for the wind is moving faster than you are. You'd better get that yoke forward and be extra careful, because things could get really exciting really fast. Any deviation from a direct downwind heading will immediately cause the plane to weathercock, and you'd better be prepared to deal with it one way or another.

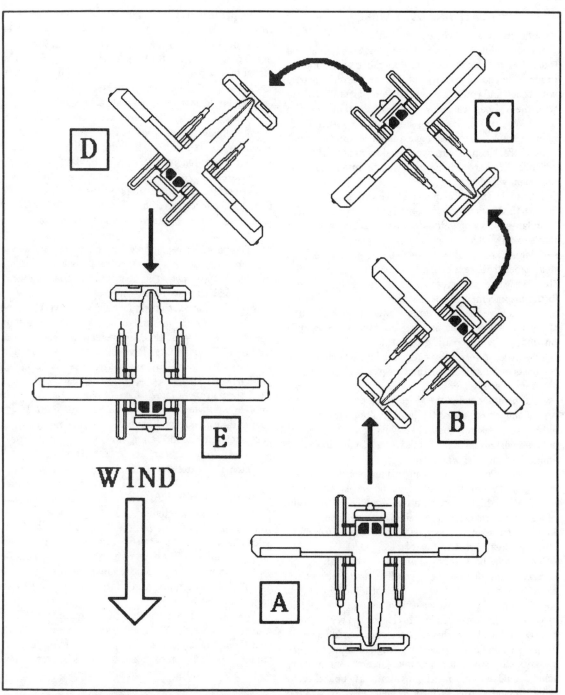

Fig. 9-5. Turning the plane with a strong wind. Start facing into the wind (A), turn to the right (B), apply full left rudder and it will swing to the left (C). As it passes through its original upwind heading, apply power to raise the nose and shift the centers of buoyancy and resistance to lateral motion aft. Continue to hold the plowing turn as the plane turns downwind (D). Stop the turn when you are heading directly downwind (E).

BOATS AND BOAT WAKES

As a floatplane pilot, you may be the master of your environment while you are airborne, but as soon as you touch the water, you become a member of a minority group. The people in charge of the water are the people with boats, and you're going to have to learn to get along with them. Boats can move much faster than you can unless you're on the step, and they're much more maneuverable. They also have a habit of appearing out of nowhere. Keep a sharp eye peeled for boat traffic, and practice defensive driving by trying to anticipate what the boats will do.

Actually, the problem you'll have with boats will not be with the boats themselves, but with their wakes. Most floatplanes cannot operate safely in very rough water, and that's exactly what a boat wake is: rough water. As we'll see later, boat wakes pose the greatest threat to floatplanes that are taking off, landing, or taxiing on the step, but wakes can create problems for planes taxiing in the displacement mode, too.

Boats have the same three forward speeds through the water as floatplanes, and the size of the wake depends on what speed the boat is going at the time. Boats moving slowly leave very little water disturbance behind them. Sailboats under sail fall into this category, and their wakes are almost negligible.

At the other end of the speed scale, powerboats that are planing across the water don't generate large wakes, either. The reason is that, like a floatplane on the step, only a small portion of the boat's hull is actually touching, and disturbing, the water.

The problem lies with boats that are being driven fast through the water, but not fast enough to plane. The result is a bow-high, plowing attitude which moves a lot of water and creates a large wake. The swells pushed up by a boat travelling at this speed can be several feet high, and are a real threat to floatplanes.

As a rule, boat wakes of any kind should always be crossed at the slowest speed possible, as it's often hard to tell just how big the swells are until you're right on top of them. If the boat wake is a big one, it's best to cross it at a 45-degree angle. This choice is a compromise between taking the waves head on, which could pitch the airplane up and down violently enough to cause the propeller to strike the water, and taking them from the side, which could set up a rocking motion that could drive a wing tip beneath the surface. Remember, with its high center of gravity, narrow "wheelbase," and long, momentum-generating wings, your floatplane is a somewhat "tippy" machine.

Be particularly careful not to take a large boat wake from the side while you are taxiing in a crosswind. The wind would very much like to get under your upwind wing and flip you over, and the side-to-side rocking motion induced by the boat wake may give the wind its chance.

It's important that you understand the proper procedures for dealing with boat wakes, because you should always try to pass behind a boat that's crossing your path. Many skippers get nervous at the thought of being on a collision course with a whirling propeller; so an early indication that you intend to pass behind them is usually appreciated. There's no way of knowing which way a power boat or sailboat is going to turn, or if it's going to suddenly accelerate, but it's a pretty safe bet that it isn't going to instantly reverse its course or start backing up.

The past few years, however, have seen the growing popularity of a boat that has given new meaning to the word *unpredictable*. This boat is the sailboard, or windsurfer, and if they are popular in your area, be very wary of them. They are extremely fast and maneuverable, and can reverse directions and accelerate almost instantaneously. On top of this, the person sailing the boat stands up behind the sail, which greatly restricts the visibility to leeward. He may not even see you coming.

The worst thing about sailboards is that they tip over a lot, and you never know when, or where, they're going to do it. Just when you think you have the darn thing's course figured out, and have turned your floatplane to pass behind it, the kid sailing it spins it around, crosses directly in front of your nose, and falls over.

To make matters worse, when a sailboard is down, it's almost impossible to see. The owner is in the water with it; the board itself is only a few inches thick; and the mast and sail are hinged to lie flat on the surface. If you're concentrating on the other boat traffic in the area, a downed windsurfer is easy to overlook. The first indication you will probably have of its presence is when the owner scrambles back onto it, yanks the mast and sail up out of the water, and accelerates out in front of you, only to fall over again.

The antics of windsurfers can be quite amusing to watch, but be very careful when maneuvering a floatplane near them. Standing on that small board, their "crews" are not very well protected, and a collision between windsurfer and a floatplane could be disastrous.

RIGHT-OF-WAY RULES: WATER OPERATIONS

Let's say you're taxiing your floatplane toward the takeoff area, and a boat approaches you from the left. At your present speeds and headings, your courses will intersect, and a collision may result. Obviously, one of you must give way to the other, but who has the right of way?

The answer is found in Part 91, Section 69, of the Federal Aviation Regulations (FAR's), entitled Right-of-Way Rules: Water Operations. The rules in this section are as follows:

(a) *General.* Each person operating an aircraft on the water shall, insofar as possible, keep clear of all vessels and avoid impeding their navigation, and shall give way to any vessel or other aircraft that is given the right of way by any rule of this section.

(b) *Crossing.* When aircraft, or an aircraft and a vessel, are on crossing courses, the aircraft or vessel to the other's right has the right of way.

(c) *Approaching head-on.* When aircraft, or an aircraft and a vessel, are approaching head-on or nearly so, each shall alter its course to the right to keep well clear.

(d) *Overtaking.* Each aircraft or vessel that is being overtaken has the right of way, and the one overtaking shall alter course to keep well clear.

(e) *Special circumstances.* When aircraft, or an aircraft and a vessel, approach so as to involve risk of collision, each aircraft or vessel shall proceed with careful regard to existing circumstances, including the limitations of the respective craft.

So the answer to our right-of-way question lies in paragraph (b) of FAR 91.69. If a boat approaches you from your left, *you* have the right of way, since you are to the boat's right.

These rules apply to all aircraft that are operating on the so-called *inland waters* of the United States, which include the country's lakes, rivers, harbors, and anything else lying within the boundary line dividing the inland waters from the international waters, or *high seas*. Seaplane operations conducted on the high seas outside these boundary lines fall under the jurisdiction of the United States Coast Guard, while seaplane operations conducted on the inland waters are under the jurisdiction of the FAA.

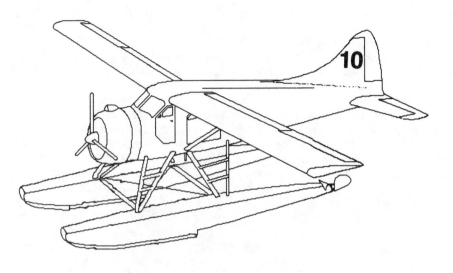

The Takeoff

I T'S VERY DIFFICULT TO PAINT WHITE LINES ON THE surface of the water, let alone expect them to stay there, so it's going to be up to you to determine the location of your "runway," or takeoff lane. There are a few seaplane facilities, Lake Hood in Anchorage, Alaska, for example, that have permanent takeoff and landing lanes marked with buoys, but for the most part, it will be up to you to select the best and safest place to take off.

This is one of the advantages you, as a floatplane pilot, have over your wheel-bound friends, because you can almost always take off into the wind. Sometimes it seems the approved method of designing an airport is to first determine the direction of the prevailing winds in the area, and then lay out the runways at precise, 90-degree angles to this direction, but floatplane pilots are not limited by these unsuccessful attempts to second-guess the weather. Even on those occasions when the shoreline or other obstructions make it impossible to take off directly into the wind, you will almost always be able to take off in a direction that will at least reduce the cross-wind component.

DETERMINE THE WIND DIRECTION

By the time you have left the dock or ramp and are taxi-ing out into open water, you should already have a pretty good idea of the wind direction. Sometimes, however, the shape of a lake, bay, or harbor may be such that the wind direction near the shore is different than the wind direction out in open water. Trees, buildings, or surrounding hills can all conspire to alter the prevailing wind, so it's a good idea to double-check the wind's speed and direction as you taxi out. Fortunately, there will be lots of clues to help you out.

We've already talked about using the floatplane itself to determine the wind direction by raising the water rudders and letting the plane weathercock into the wind, but there are other indicators all around you. Trees along the shoreline will bend or sway with the wind, as will tall reeds and marsh grass. If anyone on shore is burning trash, the smoke will be an excellent wind indicator.

The water itself is probably the best wind direction indicator, once you learn to "read" it. The friction of the wind passing over the water's surface creates waves, and the direction and size of these waves indicate the direction and strength of the wind. When the wind reaches 8 to 12 miles per hour, the surface will be pushed up into wavelets that will begin to break, making it fairly easy to determine from which way the wind is coming. It's important to remember that as the wave crests move and break with the wind, they will leave a trail of foam stretching back *upwind*. While this seems very logical when you think about it, for some reason it can become very confusing when seen from an airplane, and it's easy to be fooled into thinking that the waves and the wind are going in opposite directions.

If the wind is less than 8 knots, it's a little harder to determine its direction by looking at the water. Wavelets will still be formed, but they won't break, and it may be difficult to pick them out from the other ripples and waves left over from boat wakes and the passage of other seaplanes. A very light wind will generate ripples with the appearance of scales with their rounded edges pointing downwind, but it takes a practiced eye to pick them out.

This is one time when it's nice to have boats around, because they can be very helpful in determining the wind direction. Boats, barges, or ships that are moored to a single buoy will always point into the wind unless there is a very strong current running, in which case they will line up with the moving water. Both power boats and sailboats often have flags or streamers flying from them, and while these don't help you much if the boat is under way, they are as good as wind socks if the boat is stationary.

Sailboats, both moored and under sail, make wonderful wind indicators. All of them have some form of onboard indicators ranging from simple telltales (lengths of light string tied to the mast stays), to sophisticated, masthead direction indicators. Observing a sailboat under sail is also a good way to determine the wind direction, if you know how to interpret the position of the sails.

Sailboats cannot sail, or *point*, directly into the wind. Depending on the design of the boat, the best they can do is generally about 30 to 45 degrees off the wind, and to be able to do even this, the sails must be tightly sheeted in, or positioned nearly along the centerline of the hull. The boat will also lean, or *heel*, in the direction the wind is blowing.

When a sailboat is *reaching*, or sailing across the wind, the sails are let out farther than when the boat is pointing. The boom will no longer be close to the centerline of the boat, but will be let out some distance to leeward, and the sails will have a definite curve, or *belly*.

When a sailboat is *running*, or sailing downwind, the sails will be let out all the way, and the boom may be let out almost at right angles to the boat. If you should see a sailboat with the mainsail set out to one side and the jib set out to the other, you can be sure that the boat is heading directly downwind. This configuration is known in sailing jargon as running *wing and wing*.

Another excellent, and beautiful, indicator that a sailboat is heading downwind is if it is flying a *spinnaker*, the huge and often colorful triangular sail that is set forward of the mast in place of the jib. It is generally used only when the boat is running, but there are exceptions. Spinnakers can be used from dead downwind to reaching across the wind, but the giveaway is the position of the sail. If it is evenly across the front of the boat, and the boat is upright, the boat is very close to a downwind heading. If the spinnaker is sheeted around to one side of the boat, and the boat is moving fast with a lot of heel, it is heading across the wind.

In summary, if you see a sailboat with its sails nearly flat, and the boom pulled tightly in toward the centerline of the boat, it is heading as close into the wind as it can get. By mentally adding another 30 or 40 degrees to windward of its heading, you will get a rough but usable indication of the wind's direction. If you see a sailboat with some curve, or *belly*, in its sails, and the boom is let out to leeward, it is sailing across the wind, so you can get an idea of the wind direction by adding 90 degrees to the boat's heading. Finally, if you see a sailboat standing nearly erect with its sails let way out or flying a spinnaker, it's heading downwind, and you should take off or land in the opposite direction.

You may think I've spent a lot of effort to explain something relatively insignificant, but believe me, sailboats can come in handy, especially when you are landing. At certain speeds, the wind forms streaks, or lines, on the surface of the water which are very obvious from higher altitudes. While these streaks precisely indicate the direction of the wind across the water, it's often very difficult to tell the upwind end of the streak from the downwind end.

On one particular flight, wind streaks were the only indication I could find of the wind's direction. There wasn't any smoke, and I was too high to see which way the trees were bending. Somehow, I became convinced that the wind was coming from the south, so I flew my approach and lined up with the wind streaks on final, heading south. As I approached the water, I thought I was going awfully fast, but since I was convinced I was landing into the wind, I didn't do anything about it.

Then I saw the sailboat. It was off to my right, and heading toward me at about a 45-degree angle. The sails were sheeted in tight, and it was heeling away from me. I'd done enough crewing on racing sailboats to recognize immediately that it was pointing as close into the wind as possible, and that the wind was coming from behind me, not ahead of me. It was a simple matter to add power, go around, and land down the wind streaks in the opposite direction, this time into the wind. Although, in this case a downwind landing would probably not have gotten me into trouble, the presence of the sailboat enabled me to make a safe landing into the wind, and the risks of touching down at too high a speed were completely eliminated.

CHOOSE YOUR TAKEOFF LANE

Once you've determined the wind direction, you can select the best place to put your "runway." Obviously, you'd like to be able to take off directly into the wind, and most of the time you probably can. There are, however, several things to consider first:

☐ Make sure there's enough water in front of you to take off from (Fig. 10-1). I realize this is pretty elementary, but judging by the number of floatplanes that run out of room and end up in the bushes each year, it's a rule that bears repeating. Don't stop measuring at the far shore, either. It doesn't do much good to lift safely off the lake only to hit the trees growing around it.

☐ Don't overlook the fact that your best route out of the area may not be straight ahead. If the water surface is long enough to take off from, but you don't think you can climb at a steep enough angle to clear the trees directly ahead of you, check the landscape on either side of your planned departure route. There may be an area where the trees are not so high, or a river may create a break in the forest altogether. If the obstacle in front of you is a hill or mountainside, there may be a valley off to one side you can fly through as you

Fig. 10-1. Make sure you can safely clear any obstacles that may be in front of you when you take off. This picture was taken with a telephoto lens, and the houses and apartments are actually a mile or so away from the departing Beaver. Soon after liftoff, the pilot practiced noise abatement by turning to the left and flying down the lake while he gained altitude.

climb out. There's nothing wrong with making a gentle turn after take off to avoid an obstacle, but make sure you know exactly what you're going to do before you start your take off run. The time to begin looking for an escape route is not while you're approaching a row of trees at 90 miles per hour.

☐ Make sure there won't be any boats or boat wakes crossing your path as you take off. The wakes from boats that are some distance away can end up in your take off lane, so check out *all* the boat traffic in the area, not just that which is immediately in front of you. You still have to go through your engine run-up and pre-takeoff checklists; so don't despair if someone is plowing across your chosen take off lane in a 60-foot cruiser. By the time you're ready to go, the boat and its wake should be gone.

Of more concern would be the 60-foot cruiser that is still some distance away, because it, or its wake, will probably arrive just as you get ready to take off. If you see this situation developing, you can do one of three things. You can expedite your run-up and takeoff checks as much as possible and try to get away before the monster arrives; you can pick another takeoff lane; or you can simply taxi around a while longer until the cruiser and its wake have come and gone. If you are operating from a crowded lake or harbor, this can get extremely frustrating when one boat leaves only to be replaced by another. Fortunately, this situation doesn't happen very often.

☐ You also want to make sure that the takeoff lane you have chosen is free of obstructions. Things like pilings, docks, rafts, and buoys are easy enough to see, but underwater obstructions like mud banks, gravel or sand bars, rocks, and floating logs can be impossible to spot from a floatplane on the surface. If you arrived at this location by plane, you will have spotted any obstructions from the air before landing, but if you are new to the area, you'll have to rely on your instructor, other seaplane pilots, or local boaters to point out the places where hidden obstructions are lurking just beneath the surface.

Floating logs and stumps, called *deadheads*, are a real problem, especially in the logging areas of the Pacific Northwest. As they get waterlogged, they float lower and lower in the water, until they are just about impossible to see

from a boat or plane on the surface. Add to this the fact that deadheads don't stay in one place, but drift around with the currents, and you have a real threat to both seaplane pilots and boaters. Be very wary of any small branches you see sticking out of the water, for while they actually may be nothing more than small branches, they could also be attached to a 2000-pound, float-puncturing log. Steer clear of any seagulls that appear to be standing or walking on the water, too. Seagulls can float, but they can't walk on water. If they're standing up, they have to be standing on something, and if it's big enough for a seagull to land and walk around on, it's probably big enough to put a good-sized hole in the bottom of one of your floats.

THE PRETAKEOFF CHECKLIST

Both landplane and floatplane pilots are required to perform engine runups and to check off items on a pretakeoff checklist prior to flight. The only difference is that the floatplane pilot must perform these operations while his airplane is moving. This procedure isn't nearly as tricky as it may sound, but there are a few basic rules to follow:

☐ First of all, watch where you're going. When you were taxiing away from the seaplane base, all your attention was focused outside, but during the engine run-up and pretakeoff checks, you're going to be concentrating on things inside the cockpit. It's important that you keep glancing outside as you run through the checklists so you don't run into anything.

☐ Whenever possible, perform the engine run up into the wind, especially if the wind is strong. You will be adding quite a bit of power during the magneto, propeller, and carburetor heat checks, and the plane will move from a level, displacement attitude to a nose-high, plowing attitude. As we saw earlier, your plane is somewhat unstable in this attitude, and in a strong crosswind, the right combination of waves and gusts could put your floatplane on its back.

☐ Finally, keep the control wheel or stick all the way back during the engine run up. This action will help protect the propeller from spray by holding the nose of the floatplane up. For the same reason, keep the actual run-up time as brief as possible. Perform your engine checks quickly (but don't skip any of them), and return the engine to idle as soon as possible to minimize the time the propeller is exposed to spray.

The actual engine, instrument, and control system checks will vary among planes and should be done in the order printed in the airplane's operating manual, with one exception. If you're flying a high-wing floatplane, don't lower the flaps to their takeoff setting at this time, even if the checklist calls for it. When the flaps are down, your visibility may be blocked aft of the wing, and you won't be able to tell if you're being overtaken by a boat or another seaplane, or if you will collide with one if you start to turn. The visibility restriction varies among planes, depending on the design and amount of flap used for takeoff. It's not much of a problem in a Cessna 172, which uses only 10 degrees of flap during takeoff, but if you're flying a de Havilland Beaver, a large portion of the landscape behind you will be hidden when the flaps are lowered to their takeoff setting. Keep the flaps up until you are ready to begin your takeoff run.

After you've performed the normal engine checks as called out in the manual, it's a good idea to add one more item that I've never seen included in any of the factory manuals. Pull the throttle all the way back and check the minimum idle rpm. As mentioned in Chapter 9, many floatplanes have their minimum idle rpm set as low as possible, so the plane will taxi as slow as possible; and you want to make sure the engine will continue to run when it's throttled all the way back. It might not when it's cold, but by the time you've taxied out to the takeoff are and run up the engine, it should be warm enough to continue to run at its minimum idle setting. If the engine dies when the throttle is pulled all the way back, report this fact to the flight school or the airplane's mechanic as soon as possible so the idel can be adjusted. You don't need to have the engine die on you just as you're trying to maneuver through a crowded harbor on a windy day.

After you've performed the engine run up, and run through all the items on the pretakeoff checklist, it's time to get airborne. Well, almost. If the wind conditions will safely permit it, clear the area first by making a 360-degree turn. This will give you a chance to look for any new boat traffic that might have snuck up while you were busy doing your pretakeoff checks, and also to make sure there are no other floatplanes coming in to land on the same piece of water from which you're about to take off.

After you have completed your inspection of the surrounding sky and water, make sure your takeoff lane is still free of traffic and boat wakes. If it isn't, you can either wait for a while or shift your planned takeoff path left or right to smoother or less cluttered water.

Once you've lined yourself up on the takeoff lane you've selected, you can lower the flaps to the recommended takeoff setting. Before you start your takeoff run, however, take a moment to let other pilots who might be in the area know of your intentions. Some seaplane facilities have an assigned Unicom frequency you can use, and at those that do not, broadcast your takeoff and departure intentions on the Multicom frequency of 122.9.

THE TAKEOFF

A takeoff can be divided into four distinct phases. Their names may vary slightly, but for the purposes of this book, I will refer to them as the displacement, hump, planing, and rotation phases.

The Displacement Phase

Just before you apply takeoff power, raise the water rudders. This action will prevent them from banging up and down and damaging both themselves and the floats.

Next, hold the yoke or stick all the way back and smoothly apply takeoff power. This will be full power in most modern floatplanes, but be careful if you're flying an airplane equipped with a mechanical supercharger. The Pratt & Whitney R-985 radial engine as used on the de Havilland Beaver has a supercharger that can maintain sea-level manifold pressure up to 5000 feet. Because it is not equipped with a waste gate to dump excess supercharger pressure, it's possible to overboost the engine at lower altitudes if the throttle is simply pushed all the way up; so you'll have to keep an eye on the manifold pressure gauge as you advance the throttle.

This first phase of the takeoff is called the *displacement phase* because full power will at first simply force the floats bodily through the water. Spray will be a problem because the plane will be moving relatively slowly while the floats are bulldozing water ahead of them. If the control wheel or stick is held all the way back, the blast of air striking the elevator will help push the tail down, and as the nose comes up, the propeller will be lifted clear of much of the damaging spray.

As the plane's speed through the water increases, the bows of the floats will begin to rise. This is because the weight of the floatplane is starting to be supported by the pressure of the water against the bottom of the floats, rather than the flotation qualities of the floats alone. This water, or *hydrodynamic,* pressure, is created by the floatplane itself as it accelerates through the water.

The reason full up-elevator should be applied at the beginning of the takeoff run is simply to help get the propeller out of the spray as soon as possible. Raising the nose this way also prevents the bows of the floats from digging into the waves, if there are any, but even if the elevator is kept in its neutral position, the increasing hydrodynamic pressure will force the bows of the floats to rise.

The Hump Phase

The nose-up phase of the takeoff is called the *hump phase,* because the floatplane appears to be climbing up a hump, or hill, of water in front of it (Fig. 10-2). As the plane accelerates, its nose will lift higher and higher as the hydrodynamic pressure gets stronger and the center of hydrodynamic support moves farther aft. When the center of hydrodynamic support reaches the portion of each float's bottom that is just ahead of the step, the floatplane will drop its nose to an almost level flight attitude and skim across the water, its weight supported completely by the hydrodynamic pressure on the bottom of the floats. This, the third phase of the takeoff, is called the *planing phase,* but let's not get ahead of ourselves.

The floatplane's left-turning tendency, caused primarily by P-factor, will be strongest during the nose-high, hump phase of the takeoff run, but you can't counteract it using the water rudders because they've been retracted. The only other directional control available to you is the airplane's air rudder, but it isn't very effective unless there's a rapid slipstream of air moving past it. Since the floatplane is still moving relatively slowly while it's in the hump phase, you may have to push the right rudder pedal clear to the floor in order to counter the plane's desire to swing to the left, and in some floatplanes, even full right rudder won't keep the plane heading straight (Fig. 10-3). The blast of air over the tail resulting from the engine going to takeoff power will help bring the rudder to life, but don't be surprised if the plane swings a little to the left as it raises its nose.

Fig. 10-2. A de Havilland Beaver in the hump phase of the takeoff run. The extreme nose-high attitude can restrict forward visibility; so make sure your takeoff lane is clear before adding power.

106

Fig. 10-3. This picture was taken moments after the pilot applied full takeoff power. Note the right rudder to counteract the P-factor and the up-elevator to help raise the propeller out of the spray.

The only time this swing to the left could really be a problem is when you are taking off from waters that are crowded with boats or other obstacles, or from a narrow channel. If you are flying a floatplane that, despite your best efforts on the rudder pedals, always swings a little to the left at the beginning of a takeoff run, you can anticipate it by aiming the plane a little to the right of your intended takeoff path. By the time the inevitable left turn has brought your plane around to a heading in line with your chosen takeoff lane, you will be moving fast enough for the air rudder to be fully effective, and you'll have excellent directional control throughout the remainder of the takeoff run.

Probably the most dramatic example of the effect P-factor can have on a floatplane is the experience the British had with their series of Supermarine racing floatplanes. Their engines were so powerful, and their two-bladed, fixed-pitch propellers were so immense, the planes had to be aimed at right angles to the wind before the pilot could begin his takeoff run. By the time the plane was going fast enough for its air rudder to be fully effec-

tive, the P-factor from that giant prop had pulled the plane through a full, 90-degree arc to the left. So accepted did this practice become, the pilot of the first Supermarine Spitfire dutifully pointed the prototype fighter's nose 90 degrees to the right of the runway before applying takeoff power to begin the airplane's maiden flight. Since the Spitfire was designed by the same man who had designed Supermarine's racing floatplanes, the pilot naturally assumed that the takeoff characteristics would also be the same. They weren't, and the Spitfire started its flight into history by taking off in the direction it was pointed.

The other problem you'll encounter as the plane "climbs the hump" is the reduction of your forward visibility. The nose gets quite high during the hump phase, and your forward visibility may even be blocked completely. For this reason, it's very important that you know what's in front of you before you apply takeoff power. Once the plane drops over into the planing attitude, your visibility will be restored, but for a few moments you will be vulnerable to boats wandering into your path, especially from the right, or to obstacles you failed to notice earlier. Even if you do see them, you won't have the maneuverability to avoid them; so before you advance the throttle, make sure your takeoff lane is, and will remain, clear.

As soon as the floatplane has reached its maximum nose-high attitude, return the yoke or stick to its neutral position. The idea is to get the floatplane on the step as soon as possible, and if you continue to hold up-elevator, you will only succeed in delaying the moment when the plane pitches forward onto the step and begins to accelerate to flying speed. Elevator back-pressure should only be held during the initial part of the takeoff to lift the propeller out of the spray and expedite your plane into the hump phase.

The Planing Phase

As the floatplane's forward speed increases, so will the hydrodynamic pressure under the floats, until finally the entire weight of the airplane will be supported by the pressure of the water against the float bottoms. At this point, the floatplane will pitch forward to a nearly level attitude, and begin to skim, or plane, across the surface of the water (Fig. 10-4). This is appropriately called the planing phase, and the floatplane is referred to as being *on the step*.

When the floatplane is in the proper planing attitude, only a small portion of the float bottoms just ahead of the steps will be touching the water. The forward and after sections of each float will ride above the surface, thus minimizing the wetted surface of each float, which, in turn, minimizes the hydrodynamic drag on the floats, and the plane can quickly accelerate to rotation speed.

It is very important that the floatplane remain in the correct planing attitude. Any deviation from this attitude will result in additional drag which will extend the take-

Fig. 10-4. The planing phase of the takeoff run. The plane is being supported only by the hydrodynamic pressure on the float bottoms just ahead of the step. As the plane accelerates, its weight will be transferred to the lift generated by the wings until finally, the aerodynamic lift will equal the weight of the plane, and it will become airborne.

off run. If the nose is held too low, the forebodies of the floats will begin to *rub,* or drag on the water, and if the nose is held too high, the tails of the floats will start to dig into the water.

The most common error is to hold the nose too high. If the nose is held too low, the rubbing of the forward keels will be quite obvious, and the plane will slow down and pitch forward almost as though the pilot were applying brakes. On the other hand, if nose is too high, causing the tails of the floats to drag, the only indication that something is wrong will be the extended length of the takeoff run. Since an excessive nose-up attitude may look and feel correct to an inexperienced floatplane pilot, this fault is much harder to detect because its effects are less obvious than the effects of holding the nose too low.

The only way to learn to recognize the proper planing attitude is to practice it with an instructor. Eventually, you'll be able to "sense" when the floatplane is properly on the step, but for now, concentrate on consistently establishing the proper attitude by reference to the nose as it appears in relationship to the horizon or shoreline ahead of you.

New floatplane pilots are often surprised by the roughness of the takeoff run, even on what appears to be smooth water. Water becomes a relatively unyielding substance when slammed into at speeds exceeding 20 or 30 miles per hour, and the rotation speed of your floatplane will be at least twice as fast as that. Even small waves can send quite a jolt through the airframe, and the noise can be rather unnerving to the uninitiated. You can relax, however, for despite what your ears and the seat of your pants may be telling you, a floatplane is more than a match for its environment. The floats and their supporting hardware are extremely strong, and, when properly maintained, they will stand up to tremendous punishment.

Directional Control. It's not uncommon to see a floatplane threading its way gracefully through a busy harbor as it makes its takeoff run, because once the plane is on the step, its air rudder will become quite effective. It will be easy to make turns to avoid boats or other obstacles that appear in your path, and if you should suddenly become aware of a log or some other floating debris in the water ahead of you, it's a simple matter to steer around it. Keep your turns as gentle as possible, though, because a sharp turn creates a lot of drag and will slow you down.

Helping Your Plane Over the Hump. Normally, a floatplane will make the transition from the hump phase to the planing phase of its own, but depending on the load you're carrying or the design of the plane itself, there may be times when you will need to "assist" your plane over the hump and onto the step. If, after reaching its maximum nose-up angle, the plane doesn't seem to want to pitch over into a planing attitude, first determine that the engine is developing its maximum takeoff power. If it is, and the plane still doesn't want to get onto the step, make sure you aren't keeping it from doing so by holding back pressure on the stick or yoke. If excess back pressure isn't the problem, take a quick glance at the trim wheel to make sure you haven't inadvertently left it in a nose-up setting. If the trim is set properly, you aren't holding the nose up yourself with the elevator, and the engine is developing full power, your only recourse is to try and "help" your plane over the hump and onto the step.

By applying forward pressure on the stick or control wheel, you may be able to pitch the plane over into a planing attitude. If the floatplane still refuses to get on the step, try gently rocking the plane back and forth with the elevator. The theory here is that the plane will eventually rock forward onto the step, where it can be held with the elevator until it picks up enough speed to stay there on its own. Be careful if you decide to try this, however, because you don't want to set up an oscillation that could lead to the plane's porpoising out of control.

PORPOISING

Porpoising in a floatplane can be likened to bouncing down a runway while trying to do a wheel landing in a taildragger. In both cases, it is a cyclic oscillation that can be easily aggravated by the pilot's attempts to stop it. Modern float design has considerably reduced the likelihood of porpoising, but it's still possible; so you should know what it is and how to stop it.

Porpoising is generally a result of carrying the nose too low during the planing phase of the takeoff run. Instead of riding a few inches above the water, the forebodies of the floats are forced into it, and as a result, the push up a "wall" of water ahead of them. As this wall of water becomes bigger, the bows of the floats will finally ride up over it, pitching the nose of the floatplane into the air. As the floats pass over the crest of the wave they have created, the plane will pitch back down again, and the floats will dig in even deeper, pushing up an even larger wall of water. This, in turn, will pitch the nose of the airplane even higher into the air, and so on. If these oscillations are allowed to continue, the floatplane will eventually be pitched so high that when it comes back down it will bury the bows of the floats in the water and probably flip over.

Porpoising can also be initiated by carrying the nose too high while the plane is on the step. If the plane is being forced into an unnaturally nose-high attitude, it may suddenly pitch forward, driving the forward part of the floats down into the water, and the porpoising cycle will begin.

If your plane should start to porpoise, stopping the oscillation is simply a matter of adding elevator back-pressure at the right time. The trick is to add the back-pressure just as the nose reaches its highest point. As the plane settles back down on the water in a nose-high attitude, ease off on the back pressure to return to the proper planing attitude. Proper timing is extremely important, because if you add the back-pressure too late, you will only succeed in accelerating the plane into its next oscillation.

If your plane is not under control within about three oscillations, pull the power back to idle, apply full up-elevator, and let the floatplane come to a stop. This is a better alternative than trying to continue, which will probably result in damaging the airplane. Once you are safely back in the displacement attitude, you can begin the takeoff run again.

Avoid crossing boat wakes or large waves and swells while the floatplane is on the step, for they can easily start the porpoising cycle.

THE USE OF FLAPS DURING TAKEOFF

There are several theories about the use of flaps during takeoff. Some pilots never like to use them, while others use them all the time. Each point of view has some merit.

The biggest objection to the use of flaps during take-off is that the extra drag induced by the flaps will lengthen the takeoff run. If flaps are not used, the floatplane will accelerate faster, and will go over the hump to the planing attitude and reach liftoff speed in the shortest time possible. Pilots who elect not to use the wing flaps during takeoff claim that their airplanes' increased of acceleration may make the difference between a successful takeoff and an ignominious invasion of the woods along the shore of a lake that's just a little bit too small, on a day that's just a little bit too hot.

On the other hand, proponents of flaps claim their airplanes can be taken off the water sooner, thus shortening the takeoff run and reducing the time their planes are subjected to the water's pounding. Let's briefly review the reasons flaps are put on an airplane to begin with, and perhaps this will help you decide whether you want to be pro-flap or anti-flap.

A fully loaded de Havilland Beaver floatplane weighs 5090 pounds; so to support it in flight, its wing needs to develop 5090 pounds of lift. It makes no difference whether the Beaver is flying fast or slow, the wing still needs to develop 5090 pounds of lift. Because both speed and angle of attack generate lift, the faster the Beaver flies, the less angle of attack is required to create the necessary 5090 pounds of lift. Conversely, as the plane slows down, the only way to maintain the required lift is to increase the wing's angle of attack.

As every pilot knows, there is a limit to the amount a wing's angle of attack can be increased. When this limit is reached, the air will cease to flow smoothly around the wing and will instead separate from the upper surface, causing the wing to lose its lift and stall. By using flaps to change the shape of the wing, the speed at which air separation occurs can also be changed. In other words, the use of flaps on a wing enables it to have a lower stall speed. Extending the flaps on a Beaver allows the wing to fly at a speed that would have resulted in an immediate stall had the wing flaps been left up. A lower stall speed means a lower flying speed. This means that an airplane with extended flaps can take off at a lower airspeed than the same airplane with its flaps retracted. Score one for the pro-flap pilots.

On the other hand, the generation of lift also generates drag, and as the flaps are extended, the extra lift they generate increases the total amount of induced drag on the airplane. This is not much of a problem for a landplane, but remember, a floatplane is already fighting an incredible amount of hydrodynamic drag as it struggles to first get on the step, and then accelerate to flying speed. Even a small amount of additional drag, regardless of the source, can make a big difference in the length of the takeoff run. Score one for the anti-flap pilots.

"Okay," you say, "you've succeeded in proving that both sides are right. That doesn't help me much. What should I do with the flaps when I take off?"

The answer is one of judgment and compromise. In most cases, and I emphasize the word *most,* the best procedure is to use flap, but not a lot of flap. Generally, the first half of an airplane's total flap extension yields a lot of lift for a relatively small amount of drag. The second half of the flaps' total extension doesn't add much lift, but it generates a tremendous amount of drag. In other words, half-flap lowers the stall speed, and full-flap lets you come down like a rock. The latter comes in handy during landings, but it can really mess up a takeoff. If your floatplane is equipped with flaps (some of them aren't, which solves your problem), don't use more than half-flaps when you take off. For example, the recommended flap setting for a Cessna 172 is 10 degrees, while 20 degrees is the recommended setting for a Cessna 180, 185, or 206.

The recommended flap setting for takeoff will be listed in your airplane's flight manual, and unless special circumstances dictate otherwise, you should make it a practice to use this setting for each takeoff. Some floatplanes, like the de Havilland Beaver, require that flaps be used for all takeoffs, and in fact, the Beaver won't even lift off the water unless the flaps are deployed.

While the amount of flap recommended for takeoff will not generate much drag, it will generate some, and if your floatplane is heavily loaded, or if the amount of room available for the takeoff run is limited, you can use a slightly modified flap procedure. Instead of lowering the flaps to their takeoff setting before you apply take-off power, which is the procedure called for in most flight manuals, leave the flaps up until you are over the hump and on the step. As soon as you are positively on the step and accelerating, lower the flaps to be recommended take-off setting. By leaving the flaps retracted until you are on the step, you will minimize drag during the critical transition from the hump phase to the planing phase while still retaining the benefit of a lower liftoff speed.

The only disadvantage to this procedure is that you will be performing a task inside the cockpit at a time when all your attention should be directed outside. If you are flying a floatplane with manual flaps, like a Cessna 180, a Cessna 185, or a Maule, this isn't much of a problem because the flap lever can be positioned by feel alone. Floatplanes with electric flaps require a bit more attention, since the flap position should be verified by looking at the flap indicator or out at the wing flaps themselves. It's also important to learn to apply the flaps with one hand, while not disturbing the proper planing attitude that is being held with the other hand.

The use of flaps during takeoff can shorten the take-off run and reduce the time that the floatplane is subjected to the water's pounding. The success of some future take-off may well depend on your ability to properly use the flaps, so make sure you thoroughly understand their use, and then practice what you've learned.

ROTATION AND LIFTOFF

Once a floatplane is on the step, it will accelerate rapidly to rotation, or *liftoff,* speed. If the plane has been trimmed for a climb, it may fly itself off the water, but generally you will have to initiate the rotation yourself by applying back-pressure to the stick or yoke. Try to take the plane off the water as soon as it has reached flying speed;

to remain on the step any longer than necessary only subjects the plane to a needless pounding. As the plane leaves the water, you will feel a slight acceleration as the floats shake off the last vestiges of hydrodynamic drag (Fig. 10-5).

If you are taking off from smooth, glassy water, it may take a sharp tug on the control wheel to pull the floats free of the water's suction. Water that is ruffled with wind ripples or small waves is much easier to take off from, because the irregular surface introduces air under the floats in the form of small cavities and bubbles. The air dissipates the water's suction, and the plane will lift easily off the water.

Be careful not to rotate the floatplane too much. The tails of the floats could drag in the water and slow the plane down considerably. In fact, the airplane could easily be dragged back to a speed less than its liftoff speed, causing it to stall back onto the water and extending the length of your takeoff run.

Since you will be flying the floatplane off the water as its minimum controllable airspeed, lower the nose slightly after liftoff and build up some airspeed before retracting the flaps, but don't lower the nose so much that you fly back onto the water. Wait until you have established a positive rate of climb before raising the flaps and reducing the power to the proper climb setting.

DOWNWIND TAKEOFFS

Sometimes it's more convenient to take off downwind as opposed to making a long, slow taxi to the far end of the lake or the other side of the harbor just so you can take off into the wind. If the wind is light, a downwind take-off is a perfectly acceptable procedure, but if the wind begins to get up around 10 miles per hour or so, you'd better think twice before taking off with it chasing your tail.

If you take off into the wind, your airspeed will be equal to the sum of your groundspeed and the speed of the wind. For example, if you're planing across the water at 50 miles per hour into a wind blowing at 10 miles per hour, your airspeed will be 60 miles per hour. As the wind's velocity increases, the planing speed (groundspeed) required to attain rotation speed will decrease. This, of course, is the advantage of taking off into the wind: you will spend less time on the water, and your planing speed at liftoff will be reduced. You will, therefore, significantly reduce the amount of pounding inflicted on your plane.

If you take off downwind, your airspeed will be equal to your speed across the water minus the velocity of the wind. To use the same example as before, if you are plan-

Fig. 10-5. You will feel a slight acceleration when the floats break free of the water. The standard reciprocating engine in this Cessna 206 has been replaced with a turboprop by Soloy Conversions, Inc., Olympia, Washington, and the resulting performance increase is impressive. This particular plane is mounted on Wipline amphibious floats. (Courtesy of Soloy Conversions)

ing across the water at 50 miles per hour with a 10 mile per hour tailwind, your airspeed will be 40 miles per hour. In order to attain an airspeed of 60 miles per hour, you will have to plane across the water at 70 miles per hour, subjecting your airplane to a severe pounding for a relatively long period of time.

The only thing that determines whether or not your floatplane will get up on the step is its speed through the water; airspeed is not a factor. If the tailwind was strong enough, you could conceivably skim along on the step with no airspeed whatsoever. This, then, is the danger of a downwind takeoff in a medium or strong wind. You will go faster and faster across the water, and the pounding will get worse and worse, but the airspeed indicator will appear to be broken. You'll begin to wonder if you're ever going to reach rotation speed. The hammer blows on the bottoms of the floats will be transmitted directly to your

spine, and the instrument panel will be vibrating so violently it will just be a blur. The banging, squeaking, creaking, and groaning emanating from the plane will convince you it is moments from disintegration, which, if the water is rough enough, it may very well be. If you try to pull the plane off prematurely, you'll only succeed in digging in the sterns of the floats, which will slow you down and prolong your agonizing takeoff run even more. It's not a pleasant experience.

Before you decide to make a downwind takeoff, consider the strength of the wind, the roughness of the water, and the length of the takeoff area. If the wind is light and the water is relatively smooth, a downwind takeoff will be perfectly safe if there is enough room for the takeoff run. If the wind is strong and the water is rough, a downwind takeoff will subject your plane to a severe pounding, the result of which may be a badly damaged or even capsized floatplane. In these conditions, the convenience of a downwind takeoff is not worth the risk; so take the time to taxi slowly downwind far enough to permit a takeoff back into the wind.

NOISE ABATEMENT

It has become very fashionable to live on or near a body of water. Homes which can claim even a glimpse of a distant lake are in constant demand and command substantial prices. As the number of waterfront houses, apartments, and condominiums increases, so does the number of noise complaints. Unfortunately, seaplanes seem to draw the greatest fire, and it's a sure bet that as people move into an area used regularly by seaplanes, somebody will begin to complain about the noise. The newcomers don't care that seaplanes may have been coexisting with the long-time residents for years; they want all seaplane activities banned immediately.

Seaplanes are noisy by their very nature. As we saw in Chapter 3, they require the maximum available horsepower from their engines in order to get off the water, and since horsepower is a function of rpm, long, flat-pitch propellers are used to allow the engine to spool right up to its redline speed. The noise you hear as a seaplane takes off is not the sound of the engine, but the howl of that long, flat prop as the tips of its propeller approach the speed of sound, and it is this noise that waterfront residents find so objectionable. Fortunately, there are a couple of things you can do to reduce the noise, or at least its duration, and improve community relations.

As soon as you are safely off the water and have established a positive rate of climb, pull the power back to a lower setting. For example, the engine in a Cessna 172 floatplane will spool up to 2700 rpm on takeoff if the airplane is fitted with a seaplane propeller. (By comparison, the same engine will only turn up to 2300 to 2420 rpm on takeoff when the standard propeller is installed). At 2700 rpm, the seaplane prop is quite noisy, but if the power is pulled back to 2500 rpm as soon as the plane is off the water, the noise will be reduced considerably. Obviously, the safety of the airplane is the first consideration, and if there are obstacles ahead, no power reduction should be made until they are cleared, but if the takeoff area is unobstructed, a 200-rpm reduction in engine speed can go a long way toward improving relations between the seaplane community and the residents of the area.

Takeoff noise can also be reduced by a modification to the floatplane itself. If the airplane is normally fitted with a two-bladed propeller, replacing it with a three-bladed prop will make a big difference in the amount of noise generated at full power settings. The individual blades of a three-bladed propeller are shorter than the individual blades on a two-bladed propeller; so when the engine is turning over at its maximum rpm, the blade tips of a three-bladed propeller will be moving slower than the tips of a two-bladed propeller turning at the same rpm, and the propeller noise will be reduced. Not all airplanes can be fitted with three-bladed propellers, but some of the more popular planes, like the Cessna 180, 185, and 206, as well as the de Havilland Beaver, can be converted.

Kenmore Air Harbor, in Kenmore, Washington, operates a fleet of Beavers and Cessna 180s from the north end of Seattle's Lake Washington. The area is ringed with private homes and condominiums, but after the company installed three-bladed propellers on all its Beavers and 180s, complaints about the airplanes' noise dropped off dramatically. In addition, the Kenmore Air Harbor pilots practice noise abatement procedures by reducing power immediately after takeoff and spiraling up to altitude over the lake, instead of crossing over the shoreline at low altitude under climb power. These are good procedures for all seaplane pilots to follow, for if we do everything we can to reduce the noise of our airplanes, our relationships with the communities in our areas will be vastly improved.

TAKEOFF EMERGENCIES

Most engine failures seem to occur during the first power change after takeoff. Landplane pilots who experience engine problems shortly after liftoff are often faced with the prospect of "landing" amid buildings, trees, fields, or whatever else happens to be beyond the airport fence. As a floatplane pilot, you are a lot better off. Unless the takeoff area is very restricted, the procedure after experiencing an engine failure during, or right after, liftoff is simply to land straight ahead. Since you are not restricted to a narrow ribbon of concrete, you can turn to the left or right to avoid any boats or obstacles that may lie directly in front of you. Whenever possible, however, pick a takeoff lane that is clear of any obstacles for some distance beyond your intended liftoff point, just in case you need the extra space. If you are approaching the shore, and have gained enough altitude, it may be possible to execute a sharp left or right turn and land on the water parallel to the shoreline.

The important thing is to keep your head and continue to fly the airplane. If the engine loses power immediately after takeoff, don't bother to look for the problem, but concentrate on getting your plane safely back onto the water. If you experience engine trouble after you have gained a few hundred feet of altitude, you can quickly check obvious items like the mixture control, fuel selector, fuel boost pump, mag switches, and carburetor heat, but don't become so engrossed in finding the problem that you neglect to fly the airplane or prepare for your imminent landing.

Some floatplanes, like the de Havilland Beaver, will lose airspeed rapidly if power is lost right after takeoff or during a climb. It's important to keep the airspeed up by immediately lowering the nose when the engine failure occurs. If you do not, the airplane will either stall or sink back to the surface with insufficient airspeed to initiate a landing flare. In either case, it will slam into the water with great force and will undoubtedly be damaged.

Personally, I always assume that the engine of my airplane will quit at the worst possible moment, right after takeoff. By mentally preparing myself for this occurrence, I like to think that my reaction will be quicker if I actually experience an engine failure. So far, I've always been pleasantly surprised, for I've never yet had an engine miss a beat on takeoff.

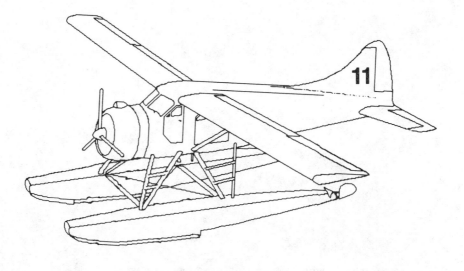

Flying the Floatplane

ONCE YOUR FLOATPLANE IS AIRBORNE, YOU WON'T notice much difference between it and the land-planes you used to fly. In fact, the most noticeable difference will probably be the sight of that big float suspended beneath you when you look out the window. The floats certainly look as though they should have a tremendous impact on the flying characteristics of the airplane, but in reality, they don't. Some airplanes even benefit from the addition of floats. For example, wheel-equipped de Havilland Beavers, Otters, and Helio Couriers tend to move around a lot in turbulent air, thanks to their huge, high-lift wings. All these planes gain a more stable and solid feel when they are mounted on floats.

If the floatplane you are flying is the same make and model as the plane you used to fly on wheels, you will find that both airplanes have virtually the same response to roll and pitch inputs. Some floatplanes, like the Cessna 172, have spring and cable interconnects between the aileron and rudder control cables, and the amount of rudder you are used to applying during a turn may now prove to be too much. The interconnects are installed to help the plane meet directional stability requirements, a subject we will look at in detail in a moment.

The next thing you may notice is that all those lines that are attached to the wing tips, the float struts, and possibly even the wing struts are behaving quite nicely. The grablines hanging from the wings will be streaming aft against the bottom of the wing, and the mooring lines on the floats will just lie quietly on top of the float decks (Fig. 11-1). Assuming the lines have been cut to the right length, nothing will be flapping in the wind or beating against the airplane.

FLOATPLANES CLIMB SLOWER

Right about the time you decide there really isn't any difference between floatplanes and landplanes in flight, you'll realize you aren't climbing as fast as you're used to. This is one of the penalties of attaching floats to an airplane. If you used to fly a Cessna Turbo-206 on wheels, don't fall into the trap of thinking that a float-equipped T-206 will climb just as fast. This kind of reasoning could get you into real trouble on the day you have to take off from a small lake and clear the inevitable trees along the shore. Using the Turbo-206 as an example, the wheeled version has a sea-level rate of climb of 1010 feet per minute on a standard day at a gross weight of 3600 pounds. On the same day, at the same gross weight, the float-

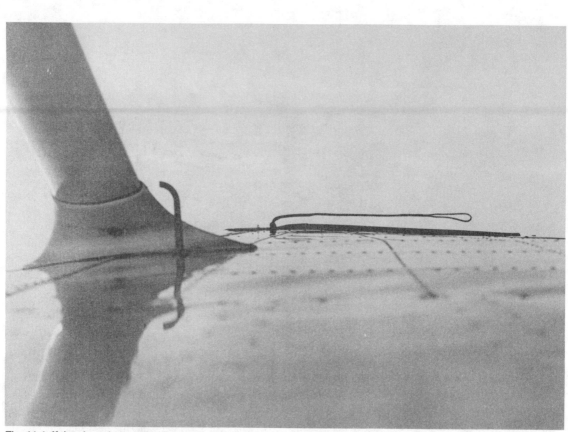

Fig. 11-1. If they have been cut to the proper length, the wing tip grablines will stream back under the wing without flapping around or beating on the bottom of the wing.

equipped T-206 has a sea-level rate of climb of only 835 feet per minute, a difference of 175 feet per minute.

Some planes are less affected than others. The popular Beaver, which has a maximum rate of climb at sea level of 730 feet per minute as a landplane, climbs at 650 feet per minute when floats are installed, or a loss of only 80 feet per minute. Regardless of the kind of floatplane you're flying, however, make sure you know its rate of climb, for someday this knowledge may keep you out of the trees (Fig. 11-2).

FLOATPLANES CRUISE SLOWER

Once you reach your cruising altitude and level off, you will experience the next big difference between floatplanes and landplanes: floatplanes are just plain slow. Unfortunately, there's no way to hide the drag of those big floats and their associated struts, brackets, pulleys, and cables, and the parasite drag they generate takes a toll on the airplane's cruising speed. Given the appearance

of all that hardware dangling into the slipstream beneath the plane, the speed penalty isn't really as great as you might think, but it's a penalty just the same, and it's something you'll have to take into consideration when planning a cross-country flight.

For example, a Cessna 172 normally cruises at 134 miles per hour at 75 percent power at an altitude of 4000 feet, but the same power setting will drag a float-equipped 172 through the air at only 109 miles per hour —25 miles per hour slower. Down at sea level, a wheel-equipped de Havilland Beaver will thump along at 125 miles per hour when the power is set for economy cruise, but the addition of floats to the airplane will lower the cruising speed to 110 miles per hour. Meanwhile, up at 20,000 feet, pilots who like to wear oxygen masks can zip along at 192 miles per hour in a Cessna Turbo-206 that's developing 80 percent power, and they will be cruising 23 miles per hour faster than anyone who happens to be up at the same altitude in a T-206 floatplane.

Fig. 11-2. A Cessna 180 climbing out after takeoff. This particular plane has been fitted with a larger engine and a three-bladed propeller.

The stalling characteristics of a floatplane are virtually identical to those of a landplane. Some floatplanes, like the Cessna 172 and 206, actually have a lower stall speed than their wheeled counterparts because of the aerodynamic characteristics of the floats, but in each case, the difference is only 2 or 3 miles per hour. On the other hand, a de Havilland Beaver always stalls at 45 miles per hour, regardless of the type of undercarriage installed — wheels, floats, or skis.

THE DIRECTIONAL INSTABILITY PROBLEM

Rate of climb and cruise speeds are not the only thing affected when a landplane is converted to a floatplane. The addition of floats has an adverse effect on a plane's directional stability, and many airplanes require stability augmentation systems, usually in the form of additional tail surfaces, to restore directional stability after the floats have been installed (Fig. 11-3).

As we saw in Chapter 9, the purpose of the vertical tail is to keep the airplane directionally stable by putting more vertical surface behind the airplane's yaw axis than in front of it. If a gust of wind or an uncoordinated turn causes the plane to yaw, skid, or slip to one side or the other, the tail presents more resistance to the air than the front of the plane. If the flight controls are returned to their neutral positions, the plane will straighten out.

If you look at a floatplane from the side, however, you will see that more of each float projects forward of the airplane's yaw axis than aft of it, thus adding a large amount of vertical surface to the front of the floatplane. The effect is a little like putting feathers on the front of an arrow as well as on the back. As long as the air is smooth, and the floatplane is kept perfectly coordinated, it will obediently follow its nose. If rough air or poor coordination of the flight controls cause the floatplane to yaw, this delicate balance will be upset.

Fig. 11-3. The ventral stability fin on a Cessna 206.

If the plane should yaw, the *relative wind,* or wind caused by the airplane's movement through the air, will begin to strike the side of the plane instead of its nose. Normally, the force of the relative wind striking the tail would straighten the plane out, but if the plane is on floats, the relative wind striking the sides of the floats out in front of the plane's vertical axis may almost, or completely, cancel the stabilizing effect of the tail (Fig. 11-4). In other words, while the tail is trying to straighten the plane out, the forward portion of the floats will be trying to slew the plane off to the side into a skid. At best, the floatplane will be very reluctant to stop skidding, and at worst, the plane may actually start to chase its tail.

This is not a very pleasant way to fly, so the airframe manufacturers came up with a simple method of restoring directional stability when their planes are put on floats. By adding more vertical surface area behind the yaw axis of their floatplanes, the destabilizing effect of the floats is overpowered, and the airplane will once again straighten itself out.

This additional surface is almost always in the form of one or more fins mounted on the empennage. Cessna 150, 172-XP, and 206 floatplanes use a single ventral fin installed beneath the tail. Float-equipped de Havilland Beavers and Otters, Twin Beeches, Maules, and some Pipers also use a single, ventral fin (Fig. 11-5). Another popular method is to install a small vertical fin at each end of the horizontal stabilizer, which can be seen on float-equipped de Havilland Twin Otters, Cessna 195s, and de Havilland Beavers as modified by Kenmore Air Harbor in Kenmore, Washington (Fig. 11-6). Another form of stabilizer fin is the "shark" fin, which mounts on top of the horizontal stabilizer (Fig. 11-7). One of the advantages of mounting a pair of fins on the stabilizer is that, unlike a ventral fin, they don't hang down lower than the tail of the airplane. They are, therefore, less susceptible to damage from docks or shoreline logs and brush.

However, and this is an important however, any additional surface installed on any airplane, be it a Piper Cub or a Boeing 757, will generate additional drag, which means the airplane will fly slower or use more fuel to fly the same speed. Over a period of time, this additional drag can make a significant contribution to the operating cost of the airplane, so the size of a floatplane's stabilizing fin, or fins, is kept to a minimum. What this means to you as a floatplane pilot is that although your floatplane is directionally stable according to the certification standards set forth by the FAA, in reality it may be flying on the ragged edge of instability.

Why all the fuss over this directional stability business in the first place? As long as the plane doesn't actually start chasing its tail, what difference does it make if the plane won't come out of a slipping of skidding condition on its own? After all, that's what the rudder is for, isn't it?

Well, yes, and if every pilot flew in a perfectly coordinated fashion all the time, we wouldn't have to worry about the directional instability of floatplanes. Unfortunately, we don't always fly with the ball dead center; so floatplane stability is a big concern to float and airframe manufacturers, as well as the FAA. One reason why the Cessna 172 floatplane has a spring-and-cable interconnect between the ailerons and the rudder is to help keep the plane coordinated as it rolls into and out of turns, even if the pilot is lax in the use of the rudder.

The problem is that even with their stability augmentation systems installed (ventral or stabilizer fins, oversized dorsal fins, etc.), many floatplanes can easily begin to skid in a turn, especially a steep turn, if the pilot doesn't pay attention to his coordination. The reason is that stabilizing fins are kept as small as possible to minimize drag. When an airplane skids in a turn, the inside wing slows down in relation to the outside wing. If the skid occurs when the airspeed is low, during a steep turn while climbing out after takeoff for example, the inside wing could slow down enough to stall. When it stalls, the plane will fall out of the turn to the inside, and begin to spin.

In fact, this is exactly what happens when you intentionally practice spins at altitude. You first reduce your airspeed until your plane is just about to stall. Then you induce a skid by applying full left or right rudder. The inside wing stalls first, and the plane drops into a spin.

The destabilizing effect of the floats replaces the application of right or left rudder to start a floatplane skidding, but the end result is the same. Because you're only likely to be making steep turns at low airspeeds right after takeoff or during a landing approach, you probably won't have enough altitude to recover from a skid-induced stall.

The easiest way to avoid a skid/stall situation is to keep the bank angles low, the airspeed up, and the ball in the center. On those occasions when you absolutely must crank in a steep turn at minimum airspeed to avoid an obstacle, keep an extrasharp eye on that ball!

Some landplanes, like most Cessna 180s and 185s and the Helio Courier, do not require any additional vertical surface at all when floats are installed because their tails are already quite large. Floats have the same effect on these planes as on any other, however, and the pilot should always pay close attention to his turn coordination, especially at low airspeeds.

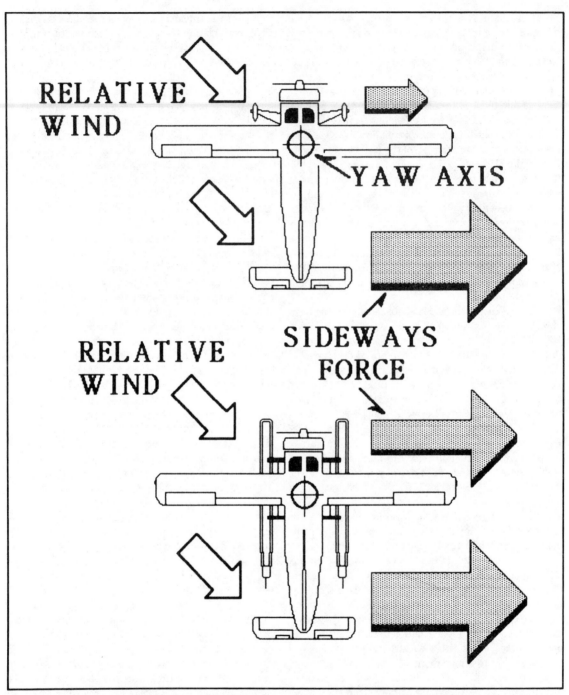

Fig. 11-4. Forces affecting the stability of a floatplane in flight. The landplane has comparatively little vertical surface in front of its yaw axis, so it will straighten itself out in the event of a slip, skid, or yaw. A floatplane, on the other hand, may have almost as much vertical surface ahead of the yaw axis as behind it, and it will not be as quick to come out of a yawing situation. The solution is to add more vertical surface behind the yaw axis.

Fig. 11-5. A de Havilland Otter in Vancouver Harbor, British Columbia. Note the ventral fin under the tail.

The de Havilland Beaver, considered by many pilots and commercial operators to be the ultimate bush plane, has acquired a reputation for being an easy plane in which to have a skid/stall accident. The story behind this reputation is an interesting one. When the plane was first certified for floats, the factory installed a large ventral fin under the tail as part of the float kit. Some pilots complained that this made the plane hard to land in a crosswind, so de Havilland, with the approval of the Canadian Department of Transport, made the ventral fin an option. Shortly after operators began flying the Beaver without the auxiliary fin, the airplane began to acquire its then deserved reputation as being prone to skid/stall accidents. Kenmore Air Harbor, a company which has probably had more experience with the de Havilland Beaver than de Havilland, flew its Beavers without auxiliary fins on the strength of the factory's advisory which made the fin an option in Canada. The Kenmore pilots, however, found

the plane to be quite directionally unstable when it was flown without the ventral fin.

Shortly after the ventral fin was made optional, the Beaver was certified for larger floats, and this time there was no question about the installation of an auxiliary fin. The fin was required when the Beaver was installed on the larger floats, and that was that. Kenmore Air Harbor received a Supplemental Type Certificate (STC) for two small fins which mounted on the ends of the horizontal stabilizer in place of de Havilland's single ventral fin, but no matter which type of fin was installed, the Beaver became a well-behaved airplane once again.

Auxiliary fins became mandatory in the United States on all float-equipped Beavers, but they were still optional on Canadian-registered Beavers equipped with the original, small floats, and reports of the big de Havillands skidding into a stall continued to trickle in. In 1983, however, the Canadian Department of Transport amended

Fig. 11-6. Twin stabilizer fins on a Cessna 195 floatplane.

Fig. 11-7. A pair of so-called shark fins mounted on a de Havilland Beaver.

its rules, and now requires auxiliary fins on all float-equipped Beavers of Canadian registry, regardless of the size and type of floats used.

If you get the chance to pilot a float-equipped Beaver, jump at it, for the airplane is an absolute delight to fly. Don't let its smooth controls and excellent handling lull you into sloppy turn coordination, though, because the skidding tendency is still there, waiting for the day you crank in a steep turn as you struggle for altitude after takeoff, or twist in through the trees on final. A Beaver will take a lot of abuse, but if you persist in ignoring the ball, that skid will eventually reach around and bite you.

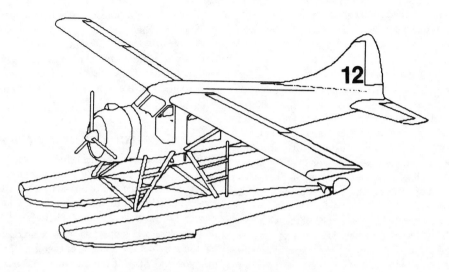

The Landing

I FIRST BECAME INTRIGUED BY FLOATPLANES DURING a trip to Alaska, when I spent the better part of a day watching the floatplanes come and go from Anchorage's Lake Hood seaplane base. A fellow who looked like a bush pilot was doing something to the engine of a Cessna 206 at the dock in front of me, and after a while I worked up the nerve to engage him in a conversation about floatplanes. When I asked him if it was difficult to learn to fly one, he thought for a minute, and then asked, "You ever flown a nose-wheel airplane? Floatplanes land just like nose-wheel airplanes. If you want to fly a floatplane, see if you can find yourself a nose-wheel plane to practice in first."

I found his answer an amusing commentary on the nature of Alaskan aviation, because while I had never flown anything but "nose-wheel planes," he talked of tricycle-geared airplanes as though they were a species of exotic bird, to be glimpsed only once or twice in a lifetime. He was correct, however, in his observation that a nose-wheel airplane closely duplicates the landing attitude of a floatplane. If you're used to flying a landplane with tricycle landing gear, you will feel very much at home while making a normal landing in a floatplane. (We'll save

rough water, crosswind, and glassy water landings for later.)

DETERMINE THE WIND DIRECTION

The first thing you need to do when you arrive over your intended landing site is to determine the wind direction. Actually, it's a good idea to practice determining the direction of the surface wind in your immediate vicinity during your entire flight. It will sharpen your wind-reading skills, and it's one way to relieve the monotony that sometimes sets in during long, cross-country trips. In the event of an emergency, knowing the wind direction in advance will save you a few precious seconds, and may even make the difference between a successful landing and an out-of-control arrival.

Some of the methods of determining wind direction discussed in Chapter 10 will also work when you are surveying a landing area from the air. Blowing smoke or dust, the set of the sails on sailboats that happen to be nearby, and windstreaks on the water are all excellent wind direction indicators that are visible from higher altitudes. *Windstreaks* appear as long, straight, narrow streaks of smooth water on an otherwise ruffled surface. They will be parallel to the direction of the unseen wind.

Windstreaks are as good as windsocks for showing the exact path of the wind, but it can sometimes be very difficult to tell the upwind end of a windstreak from the downwind end, especially if the wind is not quite strong enough to begin forming whitecaps. If this is the case, you will have to look for another clue to help you determine the direction of the wind.

WATER

A shoreline always rises higher than the water it touches. In wooded country, the trees may tower 50 to 100 feet over the water lapping the beach at their feet, while in the desert, the top of a sandy bank may be only inches above the surface of the lake it surrounds. In either case, though, the shoreline is always higher than the water. This obvious geological fact sets the stage for one of the best indicators of wind direction a floatplane pilot can have.

Waves are generated by the friction of the wind passing across the surface of the water. The stronger the wind, the greater the friction, and the larger the waves. Conversely, if the wind is weak, or if it is somehow kept from contacting the surface of the water at all, the waves generated will be small or nonexistent.

When the wind reaches the edge of a body of water, it does not immediately drop down and begin to stir up waves on the surface. Instead, it sails off the edge of the shoreline and contacts the surface of the water some distance from shore. This distance is determined by the height of the shoreline. If the shoreline is composed of a dense forest of tall trees, the trees will form a windbreak, and the wind won't hit the surface of the water until it has travelled quite a ways from shore. On the other hand, if the shoreline is composed primarily of grass, low bushes, or scattered trees, the wind will be able to start sweeping the surface of the water almost immediately after clearing the bank or beach. In either case, however, there will be a band of smooth water extending out from the upwind shore (Fig. 12-1).

The strength of the wind also helps determine how far out from the upwind shore the band of smooth water will extend. As we have seen, waves are formed by the friction of the wind on the surface of the water, but the waves do not form instantly. It takes a while for the wind to overcome the surface tension of the water and begin to pile it up into waves which it can then push along. Until the point where the waves begin to form, the water will remain smooth. A light wind will have to "rub" on the surface for a long time before it can begin to form waves; so the band of smooth water will extend quite a

ways out from the upwind shore. A strong wind, on the other hand, will begin to hump the water into waves almost immediately; so the band of calm water will be quite narrow.

Even in a light breeze, the area of smooth water extending downwind from the upwind shoreline will be quite obvious from your aerial vantage point, and the distance this smooth water extends from shore before becoming textured with ripples or waves will give you valuable information about the wind's direction and its strength.

INSPECT YOUR DESTINATION

Before you begin to pick the location of your landing lane, take a moment to overfly your intended docking or beaching site. Once you're on the water, the low perspective often makes it difficult to judge which docks are open or just how much room there is between the two planes that are already tied up. It will also be practically impossible to figure out the position of that gravel bar someone told you was just off the entrance to the channel.

From the air, the layout of the docks, the amount of space between the moored floatplanes, and the whereabouts of that elusive gravel bar will immediately become obvious. Armed with this information and what you know of the wind's direction and strength, you can decide to which dock you want to go, and figure out the best way to approach it. By doing this planning in the air, you avoid the potentially dangerous situation created by entering a crowded boat harbor or seaplane base unprepared, only to find that the dock which looked like it had enough room for you is full. By the time you're in close enough to realize you'll have to tie up elsewhere, you may be in too close to maneuver clear of the boats and planes that are already there.

If your destination is a beach or a lake shore, definitely check it out from the air before you land and taxi in. An aerial survey is the only way to spot deadheads, rocks, or reefs that may be lurking just beneath the surface, waiting to tear bottoms out of your floats as you approach the shore. Again, by knowing the direction and strength of the wind, you can determine the best approach to the beach, and then make sure that the approach is clear of underwater obstacles by inspecting the area from the air.

Don't be in a hurry to land. A floatplane is safest when it's in the air. Once you're on the water, you're dealing with a machine that has no brakes, no reverse, and is often at the mercy of the wind; so the more preplanning

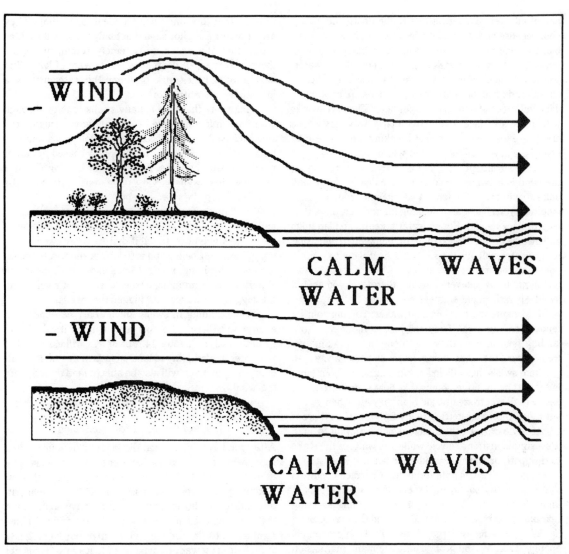

Fig. 12-1. The effect of the shoreline's profile on the wind. Regardless of the height of the shoreline, there will always be a band of smoother water extending out from the upwind shore which will be readily visible from the air.

you can do while you're safely airborne, the fewer surprises you'll get after you touch down.

CHOOSE YOUR LANDING SITE

Once you have determined where you're going to dock or beach your plane, it's time to design your "runaway." Obviously, you want to land into the wind if possible, and one of the nice things about flying a floatplane is that you almost always can do so. It would also be nice to avoid a long taxi back to shore by coming to a stop in the vicinity

of your destination. You want to make sure that your landing lane is clear of floating and underwater obstacles, too.

Determine the Water Conditions

A floatplane should always be landed in smoothest water available, at the slowest speed possible. Your goal is to minimize the amount of pounding to which the airplane is subjected. Different water conditions require different landing techniques. Absolutely flat, or *glassy*, water, is potentially very dangerous, not to the floatplane, but to you, because you will find it very difficult, if not impossible, to judge your height off the water. A special technique has evolved for making landings on glassy water, and it will be covered in Chapter 14. Water conditions considered ideal for floatplane operations are created by wind velocities of 8 to 12 miles per hour. These velocities will create a surface covered with large wavelets whose crests are just on the verge of breaking, and there may even be a few small, scattered white caps.

If the surface of the water is *covered* with whitecaps, the wind is blowing in excess of 15 miles per hour, and unless you are experienced at making rough water landings, you should start looking for another, more protected place to land. Rough water takeoffs and landings will also be covered in Chapter 14, but keep in mind that rough water will always subject a floatplane to quite a pounding, no matter how good the pilot's rough water technique is. Whenever possible, therefore, you should avoid operations under these conditions.

Make sure there are no boat wakes crossing your intended landing area. They are just as dangerous to a landing floatplane as they are to one that is taking off. Remember, too, that boats some distance away can generate swells that will end up running across your landing lane. One positive note is that boat wakes are much easier to detect from altitude than they are when you're sitting on the water getting ready for takeoff. If there is a boat wake crossing the area to which you want to land, it's a simple matter to circle while you wait for the wake to dissipate or travel beyond your landing land.

Boats are responsible for another surface condition that can really fool an unsuspecting floatplane pilot. I know, because one day, I was one of those unsuspecting floatplane pilots who got fooled. Behind the city of Seattle, Washington, is large lake called, appropriately enough, Lake Washington. There are many marinas on this 19-mile-long lake, and most of the homes that ring the shoreline also have boats tied up in front of them. The lake is popular with water skiers and sailboats, but the real problem is caused by the many big power cruisers that call Lake Washington home. The lake is connected to Puget Sound by a set of locks, and on Saturday, a constant flow of cruisers heads for the locks and a weekend on the Sound. On Sunday, they all come back. The deep wakes generated by these boats start bouncing back and forth across the lake in all directions, and as the day progresses, the result is a lumpy, confused lake surface that, to the uninitiated, looks fairly smooth from the air. Because there are no whitecaps, the pilot's tendency is

to think that the conditions are ideal for landing. They aren't and if the pilot should actually land, will find, as I did, that the water is extremely rough, and quite dangerous to small floatplanes. So beware of lakes that have a lot of boat traffic on them; the water may be a lot rougher than it looks.

Make sure there are not any swells running through your chosen landing lane. We've already discussed the swells caused by boats, but the parallel swells found in large bodies of open water are generally caused by earlier winds or distant storms. Taking off or landing in water that contains swells is very dangerous and should be avoided except in an emergency.

Swells are sometimes difficult to see from an airplane, and even if you can see them, it's hard to tell how large they are. A good way to tell if there are any swells present in the water below you is to look at the waves breaking on shore. Long, straight lines of waves breaking in a constant rhythm indicate the presence of swells, and the bigger the waves, the bigger the swells.

While landing in swells should only be done in an emergency, there is a proper technique for it, which will be described in Chapter 14. For now, I will assume that the water you're going to land on falls in the "ideal" category, and that you will also be able to land directly into the wind.

Inspect the Area for Obstacles

After you have determined the location of your landing lane, make one or more passes over the area to make sure there are no obstacles which could interfere with your landing. Your inspection passes should be made at pattern altitude or lower, and if you still have some doubt that the area is clear, don't be afraid to bring the plane right down to the surface and overfly your landing site at 50 feet. You want to make sure that the water is not only free of floating logs, branches, and other debris, but that it's deep enough for you to land in it.

If you're landing in tidal waters, look carefully for the little buoys people use to mark the locations of their crab, shrimp, and lobster pots. They can be difficult to see, and they can do a lot of damage to one of your floats or your prop if you hit one. During the shrimp season, some areas of Puget Sound become so clustered with buoys that it becomes almost impossible to find a long enough stretch of clear water in which to land.

Many of the lakes from which floatplanes operate are created by flood control or hydroelectric dams, and the water level can change overnight. If the water level is high, be extra alert for logs, stumps, and other debris that may have been picked up off the bank by the rising water. Remember that anything floating on the surface will be blown downwind. If you are landing on the downwind side of a lake, take a little extra time to check for floating debris. Be especially careful if the water is muddy, because anything from a submerged log to a rocky reef may be hidden just beneath the surface.

Extremely clear water presents a problem, too, because it can be difficult to judge its depth from the air. If you can see the bottom, pick an area that you think is deep enough, and then give yourself a safety margin by landing even further out than that.

The water is not the only place to look for obstacles that may interfere with your landing. Power and phone lines are even more of a problem to floatplane pilots than they are to landplane pilots. The lines themselves are almost impossible to see from the air; so look for the poles that hold them up. If you see any poles, it's a sure bet that they are supporting one or more lines, and it only takes one to ruin your day. Be especially careful if you are landing between an island and the mainland, between islands, or on a river. If the distances are not too great, the residents may have strung aerial power and phone lines out to the islands, and farmers may suspend a power line across a river to run pumps or other equipment on the other side. These lines are almost never indicated on any maps, and they rarely have any warning markers hanging from them, so the only way to find them is by a careful examination of the area as you fly over it.

While they are much more obvious, check for any bridges that may obstruct your landing path. Bridges often carry power lines across them, and there may be gas or water lines suspended nearby, as well. While a nearby bridge may not pose any problem to your landing pattern and final approach, remember that you may have to go around, and an obstacle that posed no threat to your landing plans could suddenly become a very real threat in the event of a go-around.

This situation brings up another point. Make sure that the body of water on which you intend to land is big enough for you to take off from later. Floatplanes come to a stop very rapidly, but their takeoff runs are longer than a landplane's; so it would be easy to land somewhere with plenty of room to spare only to find it impossible to take off again. A float-equipped Cessna 172, for example, requires only 590 feet to come to a stop after touchdown, but it will cover 1400 feet before it lifts off the water on takeoff—a difference of 810 feet. The powerful Turbo-206 floatplane will come to a stop in 845 feet,

but requires 1810 feet to take off, a difference of 965 feet. It's interesting to note that the takeoff roll of the same airplane on wheels is only 835 feet.

Of the floatplanes I am familiar with, the de Havilland Beaver is once again the champion, with a takeoff distance over a 50-foot obstacle of 1610 feet, only 100 feet more than the landing distance over the same obstacle. If you're going to be flying into small lakes, a Beaver is your best bet.

THE NORMAL LANDING

As I stated earlier, the main objective when landing a floatplane is to touch down on the water at the slowest possible speed. This is the same objective you have when landing a landplane. Also like a landplane, there are two ways to land a floatplane: power-on and power-off. Because it's difficult for pilots new to float flying to accurately judge their height above the water, the power-on method is the most recommended, since it gives the pilot more control over the sink rate and landing attitude of the airplane.

The Power-On Landing

As I mentioned at the beginning of this chapter, landing a floatplane is very similar to landing a tricycle-geared landplane. Certainly the approach is the same, with the plane flown through downwind, base, and final approach legs. Remember to verify the position of the water rudders as you run through your prelanding checklist. The rudders must remain retracted during a landing. If they are down, they will kick up violently as soon as the floats contact the water, and there is a good chance the blades will be bent, or the retraction and steering mechanism will be damaged.

Unless the wind is very gusty, you should use the maximum landing flap setting for your particular airplane to ensure that your touchdown is made at the minimum possible airspeed. Every pilot develops his own preferred procedure for flying an approach, but the important thing is that you keep the airspeed under control throughout the approach, and arrive at the touchdown point with the correct flap setting for landing. I like to put in the first increment of flaps on downwind and the second right after turning base. I save the final flap increment until I'm established on final approach and can judge my glide path to my intended touchdown point. If I'm a little too high, I can get the rest of the flaps on right away; if I'm a little too low, I can wait awhile before pumping them down. This is a pretty standard procedure and was taught by most of the instructors I've had, but there are other procedures that work just as well. The important thing is to fly your approaches as accurately and consistently as possible.

Don't get hypnotized into watching the water directly in front of you on final approach. Doing so will severely impair your ability to judge the proper time to begin your landing flare. Instead, watch the shoreline out ahead of you or use your peripheral vision to judge your altitude by looking at the shoreline next to you. If boats are in the vicinity, it will also be easier to judge your height above the water.

The surface of the water can also fool you into thinking that you're drifting sideways, when in reality, you aren't. When the wind shifts, it may take some time before the waves on the water reflect this change, and it's possible to land into the wind, but diagonally across the waves. If you become fixated on the waves directly in front of you, you may start to think you're landing in a crosswind, and if you roll in some compensation for this nonexistent crosswind, you'll get a big surprise when you touch down. If you are landing in a crosswind, only your position relative to the shoreline ahead of you can be relied upon to indicate your true rate of drift.

The actual flare and touchdown are a little like doing a soft field landing in a wheelplane. As you flare, bring in just enough power to hold the floatplane in the correct attitude for touchdown (Fig. 12-2). Ideally, you want the plane to touch down on the steps of the floats, with the nose a little higher than it is during the planning phase of the takeoff. In fact, it's okay if the plane touches down on both the step and the afterbody of each float at the same time (Fig. 12-3). The important thing is to keep the nose up so the bows of the floats won't dig into the waves. The correct touchdown attitude is not unlike that of a tricycle-geared airplane which touches down on its main wheels while the nosewheel is held off the runway.

After you have established the proper touchdown attitude and are holding the floatplane just off the surface of the water, a slight reduction in power will allow the plane to settle smoothly onto the water.

I received my single-engine sea rating with a man who has been flying floatplanes since 1928, and he has a unique way of teaching power-on landings. After I had flared the floatplane to the correct touchdown attitude, he would have me add power until the plane was slow-flying a few feet above the surface of the water. The plane's attitude was to remain constant; any altitude corrections were to be made with power. If a gust of wind ballooned us upwards, I reduced power. If we started to sink towards the surface, I added power. Once I had the

plane firmly stabilized a few feet off the water in the correct touchdown attitude, my instructor had me reduce the power by a hundred rpm or so and count to 6, without changing the airplane's attitude. I'm not sure if he wanted me to count to 6 because that's how long it took the plane to settle onto the water, or if it was simply to give me something to do so I wouldn't get impatient and try and force the plane down, but whatever the reason, the resulting touchdowns were the smoothest I have experienced. This method uses up more water than other power-on procedures, but if you have the space and plane your approaches accordingly, the touchdowns are real passenger-pleasers.

Some floatplanes, like a heavily loaded de Havilland Beaver or Cessna 206, have a tendency to sink right through the flare, and if you don't anticipate and prevent this tendency with a little burst of power, the plane could arrive on the water with a resounding whack—a touchdown which will definitely *not* please the passengers.

As soon as the floats touch the water, close the throttle. This step is important because, unless you intend to step taxi, any further application of power will only prolong the landing runout.

When the floats touch the water, they will be subjected to a lot of drag, and the plane will tend to pitch forward. The severity of this sudden forward pitch depends primarily on the speed you're travelling when you touch down. The faster you're going, the greater will be the water's drag, and the more the plane will want to pitch over—another reason why it's important to touch down at the slowest speed possible. If your floatplane is traveling fast enough, it's conceivable that contact with the water could nose it over far enough to enable the float bows to dig in. The end result would probably be a graceful forward somersault as your plane trips over its float bows and pitches onto its back.

Be prepared to bring in a little back-pressure when your plane touches down to counter this tendency to pitch forward, but don't get carried away and suck the yoke or stick back into your stomach. Too much back-pressure too early can rock the plane back onto the tails of the floats, which will cause the float bottoms to smack into the waves instead of cutting through them. Maintain the same, slightly nose-high, attitude during the first part of the landing runout that you established for the touchdown itself, and only apply enough back-pressure to offset the plane's tendency to pitch forward.

If the water is smooth, its suction will contribute greatly to the drag on the floats, and the tendency of the floatplane to pitch forward will be magnified. It may take

Fig. 12-2. Moments before touchdown. The floats are being held slightly nose-high, and contact will be made just ahead of the step.

Fig. 12-3. A perfect landing. The bows of the floats are high enough to prevent them from digging in, but not so high that the sterns of the floats strike the water and pitch the plane forward.

quite a bit of back-pressure to overcome the nose-over force experienced right after touchdown on smooth water. On the other hand, if the water is choppy or covered with waves, the nose-over tendency may be very slight, because the air introduced under the floats by the irregular water surface will reduce the water's friction on the float bottoms. In fact, if the water is choppy, it's sometimes advisable to gradually apply *forward* pressure during the planing phase of the landing runout to take advantage of the wave-cutting ability of the float keels and give the plane and its occupants a smoother ride. This procedure takes practice, however, because you don't want to push the float bows down to the point where they are in danger of digging into the waves.

When a floatplane lands, it goes through the same phases it did during takeoff, only in reverse order. After touchdown, the plane will run along on the step for a short distance. As the airplane's speed decreases, so will the hydrodynamic pressure that is supporting it, and it will settle deeper into the water. Soon, it will fall off the step

completely, and come back down over the hump to the displacement phase. As the floatplane slows down and begins to come back over the hump, the yoke or stick should be brought all the way back to help keep the nose up and the propeller clear of the spray that will be thrown out as the plane settles back into a displacement attitude (Fig. 12-4). When the landing runout is completed and the plane has slowed to an idle taxi speed, lower the water rudders and head for the dock, ramp, or beach that is your destination for this flight.

The Power-Off Landing

Power-off landings are different from power-on landings only in the fact that no power is used to ease the plane onto the surface of the water. Instead, the throttle is closed before or during the flare, and the plane is landed in a full stall. The advantages of the power-off, full-stall landing are that it uses much less space than a power-on landing, and the touchdown is made at the slowest airspeed of which the airplane is capable. The disadvan-

Fig. 12-4. This Beaver has just landed, and it is coming back down over the hump to the displacement attitude.

tage of this type of landing is that it is often difficult for an inexperienced floatplane pilot to accurately judge his height above the water. The common tendency is to flare the airplane too soon, and it may run out of flying speed while it is still some distance above the surface. If power isn't added immediately, the plane will drop onto the water hard enough to possibly break one or more of the float strut, spreader bar, or brace wire fittings. A hard landing can easily become a sinking, which does amazing things to your insurance rates.

The landing runout after a power-off, full-stall landing will be identical to the runout after a power-on landing, only it will be a little shorter thanks to the floatplane's lower touchdown speed.

WIND GUSTS AND JUMPING FISH

One of the advantages floatplane pilots have over landplane pilots is the ability to see and correct for wind gusts during landings. While landplane pilots can only react to gusts after their airplanes have flown into them, floatplane pilots can see the gusts coming and take corrective action before the gusts reach their planes.

Wind gusts appear as darker patches on the surface of the water. It's important to remember that the leading edge of the gust will be slightly in advance of the dark patch on the surface; so don't wait until you are right on top of the patch before making your power adjustment. An airplane will tend to balloon upwards when it is hit by a gust, and then sink back down as the gust passes. If you are landing on a body of water where dark patches of ruffled water are announcing the presence of wind gusts, reduce power just as one of these gusts approaches, and then put the power back in again as the gust passes by. Your objective is to cancel out the ballooning and sinking effects the gusts have on your airplane. The ability to see and correct for wind gusts is especially helpful as you are flaring your airplane for landing because, by adjusting the power, you can reduce the risk of being ballooned back into the air in a nose-high attitude with no airspeed.

Landing with full flaps in gusty conditions increases the risk of getting ballooned back up into the air, so if the wind is gusty, you may want to land using something less than the maximum flap setting for your particular airplane. In a Cessna 180, for example, you may want to use only two notches of flap, or 20 degrees, instead of the usual four notches, or 40 degrees. If you're flying a Beaver, pumping the flaps to a point midway between the "Takeoff" and "Climb" settings, instead of all the way down to the "Landing" setting, will reduce the ballooning tendency of the airplane.

There is one other hazard to water-borne floatplanes about which none of us can do anything: fish. You would think that the only time fish would present a problem to us floatplane types would be when we unsuccessfully try to catch them, but in some parts of the country, fish have been known to do some rather severe damage to floatplanes. Certain species of large fish like to jump out of the water occasionally, and if one of them should choose to become airborne at the same time and place you are trying to do the same thing, your floatplane could end up spending some time in the shop.

In the Pacific Northwest, the salmon return in the Autumn to the rivers they left several years earlier, and when they first enter fresh water, many of them leap high into the air and fall back with a resounding smack. One theory is that they are trying to knock off any parasites that may have been picked up during their stay in salt water, but whatever the reason, the sight of a 40-pound Chinook salmon launching itself 3 or 4 feet out of the water is impressive. It's unlikely that one of these fish would come up under a taxiing floatplane that was moving slowly, but if some were to jump into the propeller of your floatplane as you were taking off or landing, the damage to the prop, and possibly other parts of the plane as well, could be substantial.

Another fish that is notorious for jumping high out of the water is the paddlefish, found in many lakes of the southcentral United States. Sometimes called the *spoonbill catfish*, these primitive fish can grow to a length of 5 to 6 feet, and weigh up to 100 pounds. I've read of one case where a large paddlefish jumped up in the path of an approaching seaplane, splintered the propeller, and cracked the windshield. The pilot was startled, to say the least.

There really isn't anything you can do to avoid hitting an aerobatic fish since you have no way of knowing when one is going to launch itself out of the water in front of you, but fortunately, collisions between fish and floatplanes are relatively rare.

NO TWO LANDINGS ARE THE SAME

At the beginning of this book, I said that one of the best things about flying a floatplane is the fact that you are on your own, and that the success of your flight depends solely on the decisions you make as a pilot. To me, the landing is the most challenging and rewarding aspect of flying floats, since each one requires a different set of decisions, based on a different set of observations. No two landings are ever the same, even if they are made in the same place. Wind and water conditions are constantly changing, to say nothing of the varied and unpredictable surface traffic with which you may have to contend. There is no such thing as a routine water landing, but the sense of satisfaction you will experience each time you plan and execute a smooth, safe, and accurate approach and landing is difficult to match in any other type of flying.

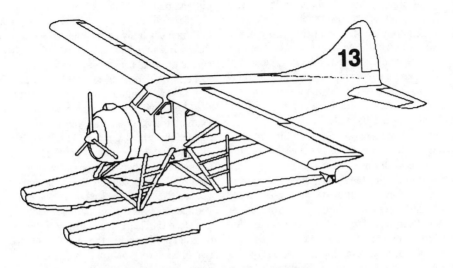

After the Flight

U NLESS YOU'RE LANDING AN AMPHIBIAN AT AN airport, your ultimate destination in a floatplane will either be a ramp, a dock, a buoy or anchor line, or the shore itself. It's said that most accidents occur in the home, and I think this statement applies to floatplanes, too. More floatplanes are dinged, dented, bent, scraped, scratched, holed, or sunk at their mooring than anywhere else. No matter where you plan to secure your floatplane, there are some basic, proper procedures to follow. As long as you follow these procedures, think through the consequences of each action, and plan for the unexpected, the odds that you will damage a floatplane will be slim indeed.

RAMPING

Ramping a floatplane is pretty easy. You simply hit the ramp head-on, slide up it, and stop. Because you carry power all the way to the ramp, the wind won't effect your plane as much as it will when you coast up to a dock with the engine cut. As easy as it seems, however, there is a right way and a wrong way to ramp a floatplane.

First, make sure there is enough room for your plane on the ramp. This seems a fairly obvious step to take, but you'd be surprised at the number of pilots who taxi in only to discover, sometimes too late, that the ramp is full, or that their airplanes won't fit between the other planes already there. If you've checked out the area from the air prior to landing, you should already know what kind of space is available on the ramp.

As you taxi in, maneuver your floatplane so that you will be able to approach the ramp head-on. Make sure no one is standing on the section of the ramp you intend to use, and that there are no mooring lines from adjacent floatplanes stretching across your path. Approach the ramp at minimum speed, but when you are about 15 or 20 feet out, bring the yoke or stick all the way back and apply enough power to raise the bows of the floats (Fig. 13-1).

As the bows of the floats come up, they will bulldoze a wall of water ahead of them onto the ramp, which will accomplish three things. First it will help the floats ride up onto the ramp. Second, it will help cushion the impact when the float keels contact the boards. Third, by lubricating the surface of the ramp, the water will enable the floatplane to slide up the ramp to the point where it will be in no danger of sliding back down again.

The critical thing here is the timing. If you apply the power too late, or if you don't put enough in, your plane may just barely get its floats up onto the ramp before it stops. If it doesn't slide back into the water right away, the movement caused by your getting out may be enough to start the plane slipping backwards. This is a potentially dangerous situation, because if you do slide back into the water, you're immediately at the mercy of the wind, and if it turns you at an angle to the ramp, restarting the engine won't do you any good, especially if there are floatplanes on either side of you. The only thing you can do in this case is to get the paddle out and fend yourself off as best you can until you drift far enough out to restart the engine and try again.

I received my floatplane rating at a facility that had a long, floating, double-sided ramp. The floatplanes were pulled up nose-to-nose down the length of this ramp, with only about 5 feet separating the spinner of one plane from the spinner of the plane facing it. It was nerve-racking enough to deliberately taxi in toward the nose of another very expensive floatplane, but it was far worse to slide up the ramp, propeller whirling, headed for what seemed like an imminent collision. As a result, I was very timid about putting in enough power to get us properly up on the ramp. As we precariously clung to the edge of the ramp, my instructor would gingerly ease himself out of the plane and onto the slippery boards so he could fasten a dock line to the bow cleat on one of the floats. Sometimes I slid off the ramp before he could get a line on the float, and I'd have to scramble out and catch the line he'd throw before I drifted into the plane next to me. My instructor was a firm believer in letting his students know when they screwed up, and although I eventually learned to ramp the plane properly, I'll never know if it was through practice, or simply because I couldn't face the consequences of yet another humiliating backwards slide off the ramp. I never did get used to sliding up to within a few feet of another floatplane, however.

The other thing you can do if you hit a ramp too lightly is power yourself up it, but bear in mind that without that wave of water preceding you up the ramp, it will take a lot of power to slide the floats up the dry boards. Make sure that the top of the ramp is free of obstacles, because the floats may wait until you're practically at full power before suddenly becoming unstuck, and the plane could surge forward quite a distance before you are able to get it under control again.

Adding power too early as you approach the ramp is just as bad as adding it too late. If you put the power in too soon, the plane will have time to overcome the water's resistance, and it will begin to accelerate before it reaches the ramp. Depending on your speed and the angle

of the ramp, you may strike the ramp too hard, slide up the ramp too far, or both.

If you've added power at the right time, don't chicken out and pull it off just as you get to the ramp. If you do, the plane will pitch forward as it decelerates, and instead of sliding smoothly up the ramp, the float bows will strike the boards quite hard as they nose down. Keep the power on and the yoke back until you are far enough up the ramp to be in no danger of sliding back again (Fig. 13-2).

Be very careful if the ramp is covered with ice. Your float keels will become a pair of giant ice skates, and if you use too much power, you'll slide right up over the top. On the other hand, you'll be more likely to slide back into the water if you don't get the plane firmly onto the icy boards, so the whole operation becomes a real judgment call. Once you get the plane on the ramp, watch your step, because the icy boards will be delighted to send you sliding, arms flailing, into the equally icy water below.

Once the floatplane is firmly on the ramp, shut down the engine and secure the plane to the dock with at least two lines. Every floatplane pilot has his or her own favorite way of securing a floatplane, so I will describe the method we used on the ramp mentioned earlier by way of an example. We ran a line from the bow cleat on each float to a single, large cleat set in the top of the ramp directly in front of the plane. We then ran a long line from the stern cleat on each float to ramp cleats set 15 or 20 feet to each side of the center cleat. In the event of a strong wind, the bow lines would hold the nose of the airplane down, and the stern lines would keep the plane from pivoting on the ramp (Fig. 13-3).

Incidentally, the ramping procedure described here should only be used on wood-decked ramps. Do not try to power a floatplane onto a concrete boat ramp. The concrete is quite rough and you will severely abrade the keels of your floats. If you should have to put your plane on a boat ramp for some reason, treat the concrete ramp like a beach, and use the beaching procedures described later in this chapter.

DOCKING

Other than an elevator or railcar ride to dry storage, ramps are the most ideal way to secure a floatplane, but they are only found at those facilities which cater specifically to floatplanes. These facilities are relatively few and far between, so most of the time you will be tieing your plane to a dock. Docks come in all shapes and sizes, ranging from sturdy, floating platforms lined with tires to protect your floats from damage, to a couple of boards nailed to some logs sticking out from shore. The only requirements

Fig. 13-1. Ramping a de Havilland Beaver. Note the use of full up-elevator. The small tubes sticking out of the sides of the float just forward of the step are attach points for beaching gear.

Fig. 13-2. Properly tied down on the ramp. The plane was powered up far enough to prevent it from sliding back into the water, after which lines were attached to keep it securely in place.

are that the dock must be low enough to clear the floatplane's wing, wing strut, and horizontal stabilizer, and that, if the dock is in tidal waters, it is of the floating variety. While lakes are not subjected to tides, their water levels can fluctuate, either through man's manipulation or from seasonal runoff and evaporation; so many freshwater boat and seaplane facilities also use floating docks.

Most docks are equipped with mooring cleats or some other means of securing the lines from your plane, but you may have to get creative when figuring out how to tie your plane to one of the more primitive wilderness docks you may encounter. If you are going to an area where you're not sure of the docking facilities, carry plenty of extra line in the plane with you. You may end up having to pass some lines completely around the dock or even to trees on shore to secure the plane.

If you are flying in a logging region, you may have occasion to tie up to a floating log raft. These actually make pretty good docks, since they are usually bound together with stout cables to which you can fasten your mooring lines (Fig.13-4).

Unless your destination is a seaplane facility or a harbor which has docks specifically designed and reserved for seaplanes, you will most likely have to tie up to a dock that was built for boats. Unfortunately, floatplanes and boats don't share the same docking requirements because boats don't have wings that stick out over the dock. Things like pilings, buildings, light poles, railings, and equipment lockers don't get in the way of a boat, but they can play havoc with your attempts to dock a floatplane.

Pilings are the worst offenders. One of the most popular methods of keeping a floating dock from floating away is to secure it to piles the size of telephone poles driven deep into the bottom of the harbor. Loosely fitting metal rings are placed around each pile and attached to the dock to keep the dock from drifting off, while still allowing it to ride up and down with the tide. The pilings usually stick up a good 10 or 15 feet above the water, and even higher in areas of extreme tides. While they present no problem for boats, they can make it almost impossible for a floatplane to approach what would otherwise be a perfect dock.

Like landings, every docking is different, and one of the things that keeps float flying from becoming routine is the challenge of figuring out the best way to get your plane to the dock. There is not enough room in this book, or any book, for that matter, to illustrate every docking situation you could possibly encounter. Instead, we will look at docking procedures and techniques in general, and see how they apply to a few basic docking situations. Armed with this knowledge, together with plenty of good

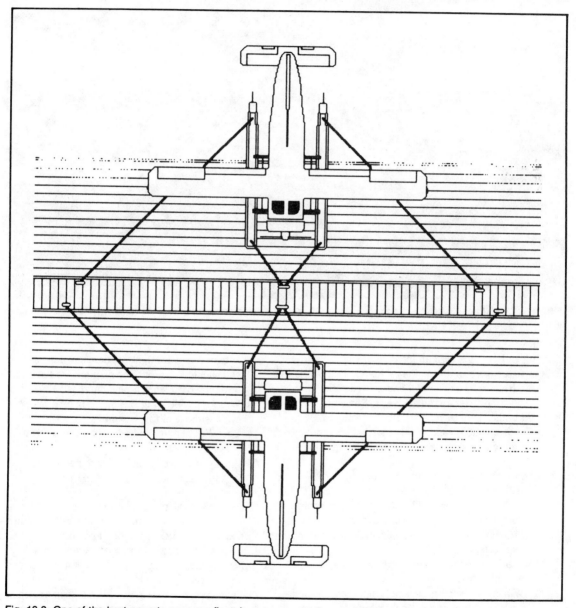

Fig. 13-3. One of the best ways to secure a floatplane to a ramp. Be careful when putting a plane onto a double-sided ramp like this one. You don't want to add so much power that you slide up over the top into the floatplane in front of you.

Fig. 13-4. Log booms (bottom left) make sturdy docks, and the cables that bind them together provide good places to fasten your mooring lines.

training and practice with an instructor, you should be able to figure out just about every situation that arises.

Rule Number One: don't let yourself be rushed into making your move before you are ready. Remember, you have no brakes and no reverse. It's very important to carefully check out a dock from the air before you land and taxi up to it. Ask yourself the following questions:

☐ Is the dock low enough for a floatplane?
☐ Is there sufficient room for me to approach the dock and stop? (You will need at least two or three floatplane lengths of open space at, or in front of, the dock before you can safely approach it, come alongside, and stop.)
☐ Can I taxi to the dock without hitting any pilings or other obstructions?
☐ Will my wings clear any boats that might be tied up to the same dock? (Don't forget, even a low-profile, open fishing boat can have a tall radio

antenna on it. It might not damage your plane if you should hit it, but you may end up having to buy the boat owner a new antenna.)
☐ Will my inside wing be able to extend over the dock without hitting anything?
☐ Once I'm tied up, will other boats or aircraft be able to get past my outside wing?
☐ Finally, if I have enough room to get to the dock, will I have enough room to depart it later?

If the answer to all these questions is yes, then you've found a good dock to tie up to. There are still questions to be answered about the direction and strength of the wind, the possible danger from boat wakes and swells, and other details, but at least you'll know you can physically get your plane alongside the dock.

Make it a practice to remove your seatbelt and open the door as you taxi in after landing, and have your front-seat passenger do the same. If it's windy, or if the dock is crowded, things could start getting hectic, and one of you may have to jump out onto a float in a hurry. The time to start fumbling with a door latch or discover that your seatbelt is still fastened is not as you are coasting inexorably towards the floatplane in front of you. As you get closer to the dock, slide your seat back far enough so you won't have to struggle to get out the door. How far you have to slide it depends on your airplane and your size. I'm 6-foot, 3-inches tall with a gross weight of a bit too much over 200 pounds, and if I'm flying a Cessna 172, I have to slide the seat all the way back before I can comfortably get out the door. I've found that by sitting on the forward edge of the seat and holding on to the V-brace above the instrument panel, I can still reach and operate the rudder pedals. I don't have this problem in a Beaver, however, since I have to put the seat all the way back anyway, just to be able to fly it. Every floatplane and every pilot is different. The important thing is that you be able to get out in a hurry if it becomes necessary.

Docking on a Calm Day

Docking a floatplane when there is no wind to contend with is relatively easy (Fig. 13-5). If there are no other planes or boats in the way, you can come straight in parallel to the dock. If the end of the dock is occupied, you'll have to approach at an angle, turning parallel to the dock at the last moment. The reason you need two or three floatplane lengths of open space at the dock will become apparent the first time you do this operation (Fig. 13-6). While you're still three or four plane lengths from the dock, shut off the engine and coast the rest of the way in. Remember to turn off the mag switch as soon as the engine stops turning over. You don't want anybody, including yourself, to get a surprise if they happen to pull on the prop for some reason.

If you've timed everything correctly, you'll drift to a stop just as you come alongside the dock, and all you'll have to do is step out and secure the plane. One of the trickiest things about learning to dock a floatplane is judging the right moment to shut off the engine. Too soon, and you'll drift to a stop before you get to the dock. Too late, and you'll be going too fast when you get there. If you stop too soon, and there's no wind, you can either throw a line to someone standing on the dock or get out your trusty paddle. Don't restart the engine to carry you those last few yards to the dock. Aircraft engines don't quit the instant you pull the mixture control back to idle

Fig. 13-5. Approaching a dock in Seattle's Lake Union. Pilot Neal Ratti has shut down the engine and has opened his door in preparation to stepping onto the dock and stopping the plane.

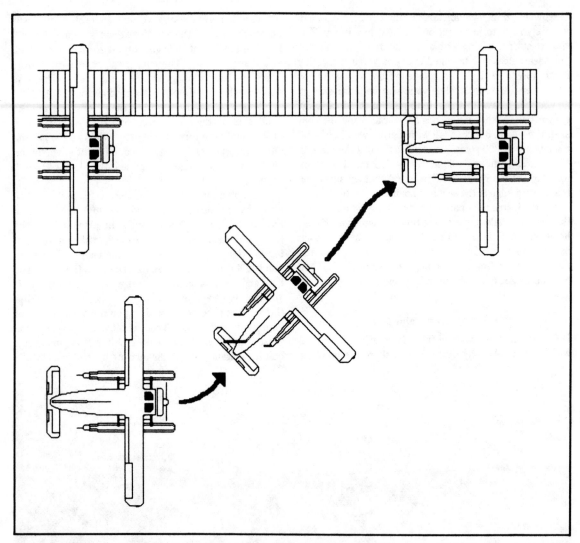

Fig. 13-6. It takes more room than you might think to bring a floatplane alongside a dock and get it stopped, especially if other planes are already there.

cut-off, and in the time it would take for the engine to shut down again, you could be carried quite a distance, assuming you didn't fetch up against a pole of something first.

Most of the time, you'll arrive at the dock carrying some degree of forward speed, and since the plane doesn't have any brakes of its own, you'll have to hop out and stop the plane yourself. You would think this would be a fairly self-explanatory procedure, but there's even a right and a wrong way to do this. The logical thing to do would be to jump onto the dock, grab the wing strut,

and pull back on it to stop the plane. That is the wrong way. When you pull back on the strut, your hands become a pivot point around which the airplane will start to rotate, and since the plane will probably be a foot or two away from the dock when you jump off, the bow of the inboard float will pivot into the dock. If it pivots into something unyielding, the float could be damaged.

The right way is to jump on the dock, grab the strut, and pull the plane in against the side of the dock while walking forward with it. When it's firmly against the dock, you can pull back slightly, and this, plus the fric-

144

tion of the inboard float against the dock, will bring the plane to a quick stop (Fig.13-7). Obviously, you don't want to pull the floats up against a dock that does not have tires or some other type of cushioning material on it. If you encounter a dock which has metal or concrete sides, you'll have to stop the plane while holding it away from the dock, but the principle is still the same. Walk along with the plane while slowing it to a stop, and don't let bow of the inboard float pivot into the dock.

If there are people on or near the dock you are approaching, someone will probably come over to catch your wing and help you stop. This is great if that person knows the correct procedure, but unfortunately, few people other than floatplane pilots understand the danger of trying to stop a floatplane by pulling back on its wing strut. If may be better to wave the helpers off and stop the plane yourself, rather than risk having your floats damaged.

If the dock you are using can accommodate several floatplanes, walk your plane as far forward as you can before cleating off the mooring lines. This will make it easier for the next pilot to get in behind you, and will make maximum use of the available dock space.

The best way to tie off, or *belay*, a mooring line to a cleat is shown in Fig. 13-8. Notice that the last turn is tucked under itself. This is called *jamming the line,* and it's frowned upon in sailboat circles, where sheets and halyards sometimes have to be uncleated in a hurry. The same tenacious qualities that make this method so unpopular with sailboaters, however, are a benefit to floatplane pilots. A line secured to a cleat in this manner will not work loose, and your plane will still be where you left it when you return.

Use at least two lines to secure your plane to the dock, and if it's going to be tied up for some time, it's a good idea to use spring lines in addition to the two dock lines. The spring lines, run diagonally from each end of the float

Fig. 13-7. The right way to stop a floatplane at a dock. Neal is holding onto the strut and one of the mooring lines as he slows the plane down, but he is not allowing the bow of the inboard float to pivot in and strike the dock.

Fig. 13-8. The best way to cleat a line. The line was brought in at the bottom of the picture, fastened to the cleat, and the free end coiled out to the right.

to a point on the dock opposite the other end of the float, act as shock absorbers, and help keep the plane from moving forward and backward.

If the dock you're tied to has tires lining its sides, you won't have to worry about protecting your floats, but if the dock has bare wood or metal sides, you'll have to use bumpers of some sort to keep your floats from rubbing up against the side of the dock. If you don't have room in the plane for a set of the popular air-filled bumpers, you can make some effective bumpers using sections of old automobile tires (see Chapter 7).

The importance of bumpers cannot be overstressed. If a float is allowed to bang repeatedly into the unyielding side of a dock, it won't be long before dents begin to appear or seams begin to open up. If the float starts rubbing on a metal dock fitting, there's a good chance a hole could be worn through the aluminum or fiberglass skin. Some docks can accommodate floatplanes on both sides. Which side you choose depends on a couple of factors. The wakes from passing boats can start a plane banging into the dock, so if there is a lot of boat traffic in the area,

try to put the dock between you and the swells. If the wind is strong and gusty, you might want to secure the plane to the downwind side of the dock. As we will see in the next section, there are definite disadvantages to approaching a dock on its downwind side, but once the plane is tied up, being in the lee of the dock has its advantages. The wind will hold the plane away from the dock, and the dock itself will protect the plane from the waves generated by the wind. If putting the plane on the downwind side of the dock will also expose it to the swells created by heavy boat traffic, however, choose the lesser of two evils, and tie up on the side away from the boat wakes.

Docking in the Wind

Docking in calm conditions can be challenging enough, but your judgment and skill will really be put to the test when the wind kicks up. Not only is the ever-present weathercocking force lurking about in the background, waiting to swing your plane in the wrong direction, but as you slow down after shutting off the engine, your wa-

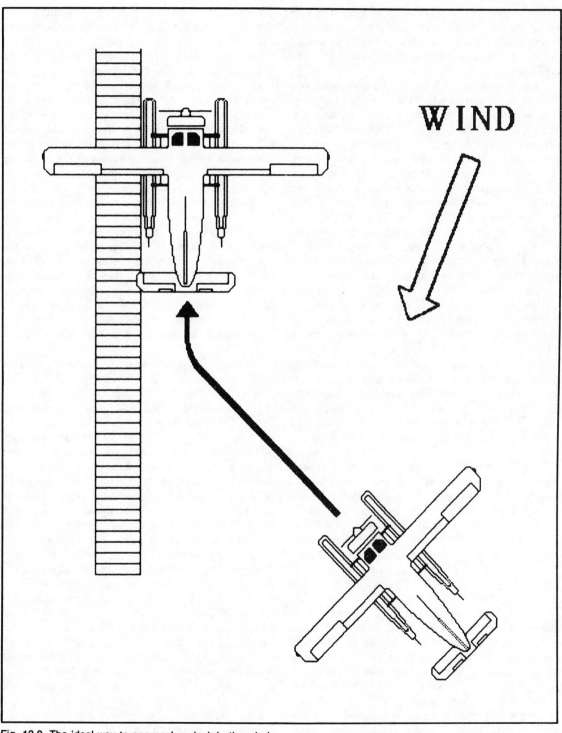

Fig. 13-9. The ideal way to approach a dock in the wind.

ter rudders will become less and less effective. Don't despair, however, because there are ways of using the wind to help you dock that are very slick and professional when properly executed, and will leave you feeling like a real pro.

The ideal way to approach a dock is on an upwind heading on the upwind side of the dock (Fig. 13-9). The wind will help you in two ways. First, it will help slow you down as you coast up to the dock after shutting down the engine. Second, it will push you into the dock and hold you there. If you shut off the engine a little too soon, and don't quite coast all the way up to the dock, it's not a big crisis, because the wind is going to push you over to it, anyway. On the other hand, if you stop short of the downwind side of a dock, the wind will immediately start to push you away from the dock and possibly into something expensive. If you aren't able to quickly throw a line to someone on the dock, all you can do is wait until you've drifted out far enough to be able to restart the engine and try again.

Whenever possible, avoid approaching a dock on a downwind or crosswind heading. For one thing, you may have to taxi faster to keep the water rudders effective. This factor, plus the fact that the wind may also be pushing you from behind, will cause you to coast in at a much higher rate of speed, and it may be difficult to get the plane stopped. This situation is especially dangerous if there is another floatplane tied to the dock ahead of you, because you run the risk of colliding with it before you can get out and drag your own plane to a stop.

It's easy to say, "Never approach a dock on a downwind or a crosswind heading," but since the wind doesn't read books like this one, the day will come when you will have no other choice but to approach a dock on a downwind or crosswind heading. If the dock is long, and there are no other floatplanes immediately in front of you, you may be able to get away with a normal docking procedure, but bear in mind your plane will be moving down the dock at a pretty good clip, and it will require extra space to bring it to a halt.

A better approach is shown in Fig. 13-10. Make your downwind approach some distance from the dock. When you are a short distance downwind of your intended parking place on the dock, start a turn toward it and pull up the water rudders. With the water rudders retracted, the wind coming from astern will weathercock your floatplane around very quickly. When the airplane is heading back upwind, lower the water rudders, and proceed with what has now become a normal upwind dock-

ing. Again, try to perform this maneuver on the upwind side of the dock, so that the wind will push you into the dock instead of drifting you away.

Another variation of a downwind docking is shown in Fig. 13-11. In this case, the dock is lying perpendicular to the wind. Approach the dock at the minimum possible speed, but be very careful not to let the wind get around to one side of you and weathercock the plane. Shut down the engine when you are two or three plane lengths out and start a turn to parallel the dock, pulling up the water rudders as you do so. If you have judged everything correctly, the plane will arrive at the dock at the same time it has pivoted around parallel to it.

Although the downwind approach illustrated in Fig. 13-11 was required because of obstructions at either end of the dock, the same docking procedure can be used in a situation where the dock itself is unobstructed, but the normal approach to it would require you to taxi across the wind. In order to maintain directional control while taxiing crosswind, you may have to taxi faster than you normally would, and you may even have to put the plane in a plowing attitude. In either case, you will arrive at the dock going much too fast. A safer alternative is shown in Fig. 13-12.

Docking a floatplane when there is a current running is not unlike docking when the wind is blowing. The same general rules apply, except that there will not be much of a weathercocking force to deal with, unless, of course, the wind is blowing, too. In fact, if the current is strong—in a fairly swift river, for example—you may be moved along fast enough to create a relative wind that will cause you to weathercock downstream. Because a current can be moving at a fairly good clip, it's best to always head into it when approaching a dock. On a river or in a strong tide, you may find that it takes more than idle power just to stay in one place, and if you were to attempt to approach a dock while heading downstream, you might not be able to stop. By taxiing into the current, you can control your forward speed quite precisely with the engine, and it's even possible to move the floatplane sideways while remaining opposite the same place on the shore. We'll look at river operations in more detail in Chapter 16, but the general rule is to always head into the current when approaching a dock.

You may have noticed that some of the illustrations in this chapter show the pilot's side of the floatplane next to the dock, while in others, the dock is against the passenger's side. Wind, current, and available mooring space, not convenience, will determine which side of the plane will end up against the dock; so you won't always

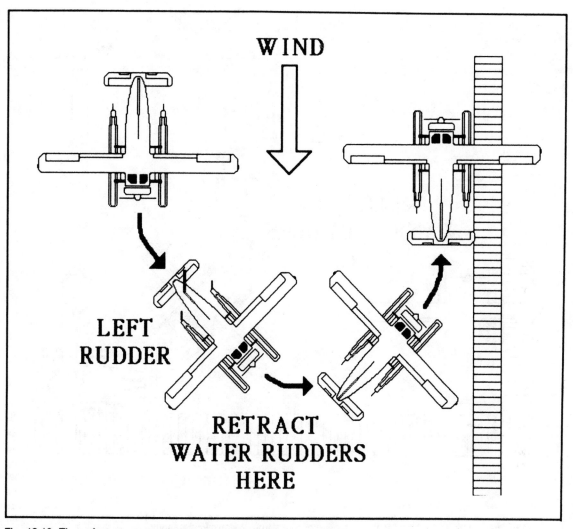

WIND

LEFT
RUDDER

RETRACT
WATER RUDDERS
HERE

Fig. 13-10. The safest way to approach a dock from a downwind heading.

be able to put it next to your door. If you're by yourself, and it looks like the dock is going to end up on the passenger's side of the airplane, all you have to do is slide over into the passenger seat and taxi the plane from there. Of course, this solution assumes that your plane has dual controls, and that there is a door on the passenger's side of the cabin. Floatplanes like the Cessna 172, 180, and 185 are very easy to dock from the passenger's side, as is the de Havilland Beaver. All of these planes have front doors on both sides of the cabin, and while not all Beavers are equipped with dual yokes, the single yoke is the throw-over type.

A Cessna 206, on the other hand, has a front door only on the pilot's side of the airplane. The plane does have nice, big, double doors on the right side of the plane, but they are for the rear seat passengers or freight. To use the rear doors, the pilot must climb over the backs of the front seats, and if the plane is full of freight, this could be a very difficult, if not impossible, task. Some 206 operators stretch a length of aircraft cable between the bow cleats on the floats. Then, if the pilot has to put a dock on the right side of the plane, he can climb out on the left float after shutting down the ending and turning off the mags, walk forward, and cross to the right float via the cable, holding onto the prop spinner for balance. From there, the pilot can step to the dock and stop the

149

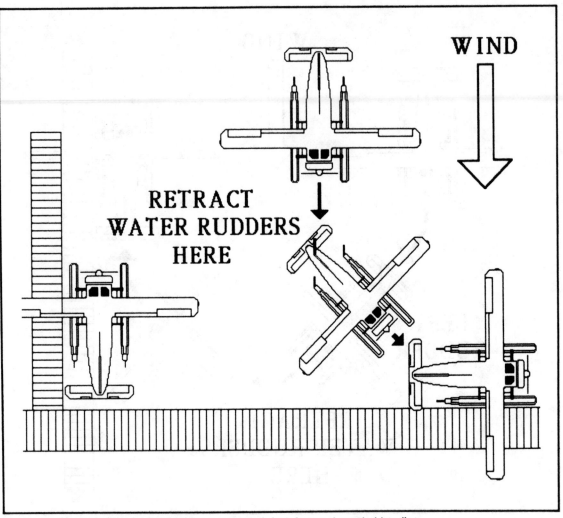

WIND

RETRACT
WATER RUDDERS
HERE

Fig. 13-11. One technique for approaching a crosswind dock from a downwind heading.

plane. Obviously, this will take more time than simply stepping out of the pilot's seat to the float and then to the dock, so pilots planning to use the cable method will have to make sure there's's sufficient space at the dock for the plane to continue coasting while they cross from the outside to the inside float.

Docking a floatplane on the passenger's side is a lot easier if you actually have a passenger sitting over there. After explaining the proper way to stop the plane, you can have your passenger step to the dock and bring the plane to a halt. As you're removing your seatbelt and opening the door while you're taxiing in after landing, have your front seat passenger do the same. This way,

he is ready to step out onto the float if you have to dock the plane on his side. If you're flying a 206 and have rear seat passengers, you can have one of them open the rear door and prepare to climb out onto the right float. As a general safety rule, instruct your passenger not to step out onto the float until the engine has stopped. If the timing is critical, you may have to make an exception to this rule, but if you do, don't let your passenger walk forward of the door until the prop has stopped.

When you kill the engine, remember to turn the mags off, too. It's an easy thing to forget as you're coasting in to what is perhaps a tricky docking situation, but as you, your passenger, or a helper on the dock scramble to get the plane stopped and some mooring lines attached, it's quite conceivable that someone could grab hold of the propeller. If the mags are still hot, you could have a real disaster on your hands.

Docking Nose First

All the docking techniques we've examined so far have assumed that you are going to moor your floatplane with one of the floats parallel to the side of the dock. While this is certainly the most recommended method, there may be times when you will be unable to approach a dock in the normal manner. For example, your aerial survey prior to landing may reveal that, although there is enough room at a particular dock for your plane, the dock itself is surrounded by high pilings which will interfere with your wings if you try to come alongside. In cases like this,

you may be able to approach nose first. The main thing to avoid in this situation is approaching too fast, because you don't want to ram the bows of the floats into the dock. The trick is to shut the engine down soon enough so that by the time you reach the dock, you are just barely moving forward. As you coast in, walk to the bow of the float and prepare to become a shock absorber. Your objective is to keep the floats from striking the side of the dock, and any technique you can come up with that accomplishes this objective is a good one.

If there is no wind to speak of, one way to ensure a gentle arrival is to stop a little ways out from the dock and paddle in. You can also use the paddle to help slow the plane down if you find you're coasting in a little too fast. Of course, if you're flying something exotic like a Turbo-Beaver, you can always bring yourself to a stop

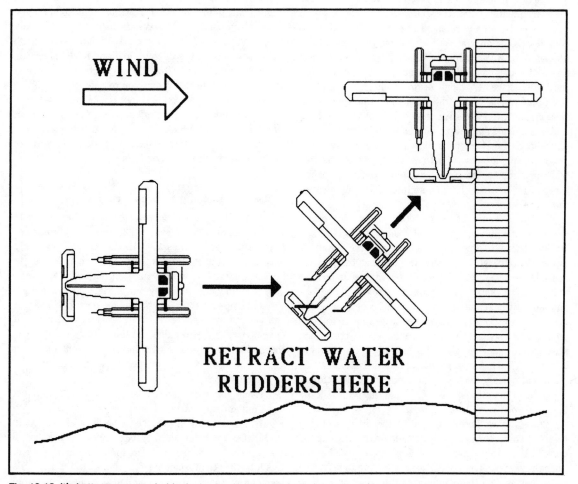

Fig. 13-12. It's better to approach this dock on a downwind heading than to approach it straight in on a crosswind heading.

at the last minute by putting the prop in reverse pitch for a moment or two.

Take a line with you when you walk forward to cushion the impact of the plane's arrival. The floats on most floatplanes project out ahead of the nose, so once you step to the dock, there won't be much to hold on to other than the floats themselves. The mooring lines that are permanently fastened to the float struts are generally not long enough to reach forward over the floats to the dock, and it will be much easier to control the plane and keep it from drifting backwards if you have hold of a line that you've attached to one of the bow cleats than if you kneel on the dock and try to hang on to the cleat yourself. Also, unless you're just dropping someone off, you're going to need to fasten a couple of mooring lines to the floats, anyway.

Pilots who operate out of crowded boat harbors where they frequently have to approach a dock head-on sometimes fasten a permanent line to the bow cleat on each float. The lines are cut long enough to reach back almost to the water rudders. If the airplane is on straight floats, the lines can be left lying on the float deck where they will behave very nicely during flight. If the airplane is on amphibious floats, the lines should be tied to the float struts with light string to keep them from getting under the floats and tangled in the landing gear. As the plane heads nose-first toward the dock, the pilot can shut down the engine, step out onto the float, pick up the line, walk forward, stop the plane, and step to the dock holding a mooring line that's long enough to reach any cleat in the vicinity.

Nosing a floatplane up to a dock can be very tricky if the wind is blowing from any direction other than straight ahead. In order to avoid damaging the floats, it's imperative that you approach the dock at the slowest possible speed. Your directional control over your airplane will decrease as its forward speed decreases, however, and a crosswind could begin to weathercock your plane away from the dock before you get close enough to jump onto it. The very fact that you have to approach the dock nose first indicates that it's probably crowded or obstructed in some way, so the chances are good that the wind will quickly push you into something unyielding. You'd be better off looking for another place to dock the plane, even if it isn't as convenient.

Once you are nosed up against the dock, you may be able to pivot the floatplane and secure it alongside the dock in the normal manner. If pilings or other obstructions prevent you from doing so, you'll have to leave the plane as it is. Pull the plane forward so the bows of the floats are against the dock, protecting them with bumpers if necessary, and run a line from the bow cleat of each float to the dock. If possible, secure the stern of the floats using the same method you would use if you were on a ramp; run a line from each stern cleat out diagonally to a cleat on the dock. This procedure will keep the tail of the plane from swinging back and forth.

If you have to depart the dock from a nose-in position, simply cast off all the lines, step onto the bow of the float on the pilot's side of the plane, and shove the plane backwards. If there isn't any wind to help you drift back, you may have to get out the paddle, but in any event, don't start the engine until you're far enough away from the dock to be able to turn away from it when you fire up. Also, be careful if there's a crosswind.

Figure out what the airplane is going to do *before* you cast off those lines. If you think the plane will be blown into a boat, piling, or other obstruction as soon as you shove off, you'll have to come up with some other way of leaving the dock. One alternative might be to attach some long lines to the upwind float and have helpers on the dock hold you away from the obstructions as you drift or paddle backwards. When you're safely clear of the obstructions, your dockside helpers can simply toss their ends of the lines in the water and you can haul them in. Of course, if you're lucky enough to be flying a Turbo-Beaver or a Twin Otter, all you have to do is put the prop or props in reverse and back out.

Docking a Large Floatplane

You will probably earn your seaplane rating in a relatively light floatplane like a Cessna 172, a Citabria, or a Piper Super Cub. These planes will coast to a stop fairly quickly once their engines are shut off, since their low mass doesn't generate much inertia. Consequently, on windy days you may have to carry power right up to the dock to avoid stopping short and being blown back before you can get out and secure the plane. Eventually, you will develop the ability to judge just the right moment to cut the engine, based on the wind and current conditions and what you know to be the deceleration rate of your airplane.

When you transition to a larger, heavier, floatplane, don't fall into the trap, as I have done on occasion, of driving the larger plane in as close to the dock as you would the smaller one before cutting the engine. If you do, you'll be in for a surprise. A Beaver, for example, will coast much farther than a Cessna 172, thanks to the Beaver's tremendous mass. At best, you'll have a hard time bringing the plane to a stop, and if it just isn't your day, you could end up shortening the overall length of the floatplane in front of you. When you start flying a larger plane, anticipate the fact that it will need more room to stop, and be prepared to pull the mixture back to idle cutoff sooner than you're accustomed to do so. It won't be long before you're used to the new plane's characteristics.

The other thing you need to be aware of when you start flying larger floatplanes is the fact that, since they present much more vertical surface to the wind, they will be blown around with much greater force than the smaller planes you're used to flying. Manhandling a Beaver at a dock on a windy day can be a real experience, especially if you're by yourself, and a huge floatplane like the de Havilland Otter requires a full dock crew to keep it under control when the wind kicks up. On the other hand, the de Havilland Twin Otter is a surprisingly easy plane to dock, thanks to its twin turboprops and reversible-pitch propellers. By manipulating the throttles and propeller controls, a Twin Otter pilot can pivot the big plane within its own length, and can maneuver into docks that a conventional, single-engined floatplane half the Twin Otter's size couldn't use (Fig. 13-13).

Docking in the Snow

In most parts of the country, winter means snow, and a heavy snowfall can severely damage an airplane. The problem is the snow's weight, which can collapse hangar roofs or overstress the skin panels, spars, and struts on planes parked outside. The only solution is to keep brushing the snow off the wings and tail before its weight can become dangerous.

In many areas, the arrival of fall signals the end of the floatplane season, but in the Pacific Northwest and southeast Alaska, the floatplane season continues year-round. While the saltwater harbors, bays, and fjords don't freeze up in these areas, late fall, winter, and early spring still brings snow, and with it comes a special threat to floatplanes.

If you visit a seaplane facility or boat harbor that doesn't have a ramp or a means of removing planes from the water, you will have no other choice but to leave the plane at a dock overnight. Regardless of the time of year, it's a good idea to check the airplane every few hours if you are in this situation, just to make sure the airplane isn't in any danger from a leaking float or a chaffing mooring line, but if the forecast is predicting snow, you'll have to take special precautions.

If the snow is wet and heavy, it can sink an unat-

tended floatplane in a very short period of time. As the snow builds up on the horizontal stabilizer, its weight will gradually force the sterns of the floats underwater. The rear float compartments will begin to fill with the water that leaks in around the access hatch covers and the rubber balls that plug the bilge-pump down tubes. This water will add even more weight to the rear of the plane, and the floats will sink even deeper. Soon, the next compartment forward will begin to fill, which will force the floats deeper still.

A friend of mine described the results of this liquid "domino" effect on a Super Cub he had seen in southeast Alaska one morning. The only thing showing above the water was the prop spinner, but only a few hours before, the plane had been bobbing high and dry at its moorings. The only sure way to prevent this situation from happening is to stay with the airplane, sweeping the snow off the wings and tail surfaces before it can accumulate.

What can you do if, for some reason, you can't stay with your airplane? Fortunately, there is something you can do to prevent the snow from submerging the floats, but first you must be able to get your plane into a boat slip between two floating docks.

Moor your plane in the slip so it can't move forward or backward. It's very important that the plane not be able to move, so use spring lines to hold the floatplane in position, and even tie the wings down if you think it will help. After the plane is securely positioned in the slip, take a heavy line at least 1/2 inch in diameter and fasten it to a dock cleat next to the tail of one of the floats. Run the line under the tails of both floats, forward of the water rudders, and to a cleat on the opposite dock (Fig. 13-14). Pull the line as tight as you can, and run it back under the floats again to the other side. Repeat this two or three times and tie off the line. If you have someone stand on the bow of one of the floats, the tail of the airplane will raise and allow you to pull the line even tighter. Now when it starts to snow, the floats will sit on the line instead of sinking beneath the surface.

This technique should not be used as an excuse for leaving your floatplane unattended, but if you must be away from the plane for awhile, it may make the difference between continuing your flight in the morning, or searching for a salvage crew.

MOORING TO A BUOY

If you mess about in floatplanes long enough, you will someday find yourself circling over your destination while

Fig. 13-13. Docking a Twin Otter in the crowded harbor at Vancouver, British Columbia. The pilot will come up to the dock nose first, stop by putting both propellers in reverse, and then pivot the plane by reversing the right propeller while pulling forward with the left one. This neat maneuver will put the plane alongside the dock and facing out, ready for its next scheduled departure.

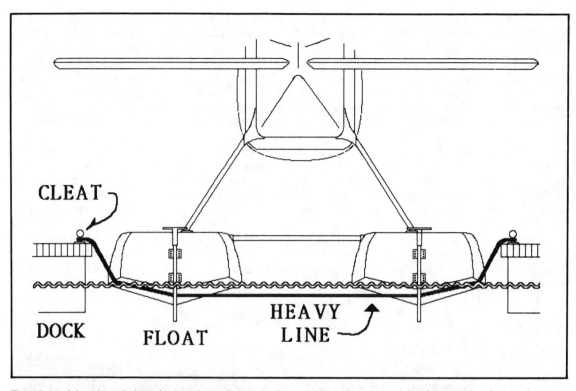

CLEAT

DOCK   FLOAT   HEAVY
                 LINE

Fig. 13-14. A handy technique for keeping a floatplane from sinking when the weight of accumulated snow threatens to drive the sterns of the floats underwater.

you look in vain for an open spot at a dock. You may even find yourself looking for a dock, period. Perhaps your destination is a beach—a beach that turns out to be covered with large, float-puncturing rocks. In cases like these, your only option will be to moor or anchor the plane offshore.

Many harbors, resorts, and marinas have permanent mooring buoys which you can use if there's no other alternative. The biggest challenge will be figuring out how you're going to get from the plane to shore and back again; the actual mooring procedure is quite simple.

First, you'll need a mooring bridle of some sort, which is simply a V-shaped harness made out of rope or cable. Each arm of the "V" should end in an eye splice just large enough to fit over the bow cleats on the floats, while a large snap hook should be fastened to the point of the "V." If you don't have a ready-made bridle, you can make a reasonable facsimile using the lines you're carrying in the plane.

Since a mooring buoy is generally located some distance from shore, you will almost always be able to head directly into the wind or current while approaching

it. Treat a buoy the same as you would a dock, and come up alongside it. Don't let the buoy get in between the floats. For one thing, it will be difficult to get hold of when it's bobbing around among the spreader bars, brace wires, and rudder cables under the plane. Also, you may have to carry power all the way up to the buoy if you're bucking a strong headwind or current, and if the buoy passes between the floats, it could be struck by the propeller.

When you're a couple of plane lengths away from the buoy, shut down the engine and climb out onto the float. You can always reach back through the door and work the rudder pedals by hand if you have to make some last-minute adjustments to your heading. If it's windy, you can leave the engine running and operate its controls from the float, too. Grab the buoy as you come up beside it (this is when a collapsible boathook can come in handy), and fasten the center of your mooring bridle to the ring on top of the buoy. If the engine is still running, shut it down and turn off the mag switches before you walk forward and fasten one of the two legs of the bridle to the bow cleat of the float on which you're standing. Toss the other half of the bridle across to the opposite float or tie it to one of the propeller blades. Just make sure you can reach it from the other float. Climb back through the cabin and secure the second leg of the bridle to the bow cleat on the opposite float.

The bridle will keep your floatplane centered on the buoy, while allowing the plane to pivot into the wind or current. Always remember to raise the water rudders after you've made fast to a buoy to enable the plane to pivot quickly in the event of a sudden wind shift and reduce the chances of capsizing.

Some pilots prefer to use a yoke around the propeller in place of a mooring bridle between the floats (Fig. 13-15). They put a loop of line around each blade close to the hub, and join the two loops together beneath the propeller. They then run a single line from the junction of the two loops of the mooring buoy. This method seems to be most popular with the pilots of small, light floatplanes with high-lift wings, like the Super Cub and the Citabria. One advantage of this system is that the nose

will be held down if the wind starts blowing hard, and the plane will be less likely to lift off the water. It's also the most convenient way to moor a floatplane that only has a door on one side. Unless you're an accomplished calf roper, or are extremely adept with a boathook, it can be very difficult to slip the other half of the mooring bridle over the bow cleat on the float you can't get to, to say nothing of getting it off again. I would not recommend, however, that you use a propeller yoke on a floatplane equipped with a variable-pitch or constant-speed propeller. The constant tugging on the propeller blades could conceivably damage the pitch-changing mechanism in the propeller hub.

To depart the buoy later, simply reverse the procedure you used when you arrived. Release the bridle from the float on the passenger's side of the plane, climb back through the cabin, and walk to the bow of the float on the pilot's side. Release the other half of the bridle and walk the buoy back alongside the float to the pilot's

Fig. 13-15. A Citabria moored with a line fastened to the propeller. Note the water rudder in the retracted position. (Courtesy of the EDO Corporation)

door. Unfasten the bridle from the buoy, put it and yourself into the airplane, and start the engine. If the buoy is back beside the plane, it will be clear of the propeller when the engine starts and you begin to taxi forward.

On a windy day, you can release the plane from the buoy right away. You'll immediately begin to drift backwards, and by the time you've removed the bridle from the floats and stowed it, you should be able to start the engine and turn away from the buoy with no danger of hitting it. Make sure, however, that you won't be blown backwards into something while you're removing the bridle and getting ready to start the engine.

If you are in danger of drifting backwards into something, first release the bridle from the floats and walk the buoy back alongside the pilot's door, as described earlier. After securing the bridle to one of the float struts to keep the plane from drifting back, fasten another line to the float strut and pass its free end through the ring on the buoy. Take up all the slack in this line and tie it off on the strut. Once this line is secured, remove the mooring bridle from the buoy and the strut and stow it in the plane. When you're ready to go, unfasten one end of the remaining line from the strut and hold on to it as you climb into the cockpit and you prepare to start the engine to keep you alongside the buoy until the engine starts. As the plane begins to move forward, allow your end of the line to be pulled through the ring on the buoy. The other end of the line will remain tied to the float strut, and you can retrieve it at your convenience.

Obviously, this whole mooring business becomes much simpler if you have a passenger on board. He can get out on the float and pick up the buoy when you arrive and release it when you depart, allowing you to concentrate on maneuvering the airplane. *Remember*, don't let your passenger walk forward of the door unless the propeller is stopped and the mag switches are off.

If a stiff breeze has made the water choppy, and you think your passenger might have trouble picking up the buoy, this little trick might make it easier for them. Kill the engine as soon as you're alongside the buoy and make a sharp turn into it. As the plane stops and begins to drift backwards, the buoy will be pinned against the side of the downwind float, and your passenger will have more time to get a line or bridle fastened to its ring.

It's important that your plane be able to swing a full 360 degrees around the buoy without hitting anything. Currents change and winds shift, and in the course of an hour, your plane can easily pass through every point of the compass. Murphy came up with a law that states, "Whatever can go wrong, will;" so your plane will in-variably swing in the direction that offers the best chance of a collision with something else.

Unfortunately, things can go wrong no matter how many precautions you take. Several years ago, the pilot of a beautiful new float-equipped Cessna 185 moored the plane to a buoy in a resort harbor in Washington's San Juan Islands. Later in the day, a large yacht arrived and anchored nearby. The captain of the yacht set the stage for the ensuing accident by putting out a stern anchor in addition to the usual bow anchor. The two anchors held the yacht in a fixed position, while the floatplane was free to pivot around its buoy. The tide turned, and the plane slowly swung around to point in the opposite direction. Its wing rode up over the unyielding yacht until the plane was pinned against the side of the hull by the current. As one wing slid up onto the yacht, the other one dipped into the water. The force of the current drove the outside wing down until it hit the bottom of the harbor. The pressure of the strong tidal current forced the waterlogged wing against the bottom until finally the outer 3 or 4 feet of the wing gave way and bent up. While this was the only serious structural damage to the plane, the owner faced an astronomical repair bill. The engine and cockpit had been immersed in the salt water, and everything, including the instruments, had to be disassembled, cleaned, and reassembled, or replaced completely.

I include this depressing account to make a point. Never go off and leave a floatplane for any length of time unless it's completely out of the water in dry storage or securely tied down on a ramp. No matter how many disasters you anticipate and guard against, there's always one more you didn't think of. Neptune and his freshwater friends have been doing strange things to boats for thousands of years, and there's no reason why their warped sense of humor shouldn't be directed against floatplanes, too. The owner of the 185 had no idea that someone would show up and park a steel island next to the carefully moored plane, but perhaps if a little closer eye had been kept on the situation developing out in the harbor, the accident could have been avoided. We'll never know, but it's something to think about.

ANCHORING

Permanent mooring buoys are generally confined to developed harbors, marinas, and waterfront resorts. If, after you earn your seaplane rating, you decide to visit one of the many remote areas the floatplane makes accessible, you'll have to use an anchor if you want to moor your plane offshore. There are several disadvantages to anchoring a floatplane, however, and you should be aware of them before you try it.

First of all, any anchor is worthless if it won't hold your plane; so you'll need one that's big enough to hold in the worst conditions you can imagine. This anchor will not be light, so don't forget to allow for it in your weight and balance calculations. You'll also have to find someplace to put it, and its sharp edges and awkward shape won't make this an easy task.

There's more to anchoring a plane than simply tying a line to an anchor and tossing it overboard, followed by a hopeful desire that it catch on something. In order for an anchor to work, it has to lie on its side so its flukes will dig into the bottom. If you let out just enough line for the anchor to reach the bottom, the pressure from the plane as it's pushed backwards by the wind or current will keep the anchor from falling over and digging in, so it will simply drag across the bottom.

The correct nautical term for anchor line is *rode,* and the recommended length of rode to properly anchor a boat is five times the depth of the water under the keel. You should adhere to this practice when anchoring a floatplane, too. If you're going to anchor in 20 feet of water, you'll need at least 100 feet of rode, which you'll obviously have to stow on board somewhere. Nylon makes the best rode, by the way, as its elasticity helps absorb shock if the wind, waves, or current start bouncing the plane around.

It's a good idea to have several feet of heavy chain at the bottom end of the rode to prevent the line from chaffing if the bottom is rocky. The chain also works like a shock absorber, enabling the anchor to hold better, but when you're not using it, it's just more dead weight the plane must carry around.

After dropping the anchor, do not simply fasten the free end of the rode to the bow cleat on one of the floats. Doing so will keep the plane from pointing directly into the wind, and it could capsize in a strong breeze. Instead, you should secure the rode to the floats with the same bridle you would use if you were mooring the plane to a buoy. In fact, it's a good idea to attach a small buoy (one more thing to carry) to the free end of the rode, and secure your plane to the buoy with the mooring bridle. If you decide to make short flights away from your anchorage during the day, you can leave your anchor in place, and the buoy will make it easy to find when you return. Approach and pick up this buoy using the same procedures described earlier.

Consider anchoring your plane only as a last resort. Beside the inconvenience of having to haul around a lot of heavy, awkward equipment, there is always the danger of dragging the anchor. Permanent mooring buoys are usually kept in position by things like 55 gallon drums filled with concrete, or old truck bodies. An anchor small enough to be carried in a floatplane is pretty puny in comparison, and will not have anywhere near the holding power of a mooring buoy's anchor. If the current or wind is strong, the movement of your plane could work your little anchor free, in which case the plane would start to drift, dragging its anchor along behind it. Once an anchor starts to drag, it usually keeps dragging, and your floatplane could very well end up on the rocks. Because of the danger of dragging the anchor, it's vitally important that you stay with or near the plane until you can make it to a ramp, dock, or beach.

HIGH WINDS AND MOORING DON'T MIX

If strong winds are forecast, do not plan to anchor your plane or moor it to a buoy, no matter how well that buoy is anchored to the bottom. Even though your plane will be free to pivot into the wind, it's just a matter of time before the combination of strong, gusty winds and large waves will turn it over.

There is one method of mooring a floatplane so it will weather most storms, but you can't carry the necessary equipment around with you in the baggage compartment. If involves taking two 55 gallon drums and filling them with just enough concrete so each one will float with its top just barely breaking the surface of the water. Each barrel is sealed, and a large ring is welded to its top. When in use, one barrel is positioned under each wing of the moored floatplane, and a nylon line is run between the ring in the top of each barrel and the tiedown ring set in the wing above it. As long as the wind and water remain calm, the wings won't have to support the weight of the floating barrels, but in the event of a storm, the barrels will act as tiedowns, and prevent the plane from lifting off the water or rocking violently from side to side. Nylon line works the best in this case because it stretches and will absorb shocks. Since the barrels are not anchored to the bottom, the plane is still free to pivot into the wind, although not as quickly.

This system will effectively guard against a capsizing, but if heavy rain, large waves, or the weight of accumulated snow on the wings and tail surfaces cause the floats to fill up with water, the plane will not be prevented from sinking. The only way to completely eliminate the threat of sinking is to put your plane in dry storage, on a ramp, or on the beach.

BEACHING

When you start to explore new territory in a floatplane, it won't be long before you'll want to put the plane on a beach. Clam digging, oyster gathering, fishing, picnicking, camping, or just sitting in front of a spectacular view are all activities made more enjoyable by a floatplane because it makes possible an escape from the ground-bound crowds. Because it's unlikely that your favorite clam beach is equipped with either a seaplane ramp or a convenient, tire-lined dock, you'll have to learn to secure your plane to the shore itself.

Aerial Surveillance

The first part of the procedure takes place in the air. Overfly the beach several times if necessary, and carefully check it over. Does it appear to be covered with rocks? If so, you may have to anchor offshore or bypass it completely, rather than risk damaging your floats.

Is the water offshore free of obstructions? Be especially alert for pilings which have been cut or broken off below the surface. If you're landing on a lake or reservoir, check carefully for deadheads and the jagged remains of tree trunks covered by a rising water level.

Will your taxi towards shore take you over, or near, large underwater boulders or ledges? They're easy to spot from the air, but impossible to see once you're on the water, and a sharp rock or jagged ledge can easily rip the bottom out of one of your floats.

Is the water offshore deep enough, or is there a chance you might run aground before you even reach the beach? It can be very difficult to accurately judge the depth of either murky, or exceptionally clear, water. Murky water obscures the bottom,while clear water may make the bottom appear closer than it really is. Many of the lakes in Canada and Alaska are so clear, that on a bright, sunny day, rocks on the bottom in 50 feet of water appear to be just inches beneath the surface.

Marine charts contain valuable information about water depths, and many topographical charts include the configuration of lake bottoms, as well as land contours. It's a good idea to keep the appropriate marine and topographical charts in your plane, along with the traditional sectional and WAC charts.

Once your plane is on the beach, will you be able to secure it to anything to keep it from being blown or washed off? If your destination is the wooded shoreline of a lake, there will be plenty of trees, logs, and stumps for you to run lines to, but if the beach is wide, or the shoreline barren, it may take a lot of line and some creative thinking on your part to keep the plane where you want it.

Which way is the wind blowing? You'll need this information anyway, to determine your landing direction, but it will also tell you in advance the safest way to approach the shore.

If you're landing in tidal waters, there is one more thing you need to know before committing your airplane to the beach. Is the tide coming in or going out? Although it's often easy to visually determine if the tide is high or low, the only accurate way to tell which way it's going is with a current, published tide table, and you should keep one with your marine and aeronautical charts. If you put your plane on the beach at high tide and leave it there, you'd better not want to leave in a hurry because you're not going to go anywhere for the next 12 hours. Conversely, if you beach your plane at low tide, you'd better not go anywhere, because if you do, your plane probably won't be there when you get back.

Beaching the Plane

The most important rule to follow when approaching the shore is to do it *slowly*. Even nice, sandy beaches are very abrasive to float bottoms and should be approached with caution. If the wind is on-shore (blowing from the water towards the shore), beaching is easy. If you're sure the bottom is free of obstructions or rocks, taxi in until you're three or four plane lengths from shore, start a turn away from it, and shut down the engine. Raise the water rudders as you turn, and the wind will weathercock your plane around until its tail is facing the beach. The wind will then begin to push it slowly backwards, so it's important that you leave the water rudders up to avoid damaging them when the sterns of the floats touch shore. When the plane runs aground, all you and your passengers have to do is walk to the rear of the floats and step onto the beach. If you're lucky, you may not even get your feet wet.

If the wind is *off-shore* (blowing from the shore towards the water), the beaching technique is different. Nose the plane gently up the beach at a 45-degree angle to allow you to quickly turn away if you find that the bottom is too rocky, or if you see that you're in danger of running aground before you reach the shore. You want to contact the beach at the slowest speed possible, so don't wait too long before shutting down the engine.

Remember to raise the water rudders before you run aground. It's an easy thing to forget, since you'll be busy watching the bottom for rocks and trying to pick the best place to bring the plane ashore, but it's important that the rudders come up before they hit, and possibly dig into, the bottom. A good way to remember to raise them is to hold the retraction handle in your hand as you coast in. Then you won't have to fumble around on the floor looking for the handle, and the fact that you're holding on to it should remind you to raise the rudders when you reach shallow water.

If you know the beach is free of sharp rocks, wait until the inshore float contacts the beach before getting out and walking forward. If you walk to the front of the float before you reach the shore, your weight will force the bow of the float a little deeper, and it will run aground farther out from the beach. Depending on the slope of the bottom, the difference may be only a few inches or it may be several feet, but it might be enough to keep the water from running over the tops of your boots when you step off the float.

Before you walk to the front of the float and step, or splash, onto the beach, secure, one of your long mooring lines to the stern cleat of the inshore float and pay out the line as you walk forward and go ashore. When you've stepped off the float, give the plane a good shove away from the beach and into deeper water, paying out the line as it goes. When the plane is out far enough to be in no danger of running aground as it turns, pull its tail back in towards you with the line until the sterns of the floats slide up on shore.

Now you can see why it's so important that the water rudders be retracted, because if they are still down as you pull the plane in backwards, they will dig into the bottom and be jammed against their stops. The rudder mechanism is not designed to take this kind of punishment, and the chances are good that the blades will be bent. The pivot and retraction system could even be broken, which would really be a disaster. If, as you're turning the plane around, you notice that the rudders are still down, wade out and retract them before pulling the plane ashore. It's far cheaper to dry out your clothes than it is to repair a set of bent, broken, or jammed water rudders.

Obscure or Rocky Bottoms

If you are unsure of the bottom near the beach, or if it's rocky, stop your plane before you get into shallow water and look the situation over carefully. If there isn't any wind, you may want to paddle the plane slowly to shore, ready to backpaddle or fend the plane off if it looks like the floats are in danger of being damaged. If muddy or murky water obscures the bottom, the only thing you can do is jump overboard and slowly pull your plane towards shore, feeling carefully for rocks and other float-damaging objects. (It's a good idea to keep a change of clothes in the plane for occasions like this.)

If the wind is blowing, or if the water is choppy, you may want to abandon the beaching attempt altogether, because the plane will be very difficult to handle, and you'll run the risk of it's being blown out of control into a rocky area or pounded against the bottom. A better decision would be to go in search of a calmer area to beach the plane. You can try the first spot again when the wind and water conditions are better.

Always Beach Tail First

Regardless of the method you use to approach the beach, your plane should always be pulled up on shore tail-first (Fig. 13-16). For one thing, you'll have to point the nose toward the water anyway when you leave; so you might as well do it now. The main reason for pulling the sterns of the floats onto the beach, however, is that the afterbodies of the floats draw much less water than the forebodies, and you will be able to pull the plane farther up on shore. With the floats solidly resting on the beach, your plane will be in much less danger of drifting away if the wind starts whipping up the waves.

The procedure for sliding the sterns of the floats onto a beach is identical to the procedure for tailing a floatplane onto a ramp. Position yourself in front of the horizontal stabilizer, facing the shore, and lift up on the stabilizer while pushing the plane backwards. Remember to place your hands under the stabilizer spar to avoid denting the aluminum skin or puncturing the fabric. Obviously, you'll be able to get a light floatplane like a Super Cub or a Citabria farther up on the beach than a Cessna 206, and you may not be able to get a big plane like a Beaver out of the water at all, even though the floats may be firmly on the bottom. The important thing is that the plane be sitting solidly on the ground, even if the ground is underwater.

Make sure the floats won't be damaged when you pull the plane up on shore. It's obvious what sharp rocks can do to the floats, and even smooth gravel can be damaging if waves cause the plane to rock back and forth. If the beach is rocky, you can help protect your floats by resting them on branches or poles cut from nearby trees. I know of at least one pilot who carries thick rubber mats for the same purpose.

When you've slid your plane as far up on shore as you can, make sure its weight isn't resting on one or both of the water rudders. Even though they're retracted, they

Fig. 13-16. A de Havilland Beaver secured tail first to the shore of a reservoir in Washington's Cascade Mountains. (Courtesy of Kenmore Air Harbor)

could be touching the beach, especially if the slope is steep. I've had to dig a little relief trench under each water rudder occasionally so the weight of the plane wouldn't bend them over.

Securing the Plane

The last step in beaching a floatplane is making sure it will stay on the beach. If you've beached your plane while the tide is ebbing, you've got nothing to worry about for awhile, but if you're on a lake, a reservoir, or a river, you'll need to get some lines ashore.

Beaches have a way of making what you thought was far too much line to carry seem like not enough. If you're going to be flying and beaching your plane in unfamiliar territory, you should carry at least 300 feet of good, strong line, and if you can fit more in with your luggage, by all means do so. You may have to run lines across a lot of sand or gravel before reaching something solid enough to tie your plane to, and while it's easy not to use all the line you have, it's impossible to use the line you didn't bring.

If you're only going to be on the beach for a short time, one line run from the tail tiedown ring to a nearby tree, log, or boulder will suffice, but if you plan to remain for several days, or if it looks like the wind and waves are going to kick up, get several lines on the plane. In addition to the line on the tail, run a line from each wing back to the beach. Finally, lines run out at an angle from each bow cleat will help keep the plane from pivoting if the wind or waves strike the plane at an angle.

If it looks like a real storm is approaching, you can fill the floats with water to keep the plane from lifting off the beach or being blown over onto its back. Remember, however, to pump the water out as soon as the danger has passed. This technique should only be used if the plane is firmly sitting on a beach or a ramp. Never fill the floats of a moored or docked floatplane with water. It does not add appreciably to the stability of the plane, but it does bring it that much closer to sinking.

If you're tailed into a sandy beach, and there's just nothing around that's solid enough to tie the plane to, you can steal a page from the four-wheel-drive enthusiasts' book, and make your own tiedown. All you need is a shovel. Find a large piece of driftwood or a big rock, and tie the lines from your floatplane to this improvised anchor. If nothing else is available, you can even use the paddle from your plane. Dig a deep hole, place your anchor with its attached lines into it, and fill the hole back in. This makes a great tie-down, although it's time-consuming to construct. Off-road drivers use this technique to provide a solid anchor for a winch line in the event they get stuck out of reach of a tree or a boulder.

If you've beached your plane in tidal waters, and only want to stay on shore for 1 or 2 hours, you don't have any choice but to move the plane every 15 minutes or so. If the water is very calm and the tide is coming in, you can run a line to a log or tree and just let the plane float off the beach. It won't go very far, and when it's time to leave, you can use the line to retrieve it. If, however, the wind or passing boats are stirring up swells, keep the plane solidly tailed onto the beach so it won't be bumped or ground against the shore by the waves.

If the tide is rising, you'll have to keep moving the plane farther up the beach to keep it from floating free, and if the tide is ebbing, you'll have to keep pushing the plane farther out so you won't get stranded. The best method of dealing with the tides is to do a little preplanning. If, for example, you want to spend 4 hours on the beach digging for clams, get a tide table for your area, and plan to arrive at the beach 2 hours before low tide. Put your plane on the beach, where it will promptly be stranded, and don't worry about it again for 4 hours, when the rising tide will float it free again. Don't neglect to put a line on the plane, however, because if you're late getting back to it, you don't want to find that it has left without you.

DRY STORAGE

The safest way to secure you floatplane after your flight is to take it out of the water completely. Unfortunately, this choice requires some expensive equipment, to say nothing of a lot of tiedown space; so dry storage is limited to the larger, established seaplane bases (Fig. 13-17). Your

Fig. 13-17. Beaver Row, Kenmore Air Harbor. Kenmore operates an average of 10 Beavers during the peak summer charter season, and is famous for its modifications to the big workhorses. Note the rubber-protected cylinders of cement used as tiedowns.

plane will be removed from the water on an elevator or a railcar and will be taken to its tiedown spot by a specially equipped forklift. Seaplane bases not equipped with elevators or railcars may pick your plane directly off the ramp with the forklift, or will position a special dolly under the spreader bars. Jacks on the dolly will raise the plane a few inches off the ground, and tug or a tractor will pull your plane to the tiedown area. If the tiedown area is paved, your plane should be set on boards rather than directly on the pavement. The boards will protect the float keels from abrasion as the plane is set down or picked up.

The parking area should be equipped with tiedown rings. They may be set directly into the pavement, in the top of large concrete weights, or welded to the top of cement-filled drums. Tie down the wings and tail of your plane just as you would a landplane. If no tiedowns are available, you can make some by lashing two water or fuel-filled, 55-gallon drums together and placing a pair under each of the wings and the tail. Your tiedown lines can be looped around the barrels and back up to the plane's tiedown rings. As a last resort, you can fill the floats with water if high winds are expected.

This has been a long chapter, but I haven't even begun to describe all the docking, ramping, and beaching situations you'll encounter as you begin to explore new territory in your floatplane. Each on will be a challenge, but as long as you take the time to thoroughly check out each situation, weigh the alternatives, and exercise good judgment, the experiences will be rewarding ones, and you will be that much better prepared to meet the next challenge. When you experience some of the breathtakingly beautiful places a floatplane can take you to, you'll really appreciate the ability to go from a downtown metropolitan dock to the sleepy wharf of a remote fishing village, a deserted beach, or the shore of a clear mountain lake. The challenges, and rewards, of float flying never cease.

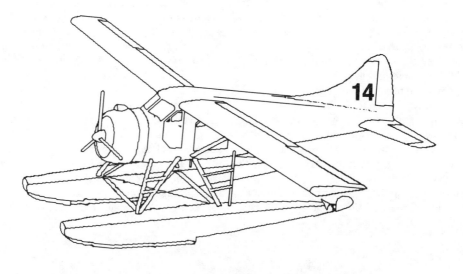

Advanced Techniques

T HE PROBLEM WITH INSTRUCTIONAL BOOKS LIKE this one is that in order to clearly describe specific techniques and procedures, it is necessary to assume that the conditions are ideal for performing these techniques and procedures. Ski books assume you're on the perfect slope in perfect snow; auto repair books assume you've got every tool known to man and a large, uncluttered garage; home improvement books assume your house was built to some standard (which never seems to be the one to which your house was built), and so far, this book has assumed the wind is light, the water is slightly ruffled, and the takeoff and landing lanes are right next to the dock. In reality, conditions are usually a little different. Sometimes, they're a lot different.

I hope you will decide to get some hands-on floatplane experience after reading this book, and if you do, your first lesson will probably be conducted under relatively "ideal" wind and water conditions. My instructor postponed my first lesson three times until the wind finally stopped whipping the lake into whitecaps, so don't be surprised, or disappointed, if you have to wait a day or two for your first logbook entry under "Single-engine, Sea." Your first lesson is not the time to be learning rough-water techniques. As your training progresses, you'll soon learn to cope with rough water, glassy water, strong winds, crosswinds, short lakes, and long taxi distances.

The floatplane's world is an ever-changing one, and you will rarely encounter the elusive "ideal" conditions. Think how boring it would become though, if every takeoff, every landing, and every docking or beaching was the same. In the next few chapters, we will look at some of the techniques designed to cope with the reality of float flying.

THE STEP-TAXI

So far, the only method we've examined for moving a floatplane from Point A to Point B on the water is the displacement, or idle, taxi. On windy days or when the water is rough, this is the safest way to taxi a floatplane, but there's no getting around the fact that it's slow. Landplane pilots don't have to worry about kicking up propeller-eroding spray; so they can taxi faster if they have long distances to cover. Not so the floatplane pilot, why not only has to worry about throwing up too much spray, but also has to keep the engine temperatures down. Both landplanes and floatplanes will taxi faster if you add power, but where the landplane's engine only has to overcome a slight increase in rolling resistance and aerodynamic drag, the floatplane's engine must work to overcome the tremendous increase in hydrodynamic drag created by accelerating the plane forward. The result is that the engines in most floatplanes will begin to overheat if a faster displacement or plowing taxi speed is maintained for any length of time.

On the other hand, it's frustrating to land a safe distance out from shore only to face a long, slow taxi to the dock. If you're renting the floatplane, a long taxi in can easily add another tenth of an hour or more to your bill. Fortunately, there's a faster way to travel across the water, and while you can't always take advantage of it, the times when you can will indeed be worth it in terms of both time and money. Besides, it's a lot of fun. It's called a *step-taxi*.

A step-taxi is simply a takeoff run that never accelerates to liftoff speed. Its advantage over a normal

displacement taxi is obvious. Instead of slogging through the water at 5 miles per hour, you skim along over it at upwards of 40 miles per hour (Fig. 14-1). Since the air rudder is very effective at this speed, the plane is quite maneuverable; so it's easy to follow a channel, thread your way through boat traffic, or avoid obstacles.

You initiate a step-taxi in the same manner as you would a takeoff run. After retracting the water rudders, hold the stick or yoke all the way back and apply full power. As in a normal takeoff, you'll probably have to add some right rudder to counteract the P-factor. When the floatplane reaches its maximum nose-up attitude in the hump phase, relax the back pressure and allow the plane to pitch forward over the hump into a planing attitude. The floats will begin to skim along over the surface of the water, supported by hydrodynamic pressure.

This time, however, you don't want the plane to take off. You want to remain on the surface, skimming along

Fig. 14-1. Step-taxiing a Cessna 206, an efficient way to cover long distances on the water. (Courtesy of the EDO Corporation)

166

like a ski boat, covering as much distance in as short a time as possible. You also want to subject the plane to as little pounding as possible, so the trick is to find and maintain the slowest speed which will still create enough hydrodynamic pressure to support the floats.

As soon as your floatplane is solidly on the step, start reducing the power. The plane will immediately stop accelerating and, as you continue to pull the throttle back, it will begin to slow down. You'll be surprised at how little power it takes to keep the plane on the step. If you reduce the power too much, however, the plane will start to fall off the step, which is inefficient and may cause an increase in engine temperature. If you do begin to fall off the step, go back to full power to get the plane back onto the step as quickly as possible, and start the power reduction procedure again. You will soon discover the minimum power setting which will keep the plane on the step, and next time, the process won't take so long.

At this speed, the air rudder is quite effective, and it's easy to make slight directional changes to avoid obstacles. Remember to hold the correct planing attitude at all times. In this respect, a step-taxi is identical to a takeoff run. If the nose is held too low, the forebodies of the floats will begin to rub, and if the nose is held too high, the sterns of the floats will dig into the water. Also as in a takeoff run, the plane is susceptible to porpoising if you don't maintain the correct attitude.

If you're going to step-taxi across the wind, remember to position the ailerons properly to keep the upwind wing from lifting. If you're on a heading between crosswind and directly upwind, hold the aileron on the upwind wing *up*. If you're on a downwind heading, the aileron position is not as critical because you should be traveling faster than the wind. If you're not traveling faster than the wind, you shouldn't be taxiing on the step in the first place, because the strong wind and rough water conditions will either pound your plane to pieces or flip it over when you try to stop.

Pay careful attention to the water ahead of you as you're skimming along. Floating logs and other debris are hard to spot when you're on the water, and at this speed a floating log or deadhead could punch a hole in one of your floats that would put your plane on the bottom in short order. Don't step-taxi into shallow water, or even water you suspect may be shallow. If you should unexpectedly touch bottom while on the step, the sudden drag on the floats will probably pitch your plane over onto its back before you can take any corrective action with the elevator. Be very alert for boat wakes and swells. Remember, a boat does not have to be in your immediate

vicinity to generate a wake that could cause you serious problems. If you see that you are going to cross some swells, stop the step-taxi immediately. Swells, whatever the cause, should only be crossed in the displacement mode with the engine at idle.

To stop a step-taxi, simply pull the power back back to idle. Since the plane is barely on the step to begin with, it will immediately come back over the hump and settle into the displacement attitude. As soon as the plane has returned to the displacement rudder attitude, lower the water rudders and taxi to your destination.

The step-taxi is most commonly used to quickly cover the distance between a landing area and a ramp, dock, or beach. To initiate a step-taxi after landing, add power as soon as the floats touch down, but be careful not to add so much power that the airplanes takes off again. Even with the power off, the plane will normally run along on the step for a short distance after touchdown, so it's only necessary to add the amount of power it will take to maintain the step-taxi. It's important that you add this power as soon as the floats touch, because if you hesitate a moment or two, the plane will have already started to fall off the step. If you're like me, however, and hesitate sometimes before putting in the power after touchdown, you'll have to put in extra power to pull yourself back up firmly onto the step before reducing the power to maintain the minimum step-taxi speed.

Some floatplanes step-taxi better than others with flaps down, but it isn't a good idea to taxi with full flaps. The drag will be considerable, and it may take more power than you really need to stay on the step. If you've landed with full flaps, raise them at least partially after you've initiated the step-taxi. Every type of floatplane will be different, and you'll just have to experiment to find which flap setting works best on the particular airplane you're flying. A Cessna 172, for example, will taxi on the step quite nicely with the flaps retracted, while a de Havilland Beaver seems to prefer the flaps partially deployed.

Don't step-taxi in too close to your destination. Allow yourself plenty of room to come to a stop after you pull the power back to idle. Whatever respect you may have garnered by executing a perfect landing followed by a flawless transition to a smooth step-taxi will probably be lost if you end the performance by slamming into the dock in a shower of spray, splinters, and float struts.

THE STEP-TURN

We've seen how the air rudder can be used to make gentle turns while the plane is on the step. It's also possible to make sharp turns, or *step-turns,* using the air rudder, but the procedure is a little more involved, and there are times when a step-turn can be downright dangerous.

There are two forces that you must contend with when you initiate a step-turn. One is the additional drag on the floats, and the other is the capsizing tendency caused by the centrifugal force generated by the turn itself.

Float Drag

When you start a step-turn by applying rudder in the direction of the turn, the floats will no longer skim straight ahead, but will start to slide sideways across the water. The keel and chines of the float will resist this slide and force the plane to move forward in the direction of the turn (Fig. 14-2). Unfortunately, the act of resisting the sideways slide also increases the hydrodynamic drag on the floats, and the plane will slow down. In addition, the centrifugal force generated by the turn will force the outside float deeper into the water, further adding to the drag, and slowing the plane even more. Since it's barely

going fast enough to stay on the step to begin with, any further reduction of speed will cause the plane to drop back off the step into the plowing attitude.

The only way to counter this decrease in speed during the turn is to add power, and the sharper the turn, the more power you'll have to add. It's important that you add the power as you begin the turn. If you wait until the turn is established, it will probably be too late, because your plane will have already started to fall off the step. To get back onto the step while the airplane is turning will require a lot of extra power, possibly even full power. It may be better to stop the turn, get back onto the step while taxiing straight ahead, and then resume the turn.

In an airborne turn, the ailerons are used to establish the desired bank angle and then returned to neutral for the duration of the turn. A step-turn will require you to hold rudder pressure throughout the turn to oppose the tendency of the float keels to travel in a straight line. To stop the turn, return the rudder to its neutral position and reduce the power back to the original setting.

A step-turn will feel very strange, to say the least,

Fig. 14-2. A de Havilland Beaver during a step-turn to the right. Note the increased amount of spray thrown out by the left, or outside float.

because unlike a boat, the plane will not lean into the turn. It will either maintain a wings-level attitude throughout the turn, or, if the turn is sharp, lean to the outside of the turn. Only your seat belts will keep you and your passengers from sliding sideways out of your seats because of the centrifugal force.

Centrifugal Force and the Wind

As the plane turns, centrifugal force will try to upset the plane toward the outside of the turn. The only thing resisting this upsetting tendency is the outside float. The tighter the turn, the greater the centrifugal force, and as the centrifugal force increases, the outside float will be forced deeper and deeper into the water. Eventually, the plane will be leaning so far over toward the outside of the turn that the outside wing tip will contact the water, and the plane will probably flip or cartwheel.

One way to help counter this capsizing tendency is to hold the wings level with the ailerons. By holding full aileron in the direction of the turn, the outside wing will be held up while the inside wing is pushed down. Initially, you'll have to rely on your instructor to tell you when your turns are getting too tight, but as you practice step-turns, you'll begin to be able to feel when you're getting close to the limit. Factors that determine how tight your airplane can turn are the width of the floats, the distance between the floats, the wingspan of your airplane, the size and effectiveness of the ailerons, and the vertical distance between the floats and the fuselage. A floatplane that sits low over a pair of wide floats set far apart will be able to make tighter step-turns than a floatplane that sits high above a pair of narrow floats set close together, all other factors being equal.

It's usually easier to make a step-turn to the left than it is to make one to the right. For one thing, you'll have a better view of where you're going. Of course, if you're flying a tandem-place floatplane like a Super Cub or a Citabria, you'll have an excellent view no matter which way you turn. The P-factor will also make it easier to turn the plane to the left, because a turn in that direction will not require as much rudder deflection as a turn to the right.

In calm air, you can make step-turns in any direction you like. The only way you can get into trouble is if you try to make your turns too tight or if you taxi into swells or rough water. It's another story when the wind starts to blow. You're okay if you turn from an upwind heading to a downwind heading, but if you try to turn from a downwind heading to an upwind heading watch out! The chances are good that you'll flip the airplane.

Let's say you're step-taxiing directly into the wind and need to make a 90-degree turn to the left into the bay toward your dock. As you begin the turn and add power, the centrifugal force generated by the turn will cause the plane to lean to the right, to the outside of the turn. This time, however, the centrifugal force will be offset somewhat by the wind, which will strike the right side of the plane and try to lift the outside wing. As a result, the floatplane will tend to remain on an even keel (Fig. 14-3).

Now let's look at the other side of the coin. Your floatplane is beached on the upwind side of a small lake, and you've decided that the wind is too strong to risk a downwind takeoff. Rather than endure a long, slow, idle taxi to the downwind end of the lake, you decide to save time and zip down the lake on the step. There's nothing wrong with this, but as you approach the other end of the lake, you decide to save even more time by doing a 180-degree step-turn on the left. Not only will this head you back into the wind, but since you're already on the step, you'll be that much farther along in your takeoff run. You begin the turn, and a short time later, as you wade ashore and look back at your capsized plane slowly sinking into the lake, you wonder what went wrong.

The explanation is simple. As you began the left turn, the centrifugal force caused the plane to lean to the right, toward the outside of the turn, as always. This time, however, instead of being opposed by the force of the wind, the centrifugal force was assisted by the wind, which pushed against the left side of the plane and lifted the left, or inside wing (Fig. 14-4). Both forces combined were more than the outside float could resist, and it was pushed deep into the water. The lean to the right was made even more severe as the wind got under and lifted the inside wing, and when the opposite wing tip struck the water, over you went.

The only thing you can do to try and save yourself if your plane starts to capsize while in a step-turn is apply full opposite rudder. If you're lucky, this action will accomplish two things. First, the centrifugal force generated by turning the plane sharply in the opposite direction will cancel out some of the forces which are trying to capsize you. Second, this new turn will take some of the pressure off the outside float, which has now become the inside float. The buoyancy of this float will bring it back up to the surface, thus righting the plane. Bear in mind that this maneuver is not something you should count on to save you, because if the plane has tipped over too far, nothing you can do will keep the plane from capsizing or cartwheeling.

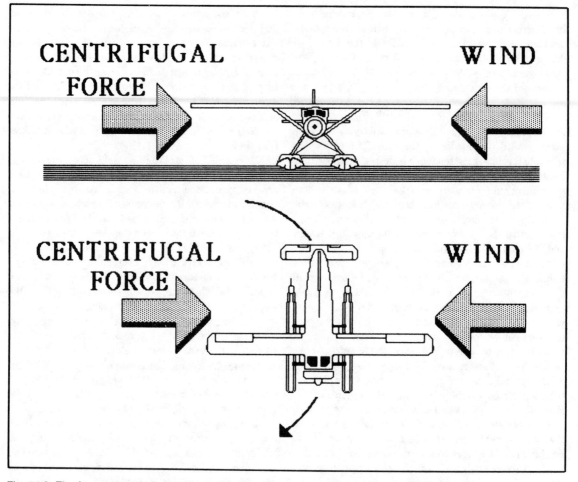

CENTRIFUGAL FORCE

WIND

CENTRIFUGAL FORCE

WIND

Fig. 14-3. The forces at work during a step-turn from an upwind to a downwind heading.

As a general rule, never make a step-turn out of a downwind heading unless the wind is very light, and even then, make the turn as wide as possible to minimize the centrifugal force. If at any time during the turn, you feel the plane is in danger of capsizing, begin a turn in the opposite direction. When the plane is back on an even keel, stop the turn and pull the power back to idle. Once you're safely back in the displacement attitude, you can figure out what to do next.

Before you start a step-turn, make sure you'll have enough room to finish it. It's very dangerous to pull the power off while the floatplane is still turning. A floatplane is laterally unstable as it comes back over the hump, and if the plane is still in a turn, the centrifugal force may capsize it as it slows down and falls off the step. If you start a step-turn and then begin to wonder if you're go-

ing to have enough room to complete it, straighten the plane out immediately and pull off the power. It's better to sedately finish the turn at idle speed than to risk slamming into the shore or capsizing the floatplane when you realize, too late, that you're not going to make it.

If there's a good breeze blowing, don't forget the weathercocking tendency. It could cause you problems if you turn to a crosswind heading and then stop the step-taxi. As we've seen, you're vulnerable as you drop off the step and back over the hump, and a strong breeze could weathercock your plane around with enough force to cause it to capsize. It may be better to make another step-turn to a direct downwind heading before stopping the plane.

It would be possible to go into a long, technical discussion of the effects the weathercocking tendency has upon the step-turn itself, but I think it's safe to say that if the wind is strong enough to generate a noticeable weather-cocking effect on your floatplane during a step-turn, the water will probably be rough enough to prevent you from maneuvering on the step in the first place. A step-turn is a real seat-of-the-pants maneuver, and chances are you won't have time to notice or think about the subtle changes in rudder pressure brought about by the wind's weathercocking effect. Your control manipulations will be based on what you see out the windshield and feel through the seat, and if the turn looks right and feels right, you're doing it correctly.

GLASSY WATER

There is nothing more beautiful than a remote wilderness lake on a calm day. The mirrorlike surface reflects the surrounding trees and mountains, and is broken only by the concentric circles of ripples spreading slowly from the spot where a feeding trout has chanced upon an unlucky bug. The lake is after bigger prey than the occasional errant insect, however, and it lies waiting for the opportunity to trap an unsuspecting or careless floatplane pilot who attempts to land on its glassy surface.

Flat, or *glassy*, water is probably the single most dangerous water condition a floatplane pilot can face (Fig. 14-5). Ironically, the danger is not to the floatplane itself, but to you, its pilot. With no waves to lend definition to the surface, it becomes almost impossible to judge your height above the water. The general tendency is to believe you are higher than you actually are, and most glassy water accidents result from pilots flying their planes

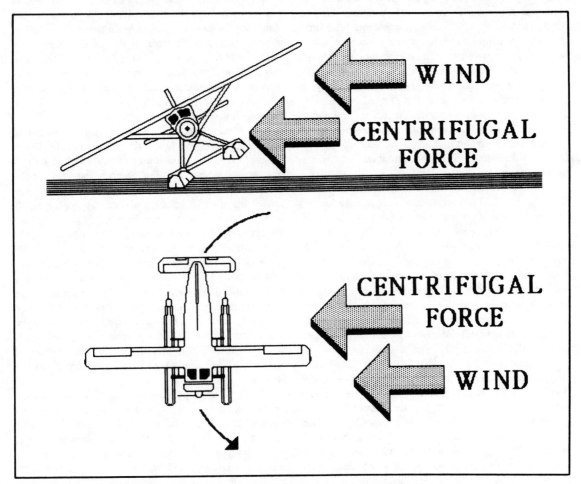

Fig. 14-4. The forces at work during a step-turn from a downwind to an upwind heading.

headlong into the water. Glassy water can also affect your perception during takeoff, and pilots have been known to lift off a mirror-smooth surface only to fly back into it again, all the while thinking they were climbing out.

If you obtain a seaplane rating and begin to fly floats on a regular basis, its's a sure bet that you will soon encounter glassy water. Every good seaplane course, therefore, puts a great deal of emphasis on the special techniques developed to deal with it.

Glassy-Water Landings

There are two methods of landing a floatplane on glassy water, and neither one of them uses the water as a reference. The first, and most commonly used, method sets up a controlled descent which will result in your plane contacting the water in a landing attitude at a a minimum sink rate. Your job is to maintain the proper landing attitude and keep the rate of descent constant. Since there is no way you will be able to judge the moment of contact, you won't even try it. The second method depends on a pattern of visual objects on the water that will enable you to judge your height off the surface. These objects can be anything from the ripples created by throwing stones out of the plane to several life jackets dropped on the surface. In some cases, you can use the shoreline as a reference. The important thing to remember is that the objects will be the focus of your attention, not the surface of the water.

The Constant Attitude/Constant Descent Rate Method. If you arrive over your destination and find the surface of the water is glass-smooth, you have at least one thing going for you. Since the surface is smooth, there is obviously no wind, so you can land in any direction you wish. As you will soon see, a glassy-water landing covers a lot more distance than a normal landing; so make sure you'll have enough room to make the long, slow descent that's required.

When you have chosen your landing lane, fly a normal approach until you are about 200 feet above the surface of the water. Both your instruments and the surrounding terrain will make it fairly easy to tell when you still have several hundred feet of air beneath your float keels. When you are approximately 200 feet up, transition your plane to a slow-flight attitude by reducing the power and raising the nose. The nose should be raised just slightly higher than the normal landing attitude to ensure that the bows of the floats will be in no danger of digging in when the plane touches down. Don't raise the nose too far, because it also could cause the floats

to dig in if their sterns strike the water with enough force to pitch the plane forward.

Your airspeed is not as important as establishing and holding the correct attitude. How much flap you use depends on the characteristics of the particular floatplane you are flying. Obviously, the slower you touch down, the better, but some planes cannot maintain the proper nose-up attitude when the flaps are fully extended. If your plane is one of these, you will have to use less flap and settle for a slightly higher airspeed in order to maintain that all-important landing attitude.

Once you've established the proper touchdown attitude, don't vary it. Use the throttle to adjust your sink rate until you are descending at a rate of 150 or less feet per minute. Now comes the challenging part. You have to accurately maintain this attitude and sink rate until the plane contacts the surface of the water. Your instruments will be the greatest aid to keeping the descent rate constant, but the best way to maintain the proper attitude is by looking at the horizon or shoreline ahead of you. Don't, however, allow yourself to become fixated on either the horizon or your instruments, and immediately correct any variations in your attitude or descent rate. Also do not, under any circumstances, try to anticipate the moment of touchdown.

When your plane approaches to within a few feet of the water, there may be a subtle change in the feel of the controls as the plane enters ground effect, but don't relax your concentration just because you sense you're within moments of touchdown. Continue to maintain the proper attitude and descent rate until the floats actually contact the surface. The touchdown will probably be a little harder than normal, since you won't be flaring the plane smoothly onto the surface.

As soon as the floats touch the water, pull the power back to idle. Your forward speed will be higher than your normal touchdown speed, and you don't want the plane to bounce back into the air. If you should happen to touch down very hard and get bounced quite a ways back up, you will be better off if you immediately apply full power and go around for another try rather than attempt to feather the plane gently back onto a surface you may not be able to distinguish.

Be prepared to pull the yoke or stick back as soon as the floats contact the surface. With no waves or wavelets to introduce bubbles and pockets of air under the floats, the glassy water will exert quite a bit of drag on the floats, and this, combined with your higher-than-normal touchdown speed, will tend to pitch the plane forward. It's important that you counteract this nose-over

Fig. 14-5. Glassy water at Princess Louisa, off Jervis Inlet on the southwest coast of British Columbia.

tendency as soon as it starts, because it could conceivably be strong enough to dig in the float tips and pitch your plane onto its back. Don't jump the gun and pull the yoke back too soon, though, or you could bounce back into the air. Wait until you feel the plane begin to pitch forward before applying up-elevator. You'll soon learn the proper timing after a little practice.

The Visual Method. The landing procedure just described is for textbook glassy-water conditions in which there are no visual aids to help you judge your height above the water. It's the procedure you would use if you had to land away from shore on a large lake or bay with a distant or indistinct horizon. While you may find yourself in this situation occasionally, most of the time you will have some degree of visual assistance while making your landing.

The main problem with the standard glassy-water landing technique is the amount of room you need to do it. A small lake can have the same confusing, glassy conditions as a large lake, but there may not be room enough to make a slow, power-on letdown from 200 feet. Fortunately, there are many visual aids available to help you get your plane safely on the water in these situations.

The most obvious visual aid is the shoreline. Since the lack of wind allows you to land in any direction you like, landing close to, and parallel with, the shoreline will make it much easier to judge your height above the water. Plan to land close to shore, but far enough out to be in no danger of hitting any underwater obstructions like fallen trees, rocks, or pilings. It will still be almost impossible to judge the proper moment to flare the airplane, but the "horizon" next to you in the form of the shoreline will allow you to fly a normal approach down almost to the water. Then when you are 30 or 40 feet above the surface, an altitude you can easily judge by referencing the nearby shoreline, pitch the nose up to the proper touchdown attitude and add power to slow your descent rate to 150 or less feet per minute. Fly the last part of the approach in the same manner you would the textbook method described previously. Maintain the proper attitude and descent rate until you touch down, reduce the power to idle, and pull back on the yoke or stick as necessary to counter any nose-over tendency.

By using the shoreline as a reference, you can fly a normal or even steep approach path down to within a few feet of the water before transitioning to the proper glassy-water landing attitude and descent rate, and you will not need anywhere near the amount of room it would take to fly a glassy-water approach from 200 feet up.

If you use a shoreline as a reference, make sure you look at the actual shoreline, and not at its reflection. Also, don't be tempted to judge your height from what seems to be the bottom just below the surface. If the water is very clear and the lighting conditions are just right, that bottom which appears to be just a few feet beneath the surface may actually be 10, 20, or even 30 feet down. If you use it to judge the right moment to flare the plane, you'll be in for quite a shock when you suddenly slam into the surface, and water you didn't even know was there starts pouring into the cockpit.

Another optical illusion that can really mess up an otherwise perfectly executed glassy-water landing is the reflection of clouds in the mirrorlike surface of the water. Since the clouds are far away, their reflections will keep pace with you, and it will appear that you are standing still, or hovering over the water. You may feel that you are about to stall, and your natural reaction will be to add power, lower the nose, or do something, *anything*, that will get your airplane moving forward again. Don't do it! Trust your instruments, look at the shoreline ahead of or beside you, maintain your attitude and descent rate, and ignore the reflections in the water. They're just part of the plot to get you to donate your plane to the Society for Homeless Fish.

There may be times when the shoreline will be unusable as a reference. In certain parts of northern Canada, thousands of lakes dot the flat, featureless landscape, while overhead, the sky is an unending pewter sheet. Gray water blends into gray shorelines, and height and distance judgments are almost impossible to make. At times like these, floatplanes pilots must create their own visual landing aids.

Water covered with ripples or waves has definition because your eyes have something on which to focus, and your depth perception enables you to accurately judge your height above the surface. The problem with glassy water is that it has no definition, and your depth perception is worthless because your eyes have nothing at which to look. The trick, then, is to put something on the surface of the water to give your sense of depth perception something with which to work.

Anything that floats or makes ripples on the surface will suffice, but try to exercise good judgment when selecting the items to be thrown into the water. Large, heavy tools generate excellent ripples when they hit the surface, but this practice can get expensive. Some pilots carry large, flat rocks in the cockpit that can be thrown out to create ripples, and others say they fire rifle or pistol shots into the surface for the same reason. The ripples created by small-arms fire are not very large, however, and they don't last very long, so I suspect the pilots who claim to use this method do so more to preserve their bush-pilot image than to actually create something that will help them land the plane. (They probably got the idea from the pilots of large flying boats during World War II who roughed up glassy surfaces by firing bursts from their forward 50-caliber machine guns into the water ahead of the plane.)

The best visual aids are those that remain floating on the water. Some pilots carry branches which act as runway markers when thrown out in quick succession as the plane overflies the water. Others advocate tossing out several crumpled-up maps. (If you decide to try this, make sure you throw out maps you won't need any more.) Probably the best things to throw into the water are life jackets, or *PFD's* (Personal Flotation Devices) as they're now called. The foam-filled life jackets will flow high on the surface of the water, and a row of two or three of them spaced some distance apart will provide an excellent means of judging your altitude. After you've landed, you can taxi back and pick them up.

Even with visual aids on the water to help you, fly your final approach very carefully. Although the objects you have tossed out of your plane will certainly make it easier for you to determine your height above the water, make it a practice to transition to a nose-up touchdown attitude while you know you are still a safe distance above the surface. If you should happen to be a little off in your altitude estimation and touch down sooner than you anticipated, you may land hard, but at least your float tips will be up.

Glassy-Water Takeoffs

Glassy water can also be a problem during takeoff. As mentioned earlier, the slick, smooth surface will exert quite a bit of drag on the floats, and it may be difficult to get the floatplane on the step, especially if it's heavily loaded. Without the lubricating effects of the bubbles and pockets of air carried under the floats by ripples and waves, the plane will feel sluggish and will accelerate slowly. A simple way to ruffle up the surface of the water is to taxi around on it for awhile. Put the plane in a plowing attitude and taxi around in circles over the area you've chosen for your takeoff lane and then return to your starting position and begin the takeoff run before the ripples and waves disappear.

If there is someone nearby with a boat, you can ask them to run down your takeoff lane ahead of you. When they are safely out of the way, make your takeoff run over the water they've stirred up, but be careful. You don't want to cross any swells that are too big for you or your plane to handle. The best thing to do is to follow exactly the same path the boat took. That way, your floats will be running over the water churned up by the boat's propeller and transom, while the large swells that make up the wake will be moving away on either side of you. If the boat is of the small, outboard-powered, cartop variety, it can run around at random through your takeoff area; its wake will not be large enough to cause you any problems.

A few pilots have experienced vertigo after taking off from glassy water, especially if the surrounding terrain is flat and featureless and the sky is hazy or overcast. The water and the sky are the same color; the horizon is indistinct, and suddenly it's not only impossible to tell how high you are, but you're not even sure if you're still climbing. While this phenomenon is most often experienced by skiplane pilots taking off from white snow into a white sky, a condition appropriately known as *whiteout,* can happen to floatplane pilots, too. The only remedy is to use and trust your instruments. Keep the wings level and maintain a positive rate of climb at a constant airspeed. Until you're high enough to positively identify a shoreline, the horizon, or some other geographic feature, don't trust what you think you see out the window. You could be flying right back into the water and have no idea you are doing so.

THE ONE-FLOAT TAKEOFF

If you're taking off in glassy water and your plane is reluctant to accelerate to liftoff speed, or if you find that you're using more of the lake than you thought you would, or if your heavily loaded floatplane just doesn't want to come unstuck from the surface and fly, there is one technique you can use that will help you accelerate a little faster. Once your plane is on the step, roll it to one side with the ailerons and lift one of the floats out of the water (Fig. 14-6). This action will reduce the hydrodynamic drag by almost half, and your plane will be able to accelerate to liftoff speed faster.

There is one school of thought that claims the additional load transferred to the other float increases the hydrodynamic drag on the float to the amount previously shared equally by both floats. In other words, the total amount of hydrodynamic drag remains the same, and you don't really gain anything. Most pilots don't share this view, and the one-float takeoff remains a popular technique.

It may take full aileron to pull the float out of the water, but once the wing starts coming up, it will come up fast. Be ready to immediately ease off a bit on the ailerons to stop the roll as soon as the float is clear of the surface. It's a tricky maneuver that requires a sensitive touch on the controls, because if you overdo it, you can easily dip a wing tip into the water, and we all know what that leads to. On the other hand, you don't want to let the float fall back onto the water because that will slow you down again. If you use the one-float technique while making a crosswind takeoff, make sure you lift the downwind float out of the water and tilt the airplane into the wind. If you lift the upwind float, the wind will be able to get under the upwind wing and capsize your plane.

Do not attempt a one-float takeoff until you've had some instruction from someone who knows how to do it properly. It's a real balancing act that will take some practice before you're able to do it with confidence, and it's nice to have a competent instructor in the other seat to keep you from getting into trouble.

ROUGH WATER

In some ways, rough water is easier to deal with than glassy water. For one thing, you can see it. Rough water is dangerous, however, because of the potential damage it can do to your floatplane. Your takeoff and landing speeds remain unchanged, but suddenly your runway has become a series of unyielding crests and troughs, and as you slam from wave to wave, the punishment inflicted on the struts, spreader bars, brace wires, and even the floats themselves can be tremendous. There is only one foolproof technique for turning rough water into smooth; sitting on the shore until the waves subside. The good thing about this technique is that it's infallible; it works every time. The bad thing about it is that you may have to sit on the shore for several days while you wait for the smooth water to appear. Since this is not always practical, techniques have been developed by which you can at least minimize the stress and strain put on your floatplane by rough water, allowing you to take off and land with relative safety.

Notice I said "relative safety." There is always an element of risk when operating in rough water. An undetected crack in a float mount, the one wave that's bigger than all the rest, the sudden gust of wind that pitches your airplane up at exactly the wrong moment— any one of these things can bring your flight to a quick and soggy end. There is no substitute for common sense and good judgment when operating in rough-water conditions, and the only person qualified to decide whether or not you or your plane can cope with a rough water situation is yourself. Don't let your passengers or anyone else make that decision for you. If the water looks too rough for you to handle, it probably is, and the best decision you can make at that point is to sit on the beach until things calm down a bit.

Rough water is generally the result of one of three things; boats, currents, or the wind. The technique for dealing with the rough water caused by boats is fairly simple. You either wait for the boats to go away, or you taxi your plane to a spot where their wakes will not interfere with your takeoff run. If you have no other choice but to take off through water stirred up by boats, use the same rough-water techniques described later in this chapter.

The second rough-water generator is the current. When two or more strong currents collide, or merge, the result is often a very rough and confused water surface. This condition is most often encountered in rivers or tidal waters where there is a considerable difference between high and low tide. The coastal waters of Washington's Puget Sound, British Columbia, and Southeast Alaska contain countless bays and channels, and the tide range can be as much as 22 feet. The tremendous volume of water pouring through these narrow channels can create extremely hazardous water conditions which would instantly destroy any floatplane foolish enough to attempt a landing (Fig. 14-7).

The Wind and the Waves

You can thank the wind for most of the rough-water conditions you will encounter. Almost everyone has heard the expression, "a Force Nine gale." Force Nine is one of the wind classifications on the Beaufort Scale of Wind Forces. The entire scale, and the way it relates to land and water conditions, is found in Fig. 14-8. The information contained in this chart can be very helpful. Aviation weather reports do not include wave heights, and the information contained in marine forecasts is aimed primarily at boat operators. Water conditions that would merely bounce a boat around a bit could do serious damage to your floatplane. Aviation and marine weather reports and forecasts do include wind velocities, however, and by relating the reported or forecast surface winds to the water conditions generally associated with these wind velocities, you will be able to make a fairly educated guess as to what sort of water surface you will encounter when you arrive at your destination.

When a breeze starts blowing across a body of calm water, the surface tension of the water will resist distor-

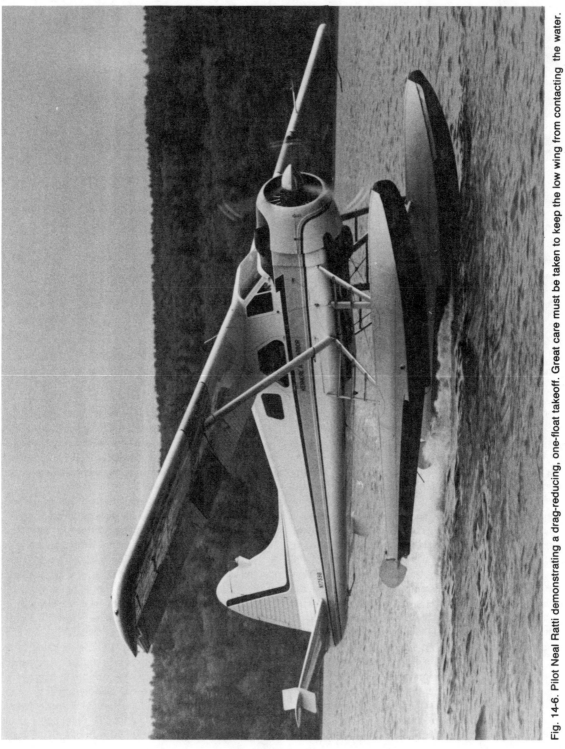

Fig. 14-6. Pilot Neal Ratti demonstrating a drag-reducing, one-float takeoff. Great care must be taken to keep the low wing from contacting the water.

Fig. 14-7. An extremely violent tidal current pouring through a narrow channel near Jervis Inlet, British Columbia. A floatplane landing anywhere near this channel would most likely be swept out of control and flipped.

tion until the breeze reaches a velocity of about 2 1/2 miles per hour. At this point, the friction between the moving air and the surface of the water will cause the water to be humped up into little ripples. If the wind velocity increases to approximately 4 1/2 miles per hour, the ripples will be pushed up into wavelets. The size and distance between these wavelets will continue to grow as the wind velocity increases. Until the wind reaches a speed of about 12 miles per hour, the waves will remain smooth in appearance. When this velocity is exceeded, the waves will begin to form crests. A bubbly froth will begin to appear on the wave crests, and the wind will blow long streaks of this froth straight downwind. Unlike the windstreaks that are sometimes formed at lower wind velocities, these streaks will be whitish in appearance, but they will be no less helpful in determining the wind direction when you're at altitude.

White wind streaks are a good indication that the water is starting to move into the "rough" category, especially if you are flying one of the smaller floatplanes. As the wind velocity begins to exceed 13 miles per hour, the wave crests will begin to break, and whitecaps will begin to appear. This is just about the limit for small

floatplanes like Super Cubs, Citabrias, and Cessna 172s. Once the wind reaches 18 or 19 miles per hour, the surface of the water will be covered with whitecaps, and the pilots of larger floatplanes like Cessna 180s, 185s, and 206s should start seriously thinking about waiting for another day.

Only the pilots of Beavers, Otters, Twin Otters, and other very large floatplanes should consider taking off or landing on water that's being whipped up by winds in excess of 20 miles per hour, and even then, their planes will have to endure quite a beating. The only reason they can get away with it is that the structural components of their floatplanes are relatively large and strong.

Another factor that helps determine the size of the waves is the distance the wind has been travelling over the water. The nautical term for this distance is *fetch,* and if the wind velocity is less than 10 miles per hour, the waves it generates will not grow beyond a certain size, no matter how long the fetch. Once the wind exceeds approximately 10 miles per hour, the waves will grow in proportion to the fetch, and the surface near the downwind shore of a lake or a bay may be far rougher than the surface near the upwind shore, even though the wind velocity is identical in both places. As a general rule, large, open bodies of water will become too rough for floatplane operations when the wind exceeds 10 miles per hour, because the long fetch will permit the formation of large waves or swells. In smaller lakes of less than 3 miles in length, floatplanes can sometimes be taken off or landed in winds of up to 25, or 30 miles per hour, since the relatively short fetch will not allow the formation of extremely large waves or swells.

Another problem encountered in rough water is spray. Even at the slowest possible taxi speed, your floats will fall off the crests of the waves into the troughs with quite a splash, and it's virtually impossible to keep the propeller clear of the spray. If you're facing a long taxi in rough water, visibility may even become a problem as the propeller picks up spray and throws it into the windshield. I was once practicing rough-water takeoffs and landings with an instructor in a Cessna 180 which had been equipped with a 270-horsepower engine (the standard engine is rated at 230 horsepower), and a three-bladed propeller. The water was extremely rough and getting rougher, but the high-horsepower 180 seemed to be holding it's own, especially on takeoff. It was a valuable experience, but when the prop started throwing solid sheets of water into the windshield, we both decided it was time to call it quits. If you have to fly in rough-water conditions, make sure you check the propeller frequently for spray erosion. If you are operating in salt water, take the time to thoroughly wash down all parts of the plane with fresh water after each flight.

The water and spray kicked up by the floats in rough water presents special problems for the designers of turbine-powered floatplanes. The inside of a turbine engine operates at extremely high temperatures, and if a large slug of water should be sucked into one of the air intakes, the thermal shock to the so-called *hot section* of the engine could be extremely detrimental to its components. Since inspection and overhaul teardowns are very expensive, the designers try to come up with intake locations that will minimize spray ingestion. The Soloy Turbine 206, for example, has small, manually operated doors that can be used to block off the forward-facing air intakes when the plane is operating on rough water. When the doors are deployed, the turbine gets its air from an alternate intake which does not connect directly to the engine intakes. Any water entering the alternate intake will not reach the engine itself (Fig. 14-9).

How can you tell if the water is too rough for your floatplane? Fortunately, rough water, and the wind that accompanies it, tends to be rather intimidating to inexperienced floatplane pilots, and the sight and sound of the wind and waves generally sends them in a search of an experienced pilot or instructor for advice. The seaplane base where I fly does not allow students or renters to fly the company's Cessna 172s if the wind exceeds 15 miles per hour, and other schools have similar policies.

The Beaufort velocity chart in Fig. 14-9 provides some general guidelines for determining water conditions, but the best way to develop an eye for the waves is to go out to your local seaplane base on a windy day and do some serious hanging around. Listen to the exaggerations the pilots are telling each other about their rough-water experiences. They're always entertaining, and there is usually enough truth in what they're saying for you to learn something. When they say the water is too rough for such-and-such a type of floatplane, they probably know what they're talking about. Try to memorize what the water looks like, and compare the planes that *are* flying with the plane that you fly. If the only things moving are de Havilland Beavers and you fly a Citabria, you'll know what to do the next time you see the same kind of waves. You'll stay inside and drink coffee with the other sensible pilots who are telling each other about the time they landed a Piper J-3 Cub on a lake in a 90-knot wind.

The larger your floatplane, the rougher the water it can handle, but that's only part of the picture. *You* must be able to handle the rough water, too, and if you don't feel you're up to it, don't try.

The Rough-Water Takeoff

Your main objective when taking off in rough water is to accelerate your plane to liftoff speed while subjecting it to the least amount of pounding possible. Always use the recommended amount of flap during a rough water takeoff. Unless your plane is very heavily loaded, you'll come up onto the step fairly quickly, and you won't gain anything by waiting to deploy the flaps until you're in a planing attitude. If the waves are large enough to cause the nose of your plane to pitch up and down, wait until the plane is starting to pitch up before adding takeoff power. If you put the power in as the nose is descending, you may drive the floats into the next wave.

Once the plane is on the step, carry the nose slightly higher than you would during a normal takeoff. This higher-pitched angle will reduce the chances of digging a float tip into a wave. Don't carry the nose too high, however, you'll only succeed in extending the takeoff run.

Most inexperienced floatplane pilots are guilty of carrying the nose too high because they are so afraid of

BEAUFORT SCALE and MAP SYMBOL	TERMS USED by the U.S. WEATHER BUREAU	VELOCITY MPH	ESTIMATING VELOCITIES ON LAND
0	Calm	Below 1	Smoke rises vertically.
1	Light Air	1 - 3	Smoke drifts; wind vanes unmoved.
2	Light Breeze	4 - 7	Wind felt on face; leaves rustle; ordinary vane moves by wind.
3	Gentle Breeze	8 - 12	Leaves and small twigs in constant motion; wind extends light flag.
4	Moderate Breeze	13 - 18	Dust and loose paper raised; small branches are moved.
5	Fresh Breeze	19 - 24	Small trees in leaf begin to sway; crested wavelets form in inland water.
6	Strong Breeze	25 - 31	Large branches in motion; whistling heard in telephone wires; umbrellas used with difficulty.
7	Moderate Gale	32 - 38	Whole trees in motion; inconvenience felt in walking against the wind.
8	Fresh Gale	39 - 46	Twigs broken off trees; progress generally impeded.
9	Strong Gale	47 - 54	Slight structural damage occurs.
10	Whole Gale	55 - 63	Trees uprooted; considerable structural damage occurs.
11		64 - 75	
12	Hurricane	75 +	

Fig. 14-8. The Beaufort Scale of Wind Forces.

ESTIMATING WIND VELOCITIES ON WATER	REMARKS
Surface like a mirror.	Check your glassy water technique before water flying under these conditions.
Ripples with the appearance of scales are formed, but without foam crests.	
Small wavelets; still short but more pronounced; crests have a glassy appearance but do not break.	
Large wavelets; crests begin to break. Foam has glassy appearance. Perhaps some scattered whitecaps.	Ideal water flying conditions in protected water.
Small waves, becoming longer; fairly frequent whitecaps.	May be too rough for small floatplanes.
Moderate waves; taking a more pronounced long form; many whitecaps are formed. Chance of some spray.	This is considered rough water for seaplanes and small amphibians, especially in open water.
Large waves begin to form; white foam crests are more extensive everywhere. Probably some spray.	
Sea heaps up and white foam from from breaking waves begins to be blown in streaks along the direction of the wind.	This type of water condition is for emergency only in small aircraft in inland waters, and for the expert pilot of large flying boats in the open sea.
Moderately high waves of greater length; edges of crests break into spindrift. The foam is blown in well marked streaks along the direction of the wind.	
High waves; dense streaks of foam along the direction of the wind. Sea begins to roll. Spray may affect visibility.	It's now time to be careful of land take-offs and landings.
Very high waves with long, overhanging crests. The resulting foam, in great patches, is blown in dense white streaks along the direction of the wind. On the whole, the surface of the sea takes on a white appearance. The rolling of the sea becomes heavy and shock-like. Visibility is affected.	

"hooking" a float tip in a wave. I certainly was. As my rented Cessna 172 bounced from crest to crest, my mind would project a slow-motion image of a floatplane digging in its floats and pitching onto its back, and I'd haul back on the yoke a little more. In doing so, I accomplished two things, both of them bad. First, by increasing the angle of attack, I increased the drag and prolonged the plane-pounding takeoff run. Second, by raising the float tips too high, I made the pounding even worse by slamming the floats flat against the front of the oncoming waves. I was, in effect, stalling from wave to wave. I have since learned to hold a less radical nose-up attitude.

By carrying the nose only slightly higher than normal, your plane will accelerate faster, and the floats will cut through the wave tops instead of slamming into them. If a wave happens to bounce the nose up too high, you may find it necessary to apply a little forward pressure to bring it back down again.

As soon as your floatplane has reached flying speed, pull it off the water. You can pull it off at its minimum stall speed or even a little slower if you remain in ground effect while you accelerate to a safe climbout speed, but don't pull it off so soon that you risk setting back onto the water in that nose-high, float-pounding attitude just described. The plane may even be bounced into the air by the waves before you can pull it off, but in either case, you'll be flying on the ragged edge of a stall, so lower the nose slightly (but don't fly back into the water) and build up some airspeed before you initiate your climbout.

If your plane is equipped with manual flaps, there is a neat trick you can do that will help you get off the water a little sooner. If you're flying a cessna 180, for example, you will normally begin your takeoff run with 20 degrees of flap, which means the flap handle will be pulled up two notches from the floor. Shortly before the plane reaches liftoff speed, extend the flaps another 5 to 10 degrees by giving a sharp upward tug on the handle to pull the plane off the water. At the same time pull back slightly on the yoke. The sudden application of flap and up-elevator will balloon the plane into the air, but now comes the hard part. The plane isn't quite ready to fly yet, and you'll need a sensitive touch on the yoke and the flap handle to keep it staggering along in ground effect while the airspeed builds up. The extra flap adds a lot of drag, and the trick is to bleed it back to 20 degrees as quickly as possible without letting the plane settle back onto the waves. You'll also have to lower the nose back to the proper takeoff attitude as quickly as you pulled it up to prevent the plane from stalling. If your plane has electric flaps, you can move the flap selector down as the plane approaches liftoff speed, but the ballooning effect won't be as great because the flaps move rather slowly.

This technique will not work in all floatplanes, and in some, it may be downright dangerous. The application of additional flap may produce so much drag that after the initial ballooning effect, the plane may simply stall and drop back onto the water with enough force to break something. Before you try this technique, make sure it's safe to do in your airplane, and get some instruction from an experienced pilot.

The first time you make a takeoff in even moderately rough water, you will be amazed at the pounding inflicted on the plane. The noise will be terrific because everything that can possibly vibrate, rattle or squeak, does. The instrument panel will be jiggling around in front of you; the engine cowl will be shaking, and you'll swear the plane is moments from destruction. You'll quickly discover that floatplanes are tougher than they look and feel, and they'll absorb a lot of punishment before giving up. Every pounding, rough-water takeoff and landing, however, contributes a little more to wear, tear, and fatigue, so give the plane the smoothest ride you can.

Avoid downwind takeoffs in rough water. The very fact that the water is rough will probably mean that the wind is strong, and you'll have to slam along over the water for a long time until you reach flying speed. If your plane's liftoff speed is 60 miles per hour, and the wind is blowing 15 miles per hour, you'll have to accelerate to 75 miles per hour before you can pull it free of the pounding waves, and the punishment inflicted may be more than the float and airframe components can take. If you take off into the wind, you'll only have to accelerate to a water speed of 45 miles per hour and your airplane will thank you for it.

Rough-Water Landings

Your goal when landing in rough water is the same as it is when taking off; subject the plane to as little pounding and stress as possible. Land in the smoothest water you can find. When you arrive over your destination, try to estimate the size of the waves as you make your aerial check of the area. When you think you know how high the waves are, double your estimation. Waves have a way of looking half their size when you're flying around over them at pattern altitude. If the water near your destination looks too rough, you may be able to find a nearby cover or bay that is more sheltered from the wind and waves. If your destination lies on the downwind shore of a lake, it may be prudent to land in the lee of the upwind shore and wait until the waves subside before mov-

Fig. 14-9. The business end of a Soloy Turbine 206. The twin air scoops can be blocked off by small doors to prevent the ingestion of spray.

ing the plane to the other side. Regardless of where you land, always land into the wind if the water is rough. If you land across the wind, the rolling and pitching of the airplane will make it easy for the wind to get under the upwind wing and capsize the plane.

While you want to contact the water at the slowest speed practical, do not make a full-stall landing. Doing so will put the airplane in a nose-high attitude, and the bottoms of the floats will smash into the crests of the oncoming waves. Instead, carry some power throughout the approach and contact the water in a relatively flat attitude. Although your touchdown speed will be slightly higher than your speed in a full-stall landing, the floats will cut through the waves rather than slam into them, and the landing will be easier on the airplane. Don't let the nose get too low, however. Digging the float tips into a wave while landing is just as dangerous as doing it while taking off.

Keep a sharp eye out for gusts. The strong winds that bring about rough water are often gusty, and your plane may be ballooned up or dropped down just as you're trying to ease in onto the waves. Gusts appear as dark patches on the water, but remember that the actual gust will slightly precede its "shadow."

If the water conditions are varied, or if you're having a problem finding a smooth touchdown spot amid a lot of boat wakes, you can skim along a few feet above the surface using power to keep the airspeed slightly above the stall. As you approach a good touchdown spot, pull the power off, and the plane will settle onto the surface almost immediately.

Ideally, rough water landings should be made with full flaps, but there may be times when this setting is not appropriate. If the wind is gusty and your floatplane has large, effective flaps, a lesser setting may keep you from being ballooned back into the air just as you're about to touch down. Some floatplanes, like the de Havilland Beaver, come down like a rock with full flaps (even the Beaver's flight manual cautions against using full flaps except in a emergency), and partial flaps will yield a better landing attitude in rough water. Again, an instructor or a pilot experienced in rough-water flying will be your best source of information regarding the ideal flap settings for your particular floatplane.

Be prepared to bring in full power and go around if you get to tossed back into the air by a large wave. It's better to go around than to attempt to rescue the landing and end up contacting the water in a nose-high, full-stall attitude. Also be prepared to put in the power and leave if you find that the water just looks too rough when you

get down close to it. Don't get desperate to land the plane—as long as there is fuel in the tanks, it's a lot safer in the air than it is in the rough water. If you feel that the water at your destination is to rough for you or your floatplane to handle, look for another place to land. It's better to land somewhere inconvenient and wait for conditions to improve than risk losing your floatplane and possibly injuring yourself or your passengers.

Once you've decided to land and your plane has contacted the water, chop the power immediately. You'll only prolong the beating your plane is about to receive by keeping the power in and attempting to "smooth out the bumps." I've tried this once or twice, and it doesn't work. You'll just have to sit there and take your lumps. As long as you're running along on the step, you'll be able to control the pitch angle, and you can keep the attitude flat so the floats will cut through the waves. (Remember, though, to keep the float tips high enough so they won't dig in.) Once the plane begins to settle off the step, however, there's not much you can do, and as the nose comes up the ride will get pretty rough. If anything is going to break, this is probably the time it's going to do it.

Things will calm down a bit once the plane is back in a displacement attitude, but you'll still have to contend with the wind and spray. You may not be able to turn out of the wind, and if your destination lies behind you, you'll have to sail the plane backwards to the dock. Before we examine the fine art of handling a floatplane in the wind, however, there is one other water condition you should be aware of, although if you're lucky, you will never encounter it.

SWELLS

Swells are no fun at all. Webster's New World Dictionary defines a *swell* as, a large wave that moves without breaking, but the definition doesn't go on to say what swells can do to a floatplane. Boat wakes are a form of swell, and if you ever have the misfortune to hit one while taking off or landing, you'll probably be amazed at the effect those seemingly innocent little lumps of water can have. The wake from a 16-foot boat can flip a floatplane, and the intersecting wakes from continuous boat traffic can make it impossible to land in a busy harbor.

Most floatplane accidents do not occur upon the first impact with the water. Usually, the plane is pitched or tipped into an attitude from which the pilot cannot immediately recover. Successive contacts with the water only worsen the situation, and eventually a structural member will break, or a float or wing tip will dig in deep enough to capsize the plane.

If you should hit a boat wake, the most important things to remember are to keep the bows of the floats from digging in and to keep the wings level. As in a rough-water takeoff, the wake will probably pitch your nose up, and you'll have to apply momentary forward pressure to get it back to the proper attitude. If you're on the step when you approach the wake, the addition of full power may enable you to take off before you reach it, or you may be able to jerk the plane out of the water long enough to stagger over the wake before settling back down again. If you settle back into the water before you've cleared the swells, however, you're liable to slam into the top of one at a high angle of attack, and you'll be worse off than you were before. Also, don't forget there are two halves to a boat wake. You don't want to successfully clear one set of swells only to run into the swells coming off the other side of the boat.

Generally, your best course of action is to pull the power off as soon as you see that you're about to run into a wake. If you're already in the swells, you'll get a pretty rough ride as you fall off the step and come back through the hump, but it may be safer than trying to power through the wake or yanking the plane off the water before it's ready to fly.

Boat wakes can almost always be seen and avoided. Far more dangerous are the big swells found in large bodies of water, or harbors and bays exposed to the sea. Most of the time, these swells are obvious from the air, but sometimes they're not visible until you approach the surface. Everything from the color of the sky to the angle of the light can affect their appearance, and you may get all the way to the end of your final approach, only to find the water covered with widely spaced swells. These swells are the remains of large waves that have been whipped up by the wind some distance away. While the wind may die, the energy stored in the waves will keep them moving for a long time, and they will gradually run together and form the rhythmic patterns of swells so familiar to boaters who venture into open water. It may take along time for swells to dissipate; the huge swells that are responsible for the excellent surfing conditions along the north shore of Oahu in the Hawaiian Islands begin life as waves whipped up by violent storms in the Gulf of Alaska, thousands of miles away.

There is really no safe way to land a floatplane on water that is covered with swells. Only the experienced pilots of large flying boats can hope to operate in and out of swells with any degree of success, and even they will be subjected to a considerable pounding. With their strong hulls and low centers of gravity, flying boats can cope with much rougher water than can floatplanes. The Japanese Shin-Meiwa PS-1, a large, four-engined, amphibious flying boat which first flew in 1967, is designed to operate in winds of up to 25 knots and seas up to 13 feet high—conditions that would make short work of even the largest floatplane.

While you should never deliberately set out to take off or land in swell-covered water, an inflight emergency may leave you no other choice but to land in whatever water lies below you, and if that water happens to be covered with swells, you'll just have to do the best you can. Fortunately, there are a few basic guidelines that will increase your chances of making a successful landing, or at least one in which no one is injured.

First, try and determine the distance between the swells. This distance, or *wavelength,* is measured from the top of one swell to the top of the next one. If the swells are close together, half the length of your floats or less, your plane will always be supported by at least two swells, and the touchdown will be relatively smooth. This isn't to say that your plane won't come apart when it starts to slow down, but the initial touchdown and runout will be smooth.

If the wavelength is between one and two times the length of your floats, your plane will only be supported by one swell at a time, and you will pitch in and out of the troughs between the swells. This is a very dangerous situation because if your plane should touch down on a crest and immediately pitch forward into a trough, the floats will dig into the face of the next swell, and you could be flipped onto your back while travelling at a fairly high rate of speed.

If the distance between the swells is four or more times the length of your floats, you can, wind permitting, land parallel to them, which will considerably lessen the chances of damaging the plane.

Since the swells were probably generated some distance away by winds that have long since dissipated, you'll often find that the swells and the local surface winds are coming from two different directions. Sometimes the local winds will be generating their own wave pattern, which will be superimposed over the swell pattern. Things can get very confusing, but whenever possible, land parallel to large, widely spaced swells. To land into them is to risk slamming into the front of an oncoming swell, sort of a monster version of making a full-stall landing into the crest of a wave. The only time you should consider landing into the swells is if the wind is blowing very hard in the same direction as the swells are moving, making a crosswind landing parallel to the swells difficult, if not impossible. If possible, try to touch down on the back of a swell or in the trough between two swells.

If the swells are moving faster than the wind, a down-wind landing may be the safest maneuver. Since you'll be landing in the same direction that the swells are moving, your speed relative to the swells will be much lower than if you landed into them. If the wind velocity is less than 12 miles per hour, however, always land parallel to the swells. The more you can head into the wind, the better, but your first consideration should be to touch down parallel to the swells.

The only guideline for taking off in water covered with large swells, or a combination of swells and other wave patterns, is to head as closely into the wind as possible, while not heading directly into any of the prevailing wave and swell patterns. Remember, floatplanes should never be operated on any body of water when swells are present, and they have no place at all on the open ocean.

The basic procedures just outlined are for emergency use only, and are in fact the same procedures that should be followed in the event you must ditch a land-plane.

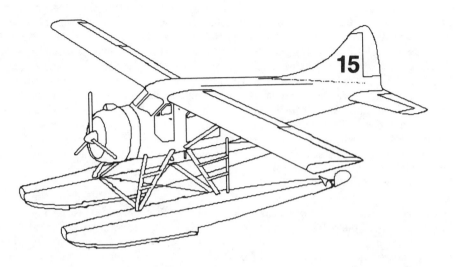

Floatplanes vs. the Wind

J UST ABOUT EVERYTHING YOU DO IN A FLOATPLANE is affected by the wind. It affects the water conditions, your steering, your takeoff and landing directions, your cruise, your taxiing, and your docking. The wind even affects you by its absence—when you have to make a glassy-water landing, for example. Much of your floatplane instruction will be spent in learning how to cope with the whims of the wind, and the more you fly, the more you'll realize that the wind's supply of tricks is infinite.

CROSSWIND TAKEOFFS AND LANDINGS

One of the advantages floatplanes enjoy over landplanes is their ability to almost always take off and land into the wind. There will, however, be times when boat traffic, obstructions in the water, or a narrow channel will dictate your takeoff or landing lane, regardless of the wind direction. The crosswind takeoff and landing procedures in a floatplane aren't that much different from the ones you're used to using in a landplane. Because of the yielding nature of the water's surface, however, it's very important not to let the wind begin to lift the floatplane's upwind wing, because this action will begin to bury the downwind float. If corrective measures aren't taken im-

mediately, the plane could capsize. Another difference will be the fact that your landing surface will be moving, which makes it very difficult, if not impossible, to judge your drift by looking at the water. The texture and movement of even the smallest ripples and wavelets may make it appear that you're drifting faster than you actually are, or maybe even in the wrong direction. The only way you can get an accurate picture of your drift is by referencing a point on shore in front of you.

The Crosswind Takeoff

If the wind is light to moderate, the takeoff run is made using the same basic procedure you would use if you were flying a landplane. Hold full aileron into the wind to keep the upwind wing from lifting, and bleed off the aileron gradually as the speed increases. Because the consequences of having the upwind wing lift out of control are irreversible, it's best to play it safe and hold some aileron into the wind all the way through the takeoff run. It's even a good practice to lift off the water with the upwind wing lowered slightly, holding the bank angle until you're well clear of the water and have established a positive rate of climb. Then if the plane should settle back onto the water after a premature liftoff, the upwind wing will still be in a position to resist being lifted by the wind. Make sure, however, that when you pull the plane off the water, you don't let the upwind wing fly down low enough to contact the surface.

You may have to hold some downwind rudder during the takeoff run to resist the wind's weathercocking force and keep the plane following a straight path. You'll have to hold more downwind rudder if the wind is coming from the left because you'll be opposing both the weathercocking effect and the P-factor. In a right crosswind, these two forces may cancel each other out. As you come up into the hump phase of the takeoff, a strong crosswind may try to weathercock your plane *downwind*. The principle is the same as the one that lets you make a plowing turn to a downwind heading, and you'll have to use the rudder to counter this tendency, too.

When you line the plane up prior to starting your takeoff run, the water rudders will keep you heading across the wind. As soon as you pull the rudders up, however, the plane will begin to weathercock into the wind, and in the short time it takes you to secure the water rudder handle to its bracket, you could be pivoted away from your takeoff lane. The solution is to turn to a heading downwind of your takeoff heading before you raise the water rudders. By the time you've gotten the retraction handle secured to its bracket (a process that takes forever when you're in a hurry), the wind will have pivoted you into line with your takeoff lane, and you can put in the power and go.

The threat of the upwind wing lifting is always present during a crosswind takeoff in a strong wind, particularly at the beginning of the takeoff run. If you have enough room, the best procedure is to start your takeoff directly into the wind. Once you're on the step and accelerating, your ailerons will be more effective, and you can turn to the required crosswind heading. The important thing is to keep that upwind wing from lifting, and your plane is most vulnerable during the transition from the displacement to the planing attitude. If you can make this transition while heading directly into the wind and waves, the chances of a capsizing will be greatly diminished.

If the upwind wing should start to lift during a crosswind takeoff and additional aileron doesn't immediately bring it back down again, pull the power back to idle and let the plane weathercock into the wind. Any attempt to continue the takeoff will probably result in burying the downwind float, which will, in turn, capsize the plane. If things go so far that the downwind float actually does become buried, pull off the power and turn the plane

downwind as hard as you can to lower the forward speed of the downwind float, and relieve some of the pressure that's forcing it to submerge. As the pressure lessens, the float's buoyancy may let it rise to the surface and level the airplane. There is no guarantee that this procedure will work; so it's best not to let the situation progress to the point where you have to hope that it does.

In severe crosswind conditions, you may be able to get the plane on the step while heading into the wind only to find that you can't hold the crosswind heading when you try to turn to it. This is the one situation when it's permissible to lower the water rudders during takeoff. They will help you hold the plane on course, but remember to raise them when you're safely off the water.

Crosswind Landings

Landing a floatplane in a crosswind is no different than landing a landplane under the same conditions. By holding the upwind wing low and applying opposite rudder, you can slip the plane sideways into the wind. Properly done, the upwind slip will cancel your downwind drift, and you will track straight down the runway, or in this case, your chosen landing lane. The touchdown will occur on the low, or upwind, float, and you should continue to hold the aileron into the wind as you decelerate to keep the wind from lifting the upwind wing. As you slow down, the plane may begin to weathercock; you'll have to counter this tendency with the rudder. As in a crosswind takeoff, your plane will be at its most vulnerable as it comes off the step and back over the hump, so be prepared to apply full aileron into the wind to keep the plane on an even keel.

As you begin your final approach, it will be difficult to judge your rate of downwind drift by looking at the water. The waves will be moving at an angle across your path, and it may even appear that you are drifting upwind instead of downwind. Since your goal is to touch down without any sideways drift at all, it necessary that you be able to see your true rate of drift so you can correct for it. The only reliable way to do so is to use a point on land as a reference. As you begin your final approach, pick a house, a dock, a tree, or any prominent object on shore and fly toward it. (If you use a boat, make sure it's anchored. Flying an approach using a moving boat as a reference could be an interesting experience.) Like the centerline on a runway, the fixed object on shore will immediately show if you're drifting downwind and whether or not you're using the right amount of correction to stop the drift.

As you get closer to the water, it will be harder to ignore the false information you may be getting from the waves, but if you continue to judge your crosswind correction using the fixed reference you've chosen, you'll make a nice, smooth touchdown on the upwind float without that sickening, sideways lurch that makes the passengers grab for the armrests.

SAILING

As we have seen, turning a taxiing floatplane from an upwind to a downwind heading can be difficult, or even dangerous, on a windy day. If the wind is above a certain velocity, it may be impossible to turn the floatplane at all, thanks to the weathercocking effect. If your destination lies directly upwind of your landing site, it's a simple matter to land and continue taxiing straight ahead. What can you do, though, if your destination lies downwind of your landing site or somewhere off your left or right wing? You'll have to resort to one of the most interesting and challenging floatplane techniques there is: sailing.

Sailing a floatplane is an art. Put simply, *sailing* is the technique of making a floatplane go in the direction the wind doesn't want it to go. It's one of the few times you'll be able to foil the wind and make it work for you instead of against you. By manipulating your plane's control surfaces and engine, you can sail the plane diagonally backwards to the left or right, or even straight sideways. By combining the different sailing techniques, you can make your floatplane go just about anywhere you want it to, even if the wind is so strong that you can only turn a few degrees to the left or right.

The techniques for sailing a floatplane are based on two principles which I call the *keel effect* and the *deflection effect*. If the force of the wind is not opposed by thrust from the engine, the plane will be pushed backwards through the water. The wind's effect will be slight, other than to produce the drift; so the plane will tend to head in the direction the floats are aimed. In other words, if there is some way to point the tail to the left or right of a dead downwind heading, the float keels will resist the wind's attempt to continue pushing the plane straight downwind, and the plane would drift (sail) backwards to the left or right. This is the keel effect.

The deflection effect is used to move the floatplane sideways. If the plane is held in position with the engine, the keels of the floats will not be moving through the water; so they will have little steering effect on the airplane. If the plane can then be turned a few degrees to the left or right, the wind will strike only one side of the fuse-lage. With more pressure on one side than on the other, the plane will be pushed, or deflected, sideways.

Most of the time, you will use a combination of both of these methods to reach your destination. The primary controls used in sailing are the air rudder, the ailerons, the engine, the flaps, and the doors. With all the flight controls in their neutral positions, the floatplane will point directly into the wind and drift straight back. To sail backwards to the left, raise the water rudders, apply full *right* rudder, and hold full *left* aileron. Right rudder will push the tail to the left. Holding the stick or yoke all the way to the left will lower the right aileron and raise the left one. Because the down (right) aileron will present more surface to the wind than the up (left) aileron, it will help the rudder swing the tail of the airplane to the left. It's important to raise the water rudders when sailing backwards, because if they are left down, they will oppose the air rudder. As the wind swings the tail to the left, the plane will begin to drift in that direction (Fig. 15-1).

You can also control your sailing speed. Lowering the flaps will present more surface to the wind, and you will be blown backwards at a faster rate. If you're still not satisfied, you can hold the cabin doors open to add even more wind-catching surface. (If you're sailing to the left, holding open only the right-hand door may help swing the tail over even farther.) Shutting down the engine will increase your sailing speed, and in moderate winds, this may be the only way you'll be able to move backwards fast enough to maintain directional control.

Be careful if the winds are strong, however. The sterns of your floats will become the bows when you start sailing backwards, but the sterns don't have as much flotation as the bows and forebodies. If you start drifting backwards too fast, you may drive the sterns of the floats deep into the water, and the wind could get under the wing and fuselage and flip the plane over its tail and onto its back. Hold the yoke or stick all the way forward when you're sailing backwards to help hold up the tail, and the sterns of the floats.

If you're sailing backwards to a dock, you can use the engine to stop your backwards drift when you get there. When you're sailing with the engine shut down, always keep it ready to start; you may need it in a hurry if you suddenly need to stop or pull forward. Some of the larger floatplanes, like the de Havilland Otter, should never be sailed backwards unless their engines are running. Because the Otter presents so much surface to the wind, it will drift backwards very quickly, but the afterbodies of its floats have very little flotation compared to

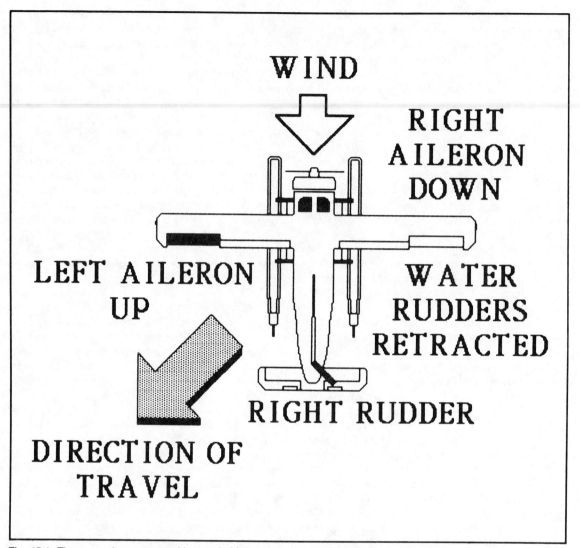

WIND

RIGHT
AILERON
DOWN

LEFT AILERON
UP

WATER
RUDDERS
RETRACTED

RIGHT RUDDER

DIRECTION OF
TRAVEL

Fig. 15-1. These are the proper positions to hold the controls to sail a floatplane backwards to the left.

the size and mass of the airplane. Without any braking action from the engine, the sterns of the floats will easily be driven under, and the wind will get under that huge wing and put the plane on its back.

There are two methods you can use to reach a dock, ramp, or beach that is directly off your wing. One is to sail backwards in the direction of your destination for awhile and then taxi forward, followed by another angled drift and another taxi forward (Fig. 15-2). Repeat this pattern until you reach your destination. The second method is to sail the plane sideways using the deflection effect. Using the engine to hold your position, apply rudder in

the direction you want to go. The water rudders should be down because they'll help the air rudder turn the plane. As you maintain your position opposite your destination, the wind will start to push you over towards it.

You'll often have to use a combination of the two sailing methods to reach your destination. A typical example is shown in Fig. 15-3. Here, the object was to put the plane into the only available space at the dock during a storm with 20-knot winds. The plane was sailed backwards into the seaplane base until it was opposite the open spot. Then the water rudders were lowered; some power was added, and the plane was sailed sideways

190

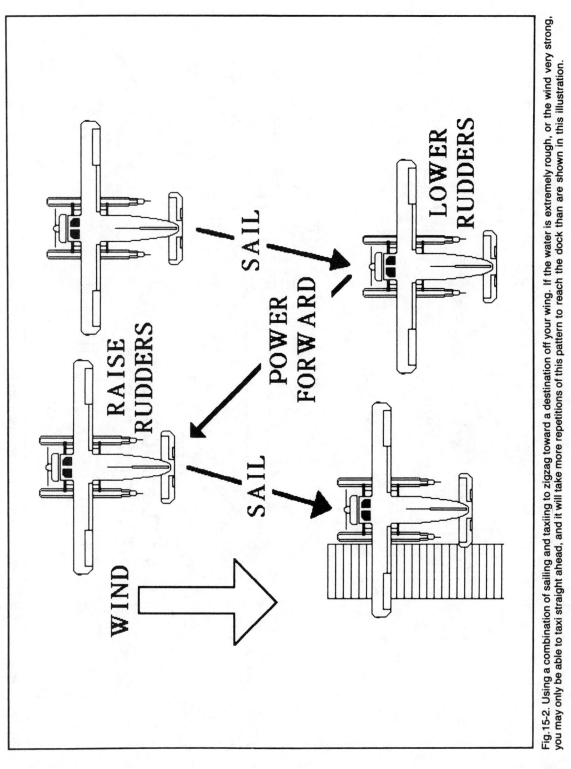

Fig.15-2. Using a combination of sailing and taxiing to zigzag toward a destination off your wing. If the water is extremely rough, or the wind very strong, you may only be able to taxi straight ahead, and it will take more repetitions of this pattern to reach the dock than are shown in this illustration.

191

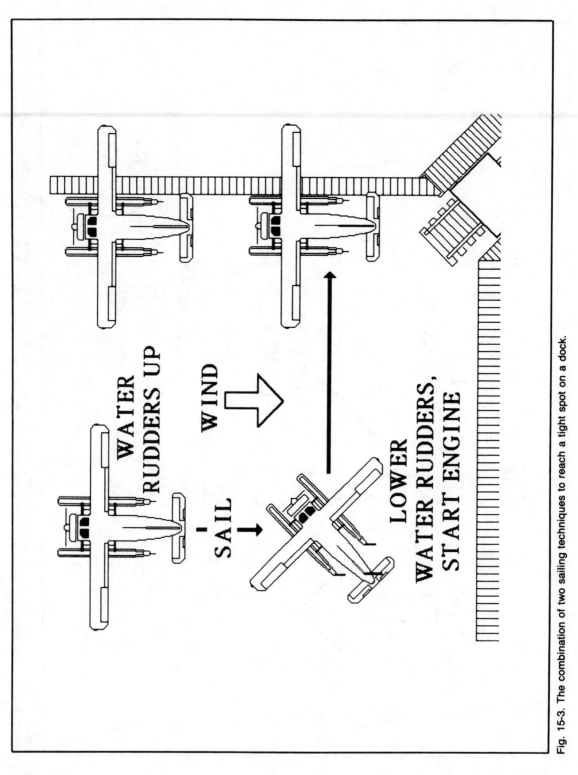

WATER RUDDERS UP

WIND

SAIL

LOWER WATER RUDDERS, START ENGINE

Fig. 15-3. The combination of two sailing techniques to reach a tight spot on a dock.

Fig. 15-4. Sailing a de Havilland Beaver backwards to the right. The water rudders are retracted, and Neal is applying full left rudder. It is important to retract the water rudders because they will oppose the air rudder when the plane is moving backwards through the water. Note also that the left aileron is down and the right one is up.

up to the dock. The flaps and the engine were used to compensate for the wind gusts and to keep from running into the plane ahead or drifting into the dock behind. If the plane moved too far ahead, the power was momentarily reduced and some flap was added. If the plane began to drift back, the throttle was advanced slightly or the flaps were retracted. This particular episode took place in a Cessna 180; so the flaps could be lowered or retracted almost instantly.

It would be impossible to illustrate all the different sailing situations in which you could find yourself. The best thing you can do is learn and practice the basics. Then, whenever the opportunity presents itself, try sailing your plane to a specific spot on a dock or a beach. It's slow, but it's a challenge to figure out just the right moves that will bring you to your destination (Fig. 15-4). Successfully sailing your floatplane to the exact spot for which you were aiming will leave you with a real feeling of accomplishment, and someday, when the wind is whistling through the trees, all that practice will really pay off.

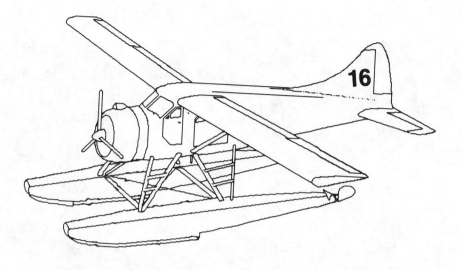

Advanced Operations

THE MAIN REASON FOR THE FLOATPLANE'S CONtinuing popularity is its versatility. From a busy downtown dock to a remote, wilderness lake, a floatplane gives its pilot an almost limitless range of destinations. The purpose of a floatplane trip is often recreation, but that great fishing or camping spot may be a little difficult to get to unless the pilot is experienced in the advanced techniques used to land a floatplane on a river or a small mountain lake. This chapter will introduce you to some of these techniques, but you should never attempt any of them on your own until you get some dual instruction from a pilot well experienced in these procedures. Rivers and mountain lakes have claimed a lot of floatplanes, and you don't want yours to be next. If you have a competent instructor in the other seat the first few times you practice these techniques, it will relieve a lot of your self-imposed pressure and anxiety, and the experience will be an enjoyable one.

RIVERS

River landings and takeoffs can be made safely if you follow a few basic guidelines. Give the section of river you want to land on a thorough going over from the air

(Fig. 16-1). Your inspection passes should be made at an altitude low enough to enable you to see any obstacles that may be in, or across, the river, and you should continue making inspection passes until you're sure the area is clear.

First, make sure the river itself is safe to land on. Determine the location of any shallow areas, sand or gravel bars, and submerged rocks or logs. These hazards will be easy to spot if the water is clear, but if the river is muddy, it will be almost impossible to tell what lies beneath the surface. Look for disturbances on the water. Ripples or waves that remain in one place are indications of underwater obstacles. Be wary of patches on the surface that are slicker in appearance than the surrounding water. They often mark the locations of underwater ledges or boulders.

Irregularities in the banks of the river will produce their own currents and back eddies. If you land or taxi into one of these eddies, it may take control of your plane and spin it into the bank.

Never land in white water. It's shallow and full of rocks and will tear the bottoms out of your floats the instant you touch down.

Check for floating debris in the water. Be especially

Fig. 16-1. Inspecting a river from the air prior to landing. This is the Snohomish River in Washington State.

careful if the water is muddy; this usually indicates that the river is receiving a lot of runoff from recent rainstorms. As the water rises, it will float downed trees and branches off the banks, any one of which could do serious damage to your floats. Take the time to check the river upstream from your intended landing site for floating debris. By the time you're on final approach, that big tree that was up around the bend could be drifting right through the middle of your landing site.

Check carefully for wires or cables strung across the river. The problem is not so much from big, high-tension power lines; they are usually marked on the map, and the wires themselves are often marked with orange balls. The danger is from smaller lines that may have been strung across the river by local residents. Farmers will often suspend a power line across a river to an outbuilding, pump, or irrigation system on the other side, and it's a sure bet it won't be on any of your maps. These single lines are almost impossible to see from the air; so rather than look for the wires themselves, look for the poles that support them. The poles are easier to see in the foliage that lines most river banks, and once you've spotted them, you can

start looking for the actual wires. Try to get a good view of the river with the sun behind you. The light will make any wires strung across the water more visible.

Check the banks for fishermen, too. While their lines can't really damage your plane, you won't help our public image much by cutting or stripping all the line off their reels or, worse yet, jerking their fishing rods out of their hands and into the river.

Make sure you'll be able to take off again before you commit yourself to a landing. Remember, you'll need a lot less room to land than you will to take off. A bridge which won't interfere with your landing may obstruct your takeoff run. Make sure the river itself will permit you to take off again. You don't want to land only to find that your takeoff run will carry you into a shallow or rocky stretch of water.

The Landing

It's just as important to determine the wind direction when preparing for a river landing as it is when preparing to land on a lake or in a harbor. Unless obstacles prevent it, always land into the wind, regardless of the

196

direction of the current. In very light or no-wind conditions, try to land downstream, with the current. The ideal landing is one which was made into the wind and with the current, but these will be rare since rivers often seem to generate their own winds which blow in the same direction as the current. By landing downstream, your touchdown speed will be reduced because both you and the river will be travelling in the same direction. If your plane normally touches down at an airspeed of 60 miles per hour and the river is moving along 15 miles per hour, your actual touchdown speed will be 45 miles per hour. An upstream landing made under the same conditions would result in a touchdown speed of 75 miles per hour.

It's important to keep the actual touchdown speed as low as possible because of the nature of the water. The surface of most rivers is very smooth, almost glassy in appearance, and a great deal of drag will be exerted on the floats when you touch down. Just as in a glassy-water landing, this drag will tend to pitch the floatplane forward, and you'll have to counter this tendency by pulling back on the stick or yoke. The faster you touch down, the greater will be the tendency to nose over, and eventually, you'll reach a touchdown speed which will cause the plane to pitch forward in spite of your holding full up elevator. The bows of the floats will dig in, and the plane will very likely end up on its back. It's extremely dangerous to make a downwind landing in an upstream direction, against the current, because your normal touchdown speed will be increased by both the speed of the wind and the speed of the current, and the result could easily be a wrecked floatplane.

An upstream landing made in no-wind conditions is like making a downwind landing on a lake. As long as the current is moving faster than a breeze blowing in the same direction, land downstream whenever possible. Once the velocity of the wind exceeds the velocity of the current, however, always land into the wind.

Whether you are landing upstream or down, always make your landing in line with the current (Fig. 16-2). Landing across the current, even slightly, will have the same effect as landing in a crab on a runway, and your plane will veer sideways. If the current is strong enough or your angle across the river great enough, your plane could easily tip up on one float, and if a wing tip contacts the surface, you'll shortly find yourself wading ashore.

The banks of most rivers have trees lining their banks, and in a crosswind, they can create downdrafts and turbulence right over the water. Always be prepared to add full power and go around for another try if things start getting too bumpy when you drop below the tops of the trees. It's best to make a power-on approach and fly a few feet off the surface carrying just enough power to keep the plane in the air. (Allow an extra margin of speed if the air is turbulent.) As you approach your touchdown spot, chop the power and let the plane settle onto the river, adding back pressure to counter the nose-over tendency. Although the water will most likely be glassy, the proximity of the banks on either side will give you a good idea of your height above the water.

One of the hardest things to get used to is the sight of the trees which line the banks whizzing past your wing tips. The photographs for this section were taken on the Snohomish River in Washington State, and it's obvious from Fig. 16-2 that there is more than enough room on this stretch of river for the Beaver to maneuver. I got an entirely different view from the cockpit, however, and during the inspection passes and the first couple of landings, I was convinced that I was going to finish the day flying the only clipped-wing Beaver in existance.

If, after you touchdown, the plane suddenly feels like it's caught in molasses, you're thrown against your seatbelt, and the nose starts to pitch down, put in full power immediately and try to jerk the plane back into the air. You've touched bottom, and if you don't succeed in getting the plane out of the water, it will probably go over onto its nose. Running aground when the floatplane is in displacement is no real problem unless the bottom is covered with rocks, but if the floats should touch bottom while the plane is on the step, the sudden drag will pitch the plane forward almost uncontrollably. This problem will be most likely to occur when the river is muddy and the bottom is obscured from view. If you are unable to locate the shallow areas, you probably shouldn't attempt a landing at all, unless you're very familiar with the river and know exactly where the deep water channels are.

Once you're off the step, lower the water rudders. Your plane can be held motionless in the river with power, or allowed to drift backwards by pulling the throttle to idle. By partially deflecting the water rudders and adding some power, you can move your plane sideways across the river to a dock or some other spot on the bank.

Turning a floatplane around on a river is an interesting visual experience. As the plane begins to turn away from its upstream heading, it will begin to accelerate downstream, and the bank of the river in front of you will appear to be going by faster and faster. You will be heading downstream at a much higher speed than you're used to going, but your actual taxi speed through the water will be the same as it always is. As you begin a turn from a downstream to an upstream heading, you will appear to slow down and stop as you swing around into the current.

When maneuvering a floatplane on a river, remember that the deepest water is almost always against the outside bank in a bend, and that's usually where the strongest current is, too. If the wind is strong, you'll have to contend with the weathercocking force as well as with the current; so it's vitally important that you carefully plan out your actions well in advance. Always approach a dock while heading upstream. If you approach on a downstream heading, you'll probably be going too fast to stop, and if you should hit something in the process, your excessive forward speed could cause considerable damage. Things could get tricky if a strong wind blowing against the current keeps you from heading the plane upstream. One solution may be to shut down the engine, lower the flaps, open the doors, and hope the wind will push you upstream

as fast as the river is pushing you downstream. Then you could sail the plane sideways up to the dock. Maybe. In any event, you can see the importance or preplanning when maneuvering on rivers.

If you're dropping people off, and there's no convenient dock anywhere in sight, you'll have to work the plane in as close to the bank as possible. Keep an eye on your wing tip. You don't want to get it tangled up in the brush or trees lining the bank. Watch the bottom as you approach shallow water. Unless the current is very slow, the bottoms of most rivers are made up of rocks or gravel. The bottoms of slow rivers are usually covered with silt and mud. If the bottom looks too rough for your floats, your passengers will have to jump out and wade ashore. Since you'll have to keep the engine running to hold your position, make sure they jump off the back of the floats, and wade straight away from the airplane. Under no circumstances let them walk forward. The same

Fig. 16-2. When landing on, or taking off from, a river, always land parallel to the current.

thing goes for picking people up. Instruct them to wade toward the airplane from the rear and climb on the after portion of the floats.

If you're going to beach the plane, try to pick an area where the current is relatively weak. If possible, position the plane upstream and let it float back onto the bank using the engine to control the speed of your backwards drift. Don't forget to raise the water rudders before you reach shallow water. Most rivers have gently sloping bottoms; so you'll probably run aground before you reach the bank. Be prepared to shut off the engine and jump out into the water to pull the plane securely onto shore. After you beach your plane, make sure the current won't keep rocking it back and forth. If the bottom is covered with small rocks or gravel, the constant motion could seriously abrade the bottoms of the floats or even wear a hole through the skin. Use the same tiedown method you use on a lake: run one line straight back from the tail and a line diagonally out from each wing tip.

The Takeoff

If there is little or no wind, a downstream takeoff is best. It will be like taking off from a lake on a no-wind day. Don't be alarmed by what looks like an excessively high ground speed during your takeoff run. Remember, the bank will be rushing past your wing tips at a higher rate of speed than your floats will be planing over the water. As far as your airplane is concerned, everything will be normal. The ideal takeoff, like the ideal landing, is made downstream into the wind. If the wind is blowing downstream faster than the current, take off upstream into the wind, but never take off upstream with a tailwind. Not only will your speed over the water be excessively high, but you will use up a tremendous amount of water before you attain flying speed. You will probably run way past the section of river you so carefully scouted earlier, and you may hit shallow water, rocks, or even a bridge before you can get airborne.

If you make an upstream takeoff into the wind, your plane will appear to be standing still when you put in full power and begin to come up over the hump. Again, this is an optical illusion, and your floats will actually be moving through the water at their normal speed. Once you're on the step, lifting one float out of the water may help you accelerate faster and get off the water sooner. There's nothing wrong with taking off or landing in a curve to follow the course of the river. The important thing is to keep the plane lined up with the current. If you have to make some turns after takeoff to stay over the river until you can clear the trees along the banks, keep them

as shallow as you can and keep the airspeed up. You don't want to risk a stall this close to the water.

River flying is both challenging and rewarding, but it can be tricky. Even if you've had some experience with rivers, always try to get some advice from an experienced, local pilot if you want to try a river you've never been to before. He will be able to point out the best places to land, and what to watch out for. You may even consider taking the local pilot with you on your flight; not only will this help keep you out of trouble, but it might even get you to the best fishing spot on the river.

MOUNTAIN LAKES

Mountain lakes can offer some of the best fishing, hunting, and camping to be had, to say nothing of the spectacular setting, but a trip to the high country should not be taken lightly by an inexperienced floatplane pilot. The combination of small lakes and high altitudes excludes all by the highest performance floatplanes, and the tricky winds and unforgiving terrain will demand the utmost skill on the part of the pilot. Mountain flying itself is something of an art, and most flight schools located in, or near, a range of mountains offer courses specifically designed to introduce new pilots to the special techniques required to fly safely in the high country. There are also several excellent books on the subject. If you are seriously interested in someday flying to the high lakes, you would do well to read the books and invest some time and money in a mountain flying course.

One of the first things you'll learn is that distances are deceiving in the mountains. The massive size of the surrounding peaks and the clear air combine to upset your sense of proportion, and a lake that looks large enough to land on may, in fact, be much too small. Even worse, it may be large enough to land on but too small to take off from. The time to find this out is not when your floats touch down on the surface, but while you are still safely flying around it at altitude. The length of the water surface is not the only thing with which you need to be concerned. The surrounding slopes may make it impossible for you to climb straight ahead after you take off; so you'll need to determine if there is enough room for you to circle over the lake as you gain altitude.

The most difficult thing to cope with besides the physical size of a small mountain lake will be the wind. The wind does strange things in the mountains, and it is possible to have winds coming from several different directions on different parts of the lake. Another problem is caused by the fact that cold air sinks. Air from higher, colder elevations will come spilling down canyons and valleys and create local wind conditions that may be completely different from the primary wind direction and strength. If there is snow on the surrounding peaks, these downdrafts of cold air will be even more prevalent. The downdrafts can be extremely dangerous, because if you fly into one while climbing out, you may be unable to clear the surrounding terrain. In addition to the downdrafts of cold air, a nearby ridge or peak may cause the prevailing wind to spill over onto the lake in a downdraft, thus adding to the problems already created by the local downdrafts. While there may be a corresponding updraft at the other end of the lake, the geography may not allow you to make use of it, and if the surrounding terrain forces you to fly into the downdrafts, you may find it very difficult, if not impossible, to climb to altitude following takeoff.

The first thing to do when you arrive over a mountain lake is to determine the wind conditions. Define the direction of the prevailing wind, and try to locate any areas which may have local winds blowing in a different direction. These will often appear as dark patches on the surface of the water, similar to gusts. Identify the areas which may contain downdrafts, and mentally project your approach and departure flight paths to see if you can remain clear of these areas. When you have a good overall picture of the wind conditions, it's time to determine if the lake is big enough for you and your floatplane.

A method of roughly calculating the length of a lake by noting the time it takes to overfly it and relating this time to your ground speed is outlined in Chapter 19. The most practical way to determine if a lake is large enough to permit safe landings and takeoffs however, is to circle approximately 500 feet above the surface. Reduce your airspeed until you are flying at your normal approach speed with the flap setting you normally use for takeoff. Fly down one side of the lake and see how many 180-degree S-turns you can make before reaching the opposite side. This will give you an idea of the lake's width. Find out if you can make a 180-degree turn at each end of the lake while remaining over the water. If not, will the surrounding terrain allow you to make the turn over land? This information will help you determine if you can turn back and circle over the lake after you take off. If there isn't even enough room for you to do these preliminary maneuvers, the lake is not for you.

Once you've determined that the lake is large enough, give it the same inspection you would any other body of water on which you were about to land. Look for shallow areas and underwater rocks or reefs, and locate the best place to beach your airplane.

Many mountain lakes are surrounded on three sides by mountains, while the fourth side is open (Fig. 16-3). If the wind is blowing in through the open end, you're in luck. If it's not too strong, you can make your approach through the open end for a downwind landing. When you leave, you'll be able to take off into the wind and climb out over the low terrain at the open end. If the wind is blowing from the other end of the lake, you'll have to take off toward the closed end and circle back towards the lake to gain altitude. The danger here is that your 180-degree turn may carry you into a downdraft area, and if it's severe enough, you may not be able to clear the rising ground around the lake. This problem is why it's so important to determine that you will have enough room for this type of maneuver *before* you commit yourself to a landing. Even if the wind is blowing in through the open end of the valley, check out the amount of flying room at the closed end. Mountain winds have a habit of shifting suddenly, and you would find yourself looking at an entirely new situation when you decide to leave.

As you make your approach to the lake, keep a sharp lookout for the dark patches on the water caused by gusts. These gusts will often be the result of downdrafts, so be prepared to add power immediately if your plane starts to sink. The water in the high lakes is often glassy, and you should always make a power-on landing to minimize your chances of misjudging your height above the water. Landing close to the shore will help you judge your altitude, but don't forget that a power-on, glassy-water landing uses up a lot more room than a power-off landing, so make sure you don't run out of lake. If you've misjudged the length, and you find yourself running out of room, your only choice is to pull the power back and increase your sink rate. Don't give in to temptation and dive for the surface, because you might find it sooner than you think. Keep those float tips up, because with the increased sink rate, you'll probably contact the water pretty hard, and you don't want to dig in the floats.

Before you take off, calculate your plane's takeoff distance based on the density altitude. Your plane won't perform the way you're used to because of the high altitude, and if the day is warm, or if you have a heavy load, your takeoff and climb performance could be pretty miserable. I've talked to several pilots who told about spending unplanned nights on the shore of a lake because the only way they could successfully take off was to wait until the next morning when the air was cold. I've also talked to pilots who left half their load in the mountains and came back for it the next day because their planes refused to become airborne with everything on board.

Fig. 16-3. A mountain lake in Washington's Cascade Mountains. The landing and takeoff must be made through the open end of the lake at the bottom of the picture. Pilots must be especially alert for downdrafts sweeping through the canyons at the far end of the lake and to the left.

201

When it's time to take off, taxi your plane all the way to the end of the lake before you turn around to start your takeoff run. The water behind you won't help you get off the lake, so use all of it. If the water is glassy, make your takeoff run close to shore so you'll have a way of estimating your height when you leave the water. Actually, it's a good idea to take off close to the shore whenever possible, because you'll have more room to make a 180-degree turn if it becomes necessary. Remember to lean the engine for the best possible performance before you begin your takeoff. Even an extra 50 rpm could make the difference between clearing the trees and hiking out of the area.

If you have any doubts about your ability to take off and climb straight out, don't even try. Plan instead to take off and circle around to gain altitude. This way, you won't hit a mountain in the process of discovering that a straight-out departure doesn't work. Some pilots advocate taking off from a small lake using a circular takeoff run. While this method looks good on paper, in reality the additional drag produced by running in a circle will only lengthen the takeoff run. If the lake is too small to let you land and take off in a straight line, it's too small, period, and you should stay off it.

On sunny mornings and afternoons, mountains and ridges will often throw deep shadows across the lakes, and the high contrast will make it difficult to see details in the shadow areas. Rather than risk flying into terrain you can't even see, it would be better to wait until the rising sun illuminates the entire lake, or until the late afternoon shadows move completely over your takeoff and climbout area.

Not all floatplanes are suitable for operations in and out of high mountain lakes. Airplanes with low horsepower-to-weight ratios or high wing loadings do not make good mountain machines, regardless of their type of undercarriage—floats, wheels, or skis. A floatplane suitable for flights into mountain lakes should have a wing that will begin flying at a relatively low speed and that will allow the plane to fly in slow, tight circles. The plane should have good low-speed aileron and elevator control to make it easy to handle in the gusty wind conditions often encountered while landing or taking off in the mountains. It should also have a powerful engine to enable it to climb rapidly and at least hold its own in the downdrafts. Among the floatplanes which meet these requirements are the Piper Super Cub, the Cessna 185, the Helio Models 700 and 800, the Soloy Turbine 206, and the de Havilland Beaver (Fig. 16-4). You should think twice about taking float-equipped Taylorcrafts, Cessna

172s, Piper Tri-Pacers, Cessna 206s, and de Havilland Otters into the high country. Some people may not agree with my inclusion of the last two airplanes, but a fully loaded 206 on floats can be a real slug on takeoff, despite its 300 horsepower, and an Otter is just too big and unwieldy.

Flying into mountain lakes is not easy. Like rivers, mountain lakes provide opportunities for flights into some spectacular country, but even more so than river flying, mountain lake flying requires the pilot to have a thorough knowledge of some very specialized techniques. The only way to obtain this knowledge is to receive expert instruction from an experienced mountain pilot, but even after you've received this instruction, don't take on something you're not sure you or your floatplane can handle. Like every other aspect of water flying, if you use good judgment and common sense, your trips to the high lakes will be rewarding ones.

ICE AND SNOW

There are a few pilots who regularly land floatplanes on the frozen surfaces of lakes or the snow-covered slopes of glaciers. These operations are very specialized, and are done only when there is no other alternative method available, or in an emergency. Although the chances that you will ever have to take off or land on ice or snow are slim, I'm including a brief description of the basic techniques because they are interesting. And who knows? In the unlikely event that you are forced down someday onto a frozen lake or a snow-covered field, the information might come in handy. For those of you who are really interested in the specialized world of glacier flying, I recommend a small book called *Fundamentals of Floatflying, Seaplanes in the Mountain Lakes, and Glacier Flying* by William D. Fisk. For several years, Mr. Fisk flew float-equipped de Havilland Beavers onto high, glacial slopes in support of geological survey teams, and he is an expert in the extremely difficult and exacting techniques needed to conduct these operations successfully and safely (Fig. 16-5).

For the purposes of this book, I will confine my descriptions to include only operations made to and from low-altitude, ice-covered lakes and areas of deep, soft snow. Sometime during each annual freeze up in the northern United States, Canada, and Alaska, there is a period when the presence of ice prevents normal float operations but isn't thick enough to support an airplane on skis. If an occasion arises that requires an airplane to be flown under these conditions, the only option is to use a floatplane, since it will at least remain on the surface as

Fig. 16-4. The Helio Model 800 is powered by a 400-horsepower, eight-cylinder, Lycoming engine, and the plane's short takeoff and landing (STOL) capabilities make it a good choice for operations in small, high lakes. This one is equipped with EDO Model 3500 amphibious floats. (Courtesy of the EDO Corporation)

it crunches its way through the ice. The two main drawbacks of operating a floatplane in conditions of breakable ice are the noise, which is considerable and not unlike the continuous smashing of a large sheet of plate glass, and the wear and tear on the floats.

As a lake freezes up, ice first forms along the shoreline, while the deeper water in the main body of the lake remains clear. A takeoff should never be attempted through ice that is more than 1/2 inch thick, so your problem will be to get to the open water through the ice that has formed in the shallow water along the shore (Fig. 16-6). As long as the plane is taxied straight ahead, the float keels will break through the ice, and the V-shaped bottom will push it out of the way. The danger lies in turning the plane. If the ice is very thin, no more than 1/2 to 3/4 inch, gentle turns can be made with little danger of the broken ice ripping through the thin skin covering

the sides of the floats. Once the ice reaches a thickness of 3/4 inch, however, it will be much less yielding, and while the keels will still break through it, the jagged edges of the ice will tear easily through the float skins if a turn is attempted. In order to turn the plane under these conditions, you will have to shut down the engine, climb out on a float and use a paddle, boathook, or some other tool to clear a patch of water large enough for you to turn the plane by hand. After you have paddled or poled your airplane around to its new heading, you can restart the engine and continue on your way.

If your takeoff lane is covered with a thin sheet of ice, the drag generated as you break through it will lengthen your takeoff run. The only way a takeoff can be made through ice that is more than 1/2 inch thick is to taxi slowly up and down your takeoff lane several times to break up the ice and clear the larger pieces out of the

Fig. 16-5. One of Kenmore Air Harbor's first uses of a float-equipped de Havilland Beaver for glacier work. (Courtesy of the EDO Corporation)

way. This is an emergency procedure only, because the pieces of floating ice will subject your floats to a severe pounding, and you may sustain damage that will have to be repaired when you reach your destination.

You should not attempt to land on ice unless you already know how thick it is. There is no way of determining thickness from the air; you'll have to rely on information obtained beforehand from local residents or other pilots who have recently used the lake. The danger lies in breaking through thick ice and puncturing your floats. If the ice is relatively thin, you can perhaps arrange to have a path broken through it by a local operator before you arrive, which can be especially helpful if you need to taxi the plane to a ramp through shallow water covered with ice thick enough to damage your floats (Fig. 16-7).

Ice exceeding 2 inches in thickness will generally support a light floatplane, and the keels of the floats will act just like the runners on a pair of ice skates. Always land into the wind so your touchdown speed will be as slow as possible. Make a power-on landing, and treat the surface as though it were glassy water. In other words, have the proper touchdown attitude set up well before you reach the surface, and control your rate of descent with power. The proper touchdown attitude for a landing on any surface other than water should be fairly flat, with the bows of the floats only slightly elevated. An excessively nose-high attitude or a full-stall landing will result in the sterns of the floats striking the ground first, and your plane may be pitched violently forward onto its nose. If the surface of the ice is covered with snow, the bows of the floats could dig in, and the plane could end up on its back.

If the surface of the ice is bare and smooth, you'll have another problem: trying to stop. With only the keels of the floats touching the ice, the likeness to a pair of ice skates will be exact. The weight of the plane will create a lubricating film of water under the floats, and you'll cover an amazing amount of distance before you stop. For this reason, always try to land toward the main body of the lake so you'll be in no danger of running into the shoreline before you come to a stop. There's not much you can do to slow your plane down if you're sliding on bare ice. Gently weaving the plane from side to side may generate enough friction to slow you down a little, and you can try applying some forward pressure on the stick or yoke to force as much of the forward keels against the ice as possible. This technique can also be used to shorten the runout after a water landing, but be careful! If you get too desperate to stop, you could force the bows too low and end up on your back.

Lack of braking is one drawback to operating a floatplane on ice. Lack of a shock absorber system is another. Unlike a ski plane, which has springs and shock absorbers to isolate the airframe from the vibration of the skis, a floatplane is rigidly connected to its floats. The shock and vibration of sliding over an uneven surface is transmitted directly to the airframe. Consequently, slightly rough surfaces or small pressure ridges that would pose no problem for a ski plane could completely destroy a floatplane if the shock of hitting these irregularities caused a major airframe component to fail. The lack of a shock absorber system effectively restricts a floatplane to takeoffs and landings on very smooth surfaces.

A floatplane will be almost as effective as a ski plane when landing in deep, soft snow. The wide footprint of the floats will provide adequate buoyancy, and because the V-shaped bottom will create a great deal more "wetted" surface than the relatively narrow, flat bottoms of the undercarriage of a ski plane, a floatplane will come to a stop very quickly. The problem occurs when you try to take off again. That same V-bottom that enabled you to stop so quickly may now cause enough drag to keep you from accelerating to flying speed. Lightening the load will help, as will employing the local residents to stamp out a runway for you. Your floats will ride higher on the packed snow, and you will accelerate must faster. Be careful not to overrotate the airplane when you lift off

Fig. 16-6. One of Kenmore Air Harbor's Cessna 180s sitting on the ice prior to departure. Open water is only a hundred yards away, but the plane faces a noisy taxi through the ice before it can take off.

Fig. 16-7. The same Cessna 180 returning through the channel cleared out by Kenmore's line crew. The ducks appreciate the channel, too.

Fig. 16-8. A Fairchild 24 lifting off a snow-covered runway, It's important not to overrotate a floatplane at liftoff or you could cause the sterns of the floats to strike the ground, resulting in possible damage to the floats or the water rudders. (Courtesy of the EDO Corporation)

Fig. 16-9. Bob Munro, owner of Kenmore Air Harbor, standing beside one of his Noorduyn Norsemans. The company used the Norsemans for glacier flying before it acquired de Havilland Beavers. (Courtesy of Kenmore Air Harbor)

(Fig. 16-8). You don't want to slam the sterns of the floats onto the ground, possibly opening up some seams or damaging the water rudders.

Landing on flat snow is like landing on glassy water, only worse. The chances are the surrounding terrain will be white, and if the sky is white, too, things could get very tricky. Try to land close to a row of trees, a fence, or anything that will help you judge your height above the ground. This is one time when some evergreen branches, blankets, maps, or life vests thrown out onto the surface will really help. If you're in contact with someone on the ground, ask them to put some empty barrels or boxes in the snow along your landing lane. If there aren't any barrels or boxes around, ask the people to stand alongside your "runway" themselves. Any visual reference will be a help. Use a power-on, glassy-water approach, and keep the nose up high enough to prevent the float tips from digging into the snow. When you touch down, expect the drag to pitch the plane forward and be ready to bring in some back pressure to maintain a flat attitude. It will be difficult to turn the airplane once it's on the snow, and you'll probably have to get several people to help you do so when it's time to leave. By tieing a long rope to the tiedown ring under the tail, your ground crew can get the leverage necessary to pull the rear of the plane around while you use the engine to move slowly forward through the snow. Do not lower the water rudders while you're on the ground. They won't make the plane any more maneuverable, and they'll probably be damaged.

Remember, operating a floatplane from ice-or snow-covered surfaces is not a routine procedure. It's hard on the plane, and the opportunities for an accident are many. The fact that it can be done, however, is a good illustration of the floatplane's versatility and strength (Fig. 16-9).

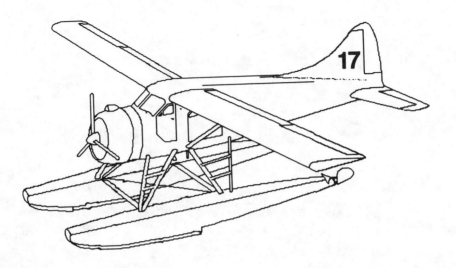

The Amphibious Floatplane

A NYONE WHO HAS SEEN AN AMPHIBIOUS FLOAT-
plane towering storklike over everything else
parked on the ramp has probably asked, "Why would
anyone want to fly something that looks like that, let alone
land it?" Amphibious floatplanes, normally called *am-
phibs*, are definitely not for everyone—not because they
are difficult to fly, but because the privilege of landing
a floatplane on dry land does not come without some
sacrifices.

The main difference between straight (no wheels) and
amphibious floats is weight. For example, a pair of EDO
Model 3430 straight floats for a Cessna 185 weighs 469
pounds, but a set of EDO Model 3500 amphibious floats
for the same airplane tips the scales at 750 pounds, a
281-pound difference. Add the weight of the hydraulic
pump, manual extension pump, hoses, and other accessories, and you wind up with about a 300-pound reduction in useful load.

Amphibious floatplanes are at their best in commercial operations where the ability to operate off both land
and water is more important than the ability to carry a
heavy load. Commercial fish-spotting, geological and
mineral exploration, medical evacuation, and law enforcement are some of the areas in which the capabilities of

the amphibious floatplane are put to good use (Fig. 17-1).
They are also becoming more popular for recreational
uses, too. The owner of an amphibious floatplane can keep
it at a convenient airport, fly to other airports, make
cross-country flights in IFR conditions if the plane is so
equipped, and still enjoy the ability to visit the remote
lakes, rivers, and bays only accessible by seaplane.

An amphibious floatplane is easier to fly than its appearance indicates. On the water, it behaves just like its
straight-float cousins. The only real difference is the
slightly longer length of the amphibian's takeoff run. This
is partly due to the fact that the floats are heavier, but
also because, with their main wheel-well cutouts behind
the step, amphibious floats don't move across the water
quite as efficiently as straight floats.

On land, however, an amphib displays some unique
handling characteristics, and it's important that you receive a thorough checkout from a pilot well experienced
with its sometimes strange behavior.

THE PREFLIGHT INSPECTION

When the amphib is on land, you'll have to add a thorough checkout of the landing gear and retraction system

Fig. 17-1. A Cessna 180 equipped with EDO amphibious floats taxiing up a steel ramp in the oil fields of Louisiana. (Courtesy of the EDO Corporation)

to the normal floatplane preflight inspection. Check all the tires for tread wear and proper inflation.

You'll be steering the plane on land with differential braking; the nosewheels are free-castering. Check the brakes carefully because they get a lot of hard use. Make sure the brake disks and pucks (pads) are in good shape and that there are no hydraulic leaks around the brake calipers. Some float manufacturers use a single main wheel on each float, and the brake components are on the outside and relatively easy to inspect. Other manufacturers prefer a dual wheel, and the brake components are mounted between the wheels, which makes them harder to inspect, but take the time to do it, anyway. There's a lot riding on those brakes, and you want to make sure they're in good shape before you start depending on them. The master cylinder for the wheel brakes is attached to the toe-brakes on the rudder pedals, and the brake lines are routed down the float struts to the main wheels. Check under the rudder pedals in the cockpit for any signs of hydraulic fluid, and, if they are visible, check the brake lines where they enter and emerge from the float struts.

The hydraulic pump that operates the landing gear may be located in the fuselage of the airplane or in one of the floats. Check the visible hydraulic lines and connections for leaks and make sure the lines are securely fastened to the airframe. Finally, check the hydraulic fluid level in the pump reservoir, and add fluid if necessary. If the level is very low, there's probably a leak somewhere in the system, and you shouldn't fly the plane until a mechanic has either located and fixed the leak or determined that there definitely isn't one. Don't forget to check the hydraulic lines leading to and from the manual extension pump in the cockpit. The manual pump itself contains rubber seals on the piston and in the cylinder, and if they are damaged or unseated, there will be traces of hydraulic fluid on the pump body.

Any hydraulic fluid seen anywhere other than in the reservoir of the primary hydraulic pump should be reported. Hydraulic systems operate under high pressure, and if fluid is starting to leak from a hose coupling or a cylinder seal, it's just a matter of time before the faulty component fails completely.

Check the visible components of the retraction mechanism for any obvious signs of damage. The main wheels of modern amphibious floats retract into a well immediately aft of the step, and the nosewheel strut either pivots up to lie flat against the underside of the bow, or is drawn up and back into the float itself (Fig. 17-2). Some of the older retraction systems pivot the nosewheel strut up and back until it lies on top of the float deck, which

Fig. I7-2. A Cessna 185 fitted with EDO MOdel 2790 amphibious floats. Note how the nose strut is drawn up flush against the underside of the bow. (Courtesy of the EDO Corporation)

contains a special recess to accommodate the nosewheel. De Havilland Beavers and Otters are often equipped with floats of this type (Fig. 17-3).

WATER OPERATIONS

If the plane is already in the water, your preflight and departure procedures will be identical to those you would use if your floatplane was equipped with straight floats. Before you begin your takeoff run, however, check the position of the landing gear and verify that it is retracted.

If the amphib you're going to fly is kept in dry storage at a seaplane facility equipped with a ramp, you can do your preflight inspection while the plane is sitting on its wheels in the parking area, and then taxi over to the ramp. Since steering is by differential braking only, it may be necessary to build up some forward momentum with a brief burst of power before you can initiate a turn, especially if the turn is to be made from a full stop.

Be careful when you taxi down the ramp (Fig. 17-4). Ease the plane slowly over the top, and then let it roll freely down the slope. Holding the plane back with the

brakes may cause the tires to skid on the boards, and if there are any nails, bolts, or large splinters projecting above the wood, the tires could be damaged. Obviously, if the ramp is a long one, you'll have to use some braking to avoid building up excessive speed, but normally you'll be able to let the plane roll down on its own. The floatplane should roll straight into the water, and if you find you do need to use the brakes, apply them smoothly and evenly. Uneven braking could cause the plane to veer to one side, and if the ramp is narrow, you might drop a wheel off the edge and have a real problem on your hands.

The bows of the floats will submerge when you hit the water, but they will quickly surface again. Lower the water rudders, retract the landing gear, and you'll be ready to proceed with a normal water takeoff. It's important that you hold the yoke all the way back when taxiing in the water (unless you're taxiing downwind in a strong breeze). Most amphibious floats are more bow-heavy than straight floats, and in rough water or when displacement taxiing with the engine above idle, the bows

211

Fig. 17-3. De Havilland of Canada's Turbo Beaver on amphibious floats. The nose struts pivot up and back to lie on the float decks. (Courtesy of the EDO Corporation)

Fig. 17-4. Kenmore Air Harbor Pilot Kevin Nelsen taxis a Cessna 185 down the ramp at Renton Airport into Lake Washington. The plane is fitted with EDO Model 3500 amphibious floats.

of the floats could be driven under the surfaces unless full up-elevator is held at all times.

You can taxi an amphib up a ramp, too. After you've made your water landing, taxi toward the ramp and lower the gear. Make sure it's down and locked before you reach the ramp. Instead of adding power just before you hit the ramp, which is the correct procedure when ramping a plane on straight floats, wait until the nosewheels contact the ramp and then add enough power to pull you up the slope (Fig. 17-5). It will probably take a lot of power to taxi up the ramp, so be prepared to back off on the throttle when you go over the top. This procedure should only be used if you're going to taxi the plane to a parking area on shore. If you're going to leave the plane on the ramp itself, use the same ramping procedure you would use if your plane was equipped with straight floats.

If you plan to leave your amphib in dry storage for some time and the facility has a forklift for moving floatplanes, have the operator raise your plane off its wheels so you can retract the gear. By storing the plane

on the keels of its floats, you'll take the strain off the gear components and the tires.

LAND OPERATIONS

The view from the cockpit of an amphibious floatplane that's sitting on its wheels is impressive. You'll look down on every plane on the ramp smaller than a Boeing 727, but the plane will not feel at all unstable. In fact, an amphibious floatplane has a more stable feel when taxiing than most low-slung, tricycle-gear landplanes, thanks to the float's wide-track, quadricycle landing gear.

The quadricycle gear is stable and smooth-riding, but it's also responsible for the amphibious floatplane's strangest tendency. When taxiing on land in a crosswind, an amphib will tend to weathercock *downwind*. In order to retain its efficiency in the water, the bottom of the float forward of the step must be smooth; so the main wheels and wheel wells are placed aft of the step. As a result, there is more vertical sheet metal in front of the main wheels than behind them. A crosswind will exert a

Fig. 17-5. Kevin taxiing the 185 back up the ramp. The turbulence on the water behind the plane gives an indication of the amount of power needed to pull the plane out of the water and up the slope.

213

sideways force on the upwind float and the side of the fuselage, and since the nosewheels are free-castering, the plane will pivot on the main wheel under the downwind float.

When you're taxiing on land, your only means of steering will be the main-wheel braking system. If you are faced with a long, crosswind taxi, the upwind brake will probably get quite hot and begin to fade, so be prepared to stop every now and then to let it cool down. Perhaps someone will come up with a practical, steerable nosewheel for amphibious floatplanes someday.

In a landplane, you are accustomed to using the rudder pedals and nosewheel steering to maintain directional control at the beginning of a takeoff roll. Amphibious floatplanes don't have nosewheel steering; so you'll have to use the brakes, and it will take several takeoffs before you develop just the right touch on the pedals. If you use too much brake, you'll keep the plane from accelerating, and if you use too little, you won't be able to stay on the centerline. As the speed increases, it will take less brake pressure to keep the plane in line, until eventually the air rudder will be all that's needed for directional control.

If a normal landplane takeoff technique is used, the amphibian may have a tendency to overrotate. This tendency isn't dangerous, but it can be a little startling, and is probably the result of air getting under the bottoms of the floats as the nose is raised.

Smooth, professional takeoffs are best made by using a soft-field technique. Begin the takeoff roll with full up elevator, and when the increasing speed lifts the nosewheels off the ground, ease off the back pressure to keep the nose from rising any farther. Continue the takeoff roll holding the nosewheels just off the surface of the runway, and when the airplane is ready to fly, it will lift off smoothly with no overrotation.

Once you've established a positive rate of climb and there isn't enough runway left in front of you to land on, retract the wheels. The main gear is hydraulically activated, and the nose gear is operated by cables attached to the main gear retraction mechanism. The landing gear is raised by moving a wheel-shaped lever on the instrument panel to the *up* position. There are three ways you can determine the position of the gear. Indicator lights on the instrument panel show blue for *up* (water landing) and brown for *down* (runway landing). When the hydraulic pump is activated, a red light on a separate circuit illuminates to indicate that the gear is in transit.

There is also a mechanical gear-position indicator in the top of each float. EDO uses a metal tab fastened directly to the landing-gear activating mechanism. As the gear comes up, the tab slides into position under a window in the float deck marked *up*. When the gear is lowered, the tab slides under the window marked *down*. In addition, most amphibious floatplanes have small, wide-angle mirrors mounted out on each wing which enable the pilot to actually see the gear under each float. The mirror on the right wing is used to check the gear under the left float, and the left-hand mirror is used to check the gear under the right float. Some amphib pilots paint the inside of their plane's wheels fluorescent orange to make them more visible against the terrain below.

LANDING PROCEDURES

If you're going to land on the water, you'll obviously leave the gear retracted. This does not mean that you can exclude a check of the landing gear from your prelanding checklist, however. If you should inadvertently land in the water with the gear down, your plane will slam over onto its back the moment it touches the water; so it's very important that you get in the habit of checking all the gear position indicators several times during the approach, regardless of the type of landing you're about to make.

If you're going to land on a runway, lower the gear before entering the traffic pattern and go through a "lever, lights, and visual" check of the gear on downwind, base, and final approach. Check the position of the gear lever on the instrument panel, confirm the gear's position with the indicator lights, and them make a visual check of the gear using the mechanical indicators in the floats and the mirrors under the wings (you'll have to get your passenger to check the indicator in the top of the right float). There is no gear-up warning horn in an amphibian since normal water landings would set it off. While a gear-up landing on a runway would not be terribly damaging, a gear-down landing on water would be disastrous. The instant the nosewheels touched the surface, the plane would somersault; so make sure you know what position the gear is in at all times.

Another good habit you should develop is to mentally relate the type of landing you're about to make with the gear position. Tell yourself, "I'm landing on land, so the gear should be down," or, "I'm landing on water, so the gear should be up." Then visually check the gear again. A lot of amphib accidents seem to occur when the pilot takes off from a runway to make a short flight ending with a water landing. The pilot either forgets to raise the gear after takeoff, or lowers it automatically before landing. Accidents also occur when a pilot is so tired after a long trip that he neglects to do a thorough prelanding

Fig. 17-6. A de Havilland Otter just prior to touchdown. Note the relatively flat attitude, which will keep the sterns of the floats from striking the ground.

systems check. These are the reasons it's so important that you get in the habit of repeating the landing gear checklist several times before every landing.

When you move the gear selector to the down position, the wheels in one float may begin to extend slightly in advance of the wheels in the other float. This will cause the plane to yaw to one side or the other, so be prepared to come in with some rudder pressure to keep the plane flying straight. As soon as both sets of gear are down and locked, the yawing tendency will disappear. Depending on the type of plane you are flying and the design of its floats, there may also be a slight pitch change as the wheels come out. The Cessna 185 pictured in this chapter is mounted on EDO Model 3500 amphibious floats, and while it displays no noticeable pitch change when the gear is lowered, it does yaw slightly to one side because the gear in one float precedes the gear in the other float.

A power-on approach and landing is the smoothest way to put an amphib on a runway. Think of it as a glassy-water landing with the transition to the touchdown attitude made right over the numbers. This method will ease

the plane down onto its main wheels while avoiding an extremely nose-high flare which could cause the tails of the floats to slam into the ground. After the mains touch, gently lower the nosewheels to the pavement and get ready to start steering with the brakes (Fig. 17-6).

You'll really have your hands (and feet) full landing in a crosswind. Use the normal wing-low method to track straight down the runway and touch down on the upwind wheel. In addition to the normal gymnastics required on the ailerons and rudder, however, you'll have to start fighting that downwind weathercocking business with the upwind brake as soon as you touch down. It can be a real adventure, and will certainly give you plenty to talk about in the next hangar-flying session.

Although the type of flying you do may not require the unique capabilities of an amphib, getting a checkout in one is a lot of fun. Not only will it give you some valuable experience in retractable gear procedures, but the challenge of mastering its steering system and the opportunity to fly the tallest, if not the biggest, thing on the ramp will make it a flight you won't soon forget.

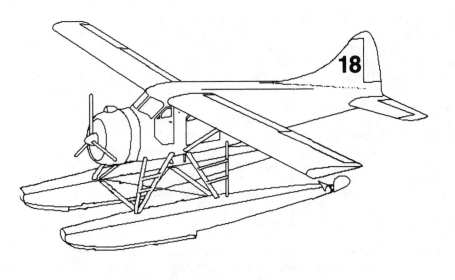

Emergencies

I F YOU HAVE TO HAVE AN ACCIDENT IN AN AIRPLANE, have it in a floatplane. That's a very negative statement, but it's true. The addition of floats makes an airplane much more crashworthy, and statistics show that your chances of walking away from a controlled floatplane crash are excellent. The key word here is *controlled*. Even if you experience a complete power failure over a dense forest, if you keep your wits about you and continue to fly the airplane all the way down to the trees, your biggest problem will most likely be figuring out how to climb down to the ground. (And you wondered why you were carrying around all that mooring line.)

There's more to surviving a crash than just making a good landing, however. If your accident occurs out in the bush someplace, you'll need adequate survival gear to keep you going until help arrives. If you end up in the water, you'll need to guard against hypothermia and revive any members of your party who succumb to it. If it's at all possible, you'll probably also want to recover your airplane. Of course, your first task is to get your airplane down and stopped with everybody intact.

LANDINGS

There are two categories of emergency landings. The first one is the actual, *I-have-to-land-right-now, emergency landing*. This is the type of landing you're faced with in the event of a complete power loss or a failure of one of the airplane's critical components. The second type of emergency landing is the *precautionary landing*. If the oil pressure starts a slow drop to zero; if you suddenly realize you've miscalculated your fuel consumption, and you shortly won't have any left to consume; or if you're running out of daylight, and you don't want to risk a night landing at your destination, a precautionary landing is your ticket to survival.

The basic procedures for making an emergency landing are the same for floatplanes and landplanes. If a total power loss is experienced, first establish the maximum-distance glide speed for your particular airplane. Then pick the best possible landing site within reach and turn toward it. If you are in contact with a radio facility, advise them of your location and situation while you try to locate the source of the problem. If you are not in radio contact, switch to the emergency frequency 121.5 MHz and broadcast MAYDAY together with your location and intentions. *Do not* let your radio broadcasts and troubleshooting efforts interfere with your flying. No one on the ground can help you at this point, and it's vital that you maintain control of the airplane as you head toward your landing site. As you prepare to land, follow the fire-prevention procedures outlined in your plane's flight manual.

The advantage of being in a floatplane now becomes apparent. Those same floats that enable the plane to land on ice or snow also work great on the ground. They are, in effect, two big skids. A freshly plowed field or soft, boggy meadow that would rip the gear off a landplane present no problems for a floatplane. Another advantage of being a floatplane pilot is that you are used to using something other than a windsock or a tower controller to determine the wind direction. Try to determine the wind direction by looking for rising smoke, blowing dust on the ground, or the direction the tree tops are bending. Doing so will not be easy under the pressure of the emergency, and you should always be looking for clues to the wind's direction during your flight so you'll be prepared in the unlikely event you have to make an emergency landing.

Pick the smoothest, most level landing site you can, and land into the wind to give you the lowest possible touchdown speed. Your landing attitude should be fairly flat, with the float tips raised just enough to avoid digging them into the ground. Try not to land in a full-stall attitude. The extreme nose-up angle could cause the sterns of the floats to strike the ground hard enough to pitch you forward onto the bows of the floats, which would then dig in and flip the plane onto its back. Even in a fairly flat attitude, the drag on the bottom of the floats will tend to pitch the nose down; so be prepared to pull the stick or yoke all the way back to keep the floats from digging into the ground. The amount of drag exerted on the floats will vary with the type of surface on which you're landing. A grass- or crop-covered field will not create nearly as much friction on the float bottoms as a field covered with bare dirt or rocks.

If you're unable to find an obstacle-free touchdown site, the fact that you are in a floatplane will really pay off. Those big floats projecting out ahead of the plane with their struts and spreader bars make wonderful energy absorbers in the event of a crash. As long as you maintain control and touch down in a normal attitude, there will be an awful lot of sheet metal between you and whatever stops the plane to soak up the impact. While the plane may end up a total mess, you and your passengers will probably walk away.

If you experience an engine failure over a forest, head into the wind and try to land in the thickest foliage you can find. Trees that are close together and have a lot of branches will help cushion the impact, as will the floats and struts. It's better to come down on top of the trees than to try and land in a clear area that's too small and risk slamming into the tree trunks. Use full flaps and touch down at the slowest possible speed, but don't stall the plane. Doing so will cause the nose to drop, and you may plummet down between the trees and hit the ground nose first.

If you land in the trees and your plane comes to a stop before it reaches the ground, be very careful getting out. You don't want to come through the landing unscathed only to break a leg falling off a branch. Your mooring lines may come in handy if you're still some distance above the ground. Unless there's an immediate danger of fire, don't be in such a hurry to get out of the plane that you forget your survival gear. You'll just have to climb back up and get it later.

NIGHT LANDINGS

Some floatplane pilots make night landings on a routine basis, but to the average pilot, a night landing should be considered only as a last resort. In fact, if you have a choice between landing on an unfamiliar body of water on a dark night or on a nearby lighted airport, choose the airport. You may have to replace the keels of your floats afterward, but landing on pavement you can see is a lot safer than landing on water you can't see.

One of the difficulties encountered when making a water landing at night is finding the water, especially if the night is a dark one. A particular lake I fly to on a regular basis has several acres of flat ground at one end, covered with shrubs and blackberry bushes. The area is crisscrossed with drainage ditches and littered with rocks. It would not be a good place to land a floatplane; yet at night, this patch of ground looks just like part of the lake. It's impossible to tell where the water ends and the ground begins. This is one reason you should plan to do night landings only on bodies of water with which you are very familiar.

The most dangerous thing about a night landing is the fact that it's difficult, and sometimes impossible, to determine if the surface of the water is a safe landing spot. Moving boats are supposed to have their running lights illuminated, but some people forget to turn them on, or they may not work at all. Running lights seem to be the first things to quit on a new boat, and the canoes and small, outboard-powered skiffs normally encountered on lakes don't have them to begin with. The only way to see all the boats, rafts, barges, and other large floating objects that may be out on the water is to position your airplane in such a way that whatever light is in the sky will reflect off the surface toward you. Any large objects will appear as black shapes against the gray or silver color of the water.

While you may be able to pick out large objects on the surface, there is no way you'll be able to spot deadheads, floating logs, and the other types of floating debris that can do so much damage to your floats. Areas of shallow water and underwater obstructions will also be hidden from your view; so always land well out from shoreline if you are unfamiliar with the area.

Night landings are made much easier if there are lights along the shore of the lake. The light reflecting off the water will give you an idea of your height above the surface, and it will tell you your distance from the shoreline. The reflections will also let you see how rough the surface of the water is, and whether or not there is an obstacle in your path. Two of the best places to land at night are New York City's East River and Seattle's Lake Union. Both these bodies of water are surrounded by apartment, office, and industrial buildings, and the reflection of hundreds of lights makes it quite easy to judge your altitude above the surface. The approach to Lake Union, with which I am very familiar, is over land, and the well-lit city streets below make it possible to fly a very accurate approach to this rather small lake. Because of the proximity to residential neighborhoods, I try to avoid taking off at night, but small planes don't make much noise when they land, so Lake Union makes a good place to end a flight that has continued beyond sunset.

Your landing should be made into the wind, but at night, this isn't as easy to do as it sounds. As a floatplane pilot, you will have learned to read the wind from all kinds of indicators—blowing smoke, bending trees, the sails on sailboats, and wind streaks—all of which are useless at night. If the sky is luminescent enough to provide a good reflection off the water, you may be able to read the wind direction from the waves, but you'll probably have to rely on the area weather reports and forecasts for a general idea of the wind conditions. If the lake or harbor is located near an airport with an operating control tower, you can get an approximate idea of the surface winds from a controller or the ATIS broadcasts. Otherwise, you're on your own.

If there are lights on the upwind shore of the lake, pick the brightest one and land straight toward it. Its reflection will make a runway of sorts, and if a boat should stray into your landing lane, you'll be able to spot it im-mediately. Even when you're at pattern altitude, lights along the shore will give you a good indication of the surface conditions. If the reflections extend a long way out from shore, the water is smooth. If they are short and indistinct, the water is rough.

The procedure for landing at night is identical to the procedure for landing on glassy water, except you'll be more dependent on your instruments. Unless the sky is very bright, you won't have a distinct horizon in front of you, so you'll have to use your plane's gyro horizon to keep the wings level and maintain the correct pitch angle during your descent.

Remember, glassy-water landings use up a lot of space. Make sure you have enough lake in front of you to complete the landing. A light on shore will help, but make sure it's really a light. I've heard stories of pilots who ran out of lake because they mistook a bright star low on the horizon for a light on shore.

It's a strange and slightly scary feeling to be sitting there in the glow from the instrument panel, maintaining a constant attitude and descent rate through the blackness that surrounds you, heading towards what you hope is smooth, unobstructed water. The last 30 seconds or so will seem like an eternity, and you'll begin to wonder if you're ever going to land. About the time you decide that all your careful calculations were wrong and that you're going to run out of lake and crash, you'll feel the plane enter ground effect and touch down smoothly on the water. Believe me, it's a nice feeling.

Turning on your landing light won't make it any easier to find the water, but it will show you if the surface is covered with whitecaps. It will also warn any boaters in the area of your intentions to land. If your light is a powerful one, it may even pick out logs or other floating debris in time for you to take evasive action, but don't count on it. In this regard, night landings are always risky. Since it will be almost impossible to tell how rough the surface of the water is, you'll just have to wait until you actually touch down to find out. Be prepared to put in full power and go around, because if you get bounced back in the air as soon as you land, the water may be too rough for your plane. Although whitecaps will be easy to see, boat wakes, swells, and waves that aren't quite big enough to break will merge into the overall blackness of the water. If the water proves to be too rough for a safe landing, you'll have no other choice but to find somewhere else to land, which could be very difficult on a dark night in unfamiliar territory.

As a general rule, you should avoid flying a floatplane at night. The risks are just too great. The Canadian government feels the same way, and passed a law making it illegal to take off or land a seaplane after what is known as "civil twilight." The law does not prohibit seaplanes from *flying* at night, only from taking off or landing; so pilots can take off in Canada just before sunset ad make a night flight to a destination in the United States if they want.

SURVIVAL GEAR

Much has been written about the type of survival gear that should be carried in an airplane, and there are several courses specifically designed to help people survive a plane crash in the wilderness. If you are planning a flight over sparsely settled country, it's essential that you carry at least a minimum of survival gear, regardless of the type of airplane you're flying. If you're going to be making the trip in a floatplane, there are some additional items you should carry, but first, let's look at the basics.

A good place to start is the list of emergency equipment the state of Alaska requires all aircraft to have on board while they are inside Alaska's borders. In the summer, from April to October, the following items are required:

- ☐ Food for each occupant sufficient to sustain life for 2 weeks.
- ☐ One axe or hatchet.
- ☐ One first aid kit.
- ☐ One pistol, shotgun, or rifle and ammunition.
- ☐ One small gill net and an assortment of tackle, such as hooks, flies, lines, and sinkers.
- ☐ One knife.
- ☐ Two small boxes of matches.
- ☐ One mosquito headnet for each occupant.
- ☐ Two small signaling devices, such as colored smoke bombs, railroad fuses, or Very pistol shells in sealed metal containers.

From October to April, the following items must be carried in addition to the basic equipment just listed:

- ☐ One pair of snowshoes.
- ☐ One sleeping bag.
- ☐ One wool blanket for each occupant over 4 years old.

Canada also has a list of required emergency equipment for aircraft operating within its borders, and while the list is similar to Alaska's, there are some additional items:

- ☐ Cooking utensils.

- ☐ One stove and a supply of fuel or a self-contained means of providing heat for cooking when you are operating north of the tree line.
- ☐ One portable compass.
- ☐ One flexible saw blade or equivalent cutting tool.
- ☐ Snare wire at least 30 feet or 9 meters and instructions for its use.
- ☐ Tents or engine and wing covers of suitable design, colored, or having panels colored, in international orange or other high-visibility color, sufficient to accommodate all persons carried when operating north of the tree line.
- ☐ A suitable survival instruction manual.
- ☐ One large panel of fabric or plastic colored in international orange or other high-visibility color to mark the crash site.

Obviously, the contents of your survival kit will depend a lot on where you're flying. Floatplane pilots in Florida and Louisiana probably won't have much use for snowshoes, but most of the items listed here would be useful anywhere. If the requirement for 2 weeks worth of food conjures up images of stuffing several bulging grocery sacks into the back of your plane, relax. The human body can survive for 2 weeks on very little food, and you can pack a lot of freeze-dried foods, raisins, and candy bars into a very small container. I have a friend who ferries floatplanes up and down the Inside Passage between Seattle and Alaska, and he carries all the required summer survival gear in one small duffle bag.

Make sure you include a good survival manual which covers the type of country over which you're going to be flying. The worst problem after a crash is recovering from the shock of the accident and organizing the survival efforts. A survival manual with step-by-step instructions will make it easier for you to begin constructing a shelter, making the site more visible from the air, organizing your food and water supplies, and so forth.

Handguns are illegal in Canada; so if you're going to be traveling in that country, you'll have to carry some other type of firearm. I've found the best survival weapon to be a single-barrel, 12-gauge shotgun. It's inexpensive, and the simple, break-open action will stand up to a lot of abuse. You can use both birdshot (for small game), and heavy, rifled slugs (in case a bear tries to participate in your survival efforts) in the same gun. The shotgun I prefer, a Harrington & Richardson Model 088, is small and light enough to fit easily into the baggage compartment with the rest of my survival gear. Not only will this weapon comply with both the Alaskan and Canadian firearm requirements, but it will provide you with a very practical survival tool.

Insect protection is extremely important. Whether you're flying in Alaska, northeastern Canada, or Louisiana, the bugs can drive you nuts. Mosquitos are not the only culprits. The northeastern and northcentral United States and Canada are home to the notorious blackfly, a small, biting fly which has been known to drive deer so insane that they literally run themselves to death. By comparison, mosquitos are friendly. Blackflies are bad enough on a regular camping trip, but in a survival situation, they could easily disrupt all your efforts to remain calm and organized. Nothing is totally effective against insects; so the solution is to carry several forms of protection. Plenty of insect repellent is a must, and it's also a good idea to carry a headnet for each occupant of the airplane, even if it's not required by law. If you're planning to wear short-sleeved shirts during your trip, carry a long-sleeved shirt with you, anyway. It will help protect you from insects if you're forced down.

The mylar "space blankets" available in many sporting goods stores take up very little room and may save the day if your sleeping bag gets soaked. A large plastic tarp doesn't take up much room either, and in the event of an emergency, it can be used as a temporary shelter or a windbreak. They are available in a variety of bright colors, and an orange or yellow tarp will make your location easier to spot from the air. Be sure to include several large, plastic garbage bags in your survival kit. In an emergency, they make excellent rain ponchos, and they will be invaluable if you have to treat someone suffering from hypothermia.

Since you're flying a floatplane, you should have a life jacket on board for each occupant. The requirements for life jackets are getting stricter in both the United States and Canada. Canada has taken the lead, and as of December 31, 1983, all aircraft operating in Canada farther than gliding distance from shore, or taking off and landing on the water, must carry an approved life jacket meeting the Federal Aviation Administration Technical Standard Order (TSO) C13c. The life jacket must be equipped with a light, and after May 1, 1987, all adult life jackets must have a buoyancy of at least 35 pounds. Older approved jackets have a buoyancy of anywhere from 9 to 20 pounds and would not always right a wearer who was face down in the water. An average adult has a buoyant weight of 10 to 12 pounds when immersed in water. Canadian law also requires that any aircraft operating more than 50 nautical miles from shore carry a life raft.

In January 1983, the FAA passed TSO C13d, which sets the standards for life jackets required in the United States. As of this writing, FAA-approved life jackets are only required on aircraft operating more than 50 nautical miles from shore. A jacket meeting the TSO C13d requirements must be able to be donned in 15 seconds, must have a 35-pound buoyancy, and must be able to right the wearer from a face-down position within 5 seconds. A light is not required unless the flight will take the aircraft more than 30 minutes flying time or 100 nautical miles from shore.

If your float flying consists of visiting lakes in the United States that are less than 100 nautical miles across, you aren't legally required to carry life jackets, but you should anyway. A 1/2-mile swim might be as impossible as a 50-mile swim for a child or someone who is out of shape.

Store the life jackets where they will be easy to reach in a hurry (not in the baggage compartment), and periodically check the CO_2 bottles for leakage. If your life jackets have lights, make sure the batteries are still good. Whenever you plan to conduct a flight at low altitude over water, you and your passengers should put on life jackets before you take off. An engine failure could put you in the water very quickly, and you may not have time to get a life jacket out of its pouch under the seat and put it on.

The airplanes I fly are equipped with life jackets, but I prefer to wear a flotation vest. The vest has a buoyancy of 15 pounds, and while it won't right me if I'm face down in the water, it will support me if I right myself. Of course, in the event of an accident, I would put a life jacket on over the vest, but by already having the vest on, I'm that much better off. The advantage of wearing a flotation vest, or one of the long-sleeve flotation coats, is that it's comfortable; so you'll be more likely to wear it. It will also offer some protection against hypothermia should you end up in the water.

HYPOTHERMIA

If your floatplane flips over or sinks, the greatest threat to your life will not be the accident itself, but the possibility of succumbing to hypothermia while you await rescue. *Hypothermia* is defined as subnormal body temperature, and many people don't realize how dangerous it can be. What's worse, many of the things we do to warm ourselves up only succeed in cooling us down even more.

Hypothermia is not as dangerous to people living in warmer, southern climates as it is to people living or traveling in the northern United States, Canada, and Alaska, but the fact that you're flying in Florida doesn't mean you can forget about hypothermia altogether. If your plane flips over on a southern lake some evening and the night is a cool one, you can succumb to hypothermia as easily as the person who falls off a fishing boat in the Gulf of Alaska. The only difference will be in the amount of time it takes for hypothermia to set in. If the water temperature is less than 50 degrees, hypothermia will occur within minutes of immersion unless the body is somehow insulated from the cold.

The critical factor in hypothermia is the temperature of the body's core where the organs necessary to sustain life are located. The normal temperature of the human body averages around 98.6 degrees, and this temperature doesn't have to drop very far before hypothermia sets in. A drop of only 2 or 3 degrees in core temperature will make a person extremely cold, and he will begin to shiver violently. This is the first stage of hypothermia. If the temperature of the body core continues to drop, but remains above 90 degrees, the victim will complain of being bitterly cold, will continue to shiver violently, and may be slightly uncoordinated. He will, however, be able to move around fairly normally, will be coherent, and, with the proper rewarming techniques, will survive. If the core temperature falls below 90 degrees, the victim will be uncoordinated and unable to walk. He will probably seem disoriented and be unable to speak coherently, and may also be very stiff. If the core temperature drops below 80 degrees, the victim will most likely lose consciousness. Statistics show that 65 percent of the victims whose core temperatures fall below 90 degrees will die if they are not treated properly during the rewarming process.

Prevention

If you find yourself in the water after an accident, there are several things you can do to delay the onslaught of hypothermia. First, try to get as much of your body out of the water as you can. When a floatplane flips over, it generally remains floating upside down if the floats have not been damaged. By climbing onto the bottom of a float, you won't lose body heat to the water. If the plane sinks, try to find some floating debris, such as a seat cushion, to help raise your body even a few extra inches out of the water.

Don't swim or thrash about in an effort to stay warm. While this activity will generate some heat, it will also speed up the pulse and increase the flow of warm blood to the arms and legs where it will be cooled and returned to the heart, lowering the core temperature even faster.

Unless the shore is very close, don't attempt to swim to it. Cold water can bring even an excellent swimmer to a stop within 3/4 mile. Remain motionless in the water or on the float until help comes. This is one reason it's so important to be wearing a life jacket. If you're in the water, the jacket will buoy you up, and you won't have to move your arms or legs to remain on the surface. If you are by yourself, bring your knees up to your chest. This will slow down the heat loss. If you're in the water with other people, group together to hold the heat in as long as possible. If you and your passengers are sitting on the bottoms of the floats, huddle close together to minimize the heat loss. These techniques can double your survival time in the water.

While it may be hard to force yourself to remain motionless and do nothing in the face of what seems like certain death, you will only hasten death by thrashing about or attempting to swim to a distant shore. If the water is 50 degrees, the survival time for an adult dressed in light clothing and wearing a life jacket is 2 1/2 to 3 hours. Children succumb to hypothermia faster than adults because their smaller size affords less insulation against heat loss. The longer you can remain alive, the greater will be your chances of being rescued.

Obviously, your actions will be dependent upon the conditions in which you find yourself. The survival times and techniques just described are based upon the 50-degree water of Washington's Puget Sound. If you find yourself bobbing around in the Gulf of Mexico, your situation, from a temperature point of view at least, won't be as serious, and if you're a good swimmer, you may be able to reach a shore you would have no hope of reaching if you were in the cold waters of the Sound.

Treatment

If you and your passengers have safely made it to shore after a capsizing or sinking, but you notice one or more members of your party showing signs of hypothermia, there are specific rules to follow when attempting to reverse the cooling process:

☐ First, do not allow the victim to exercise or move about, even if he wants to do so. This will only serve to move warm blood away from the vital organs to the extremities where it will be cooled and returned to the heart. The victim should lie still until the body temperature begins to rise. It may take well over an hour before the victim begins to show signs of recovery.

□ Handle the victim gently. Most hypothermia victims die of heart failure, and rough handling may cause ventricular fibrillation. If necessary, move the victim by stretcher, or by carrying in such a way that he is not bumped or jostled and does not have to actively hold onto the rescuer. Do not rub or massage the victim. Massaging the chest area may cause the heart to fibrillate.

□ Remove all wet clothing immediately, but remember to handle the victim gently as you do so. If you roughly turn the victim over in your haste to remove the wet clothes, the movement could be enough to cause the victim's heart to fail.

□ Replace the victim's wet clothing with dry clothing if possible, because the moisture in the wet clothes will begin to evaporate and lower the body's temperature even more. If no dry clothes are available, wring out the wet clothes thoroughly and put them back on the victim. Wool garments are especially valuable in this situation, because they will retain heat even when wet.

□ Wrapping the victim in a plastic tarp or other nonporous material will help prevent heat loss from evaporation and convection (windchill).

□ Try to place some sort of insulation between the victim and the ground. Even a plastic tarp or rain poncho will help slow the transfer of critical body heat to the soil or sand beneath the victim.

□ Protect the victim from the wind by placing him behind a boulder, log, or other windbreak. The movement of air will carry heat away from the skin, and as the body tries to replace this heat by increasing the flow of warm blood, the core temperature will begin to drop. In fact, loss of body heat from windchill alone can bring on hypothermia, and it's important that hikers, backpackers, boaters, and bicyclists protect themselves from the cooling effects of the wind. Waterproof rain gear provides excellent wind protection, and if this type of clothing is available, it should be placed over the victim.

□ The appearance of a rescue helicopter brings another problem. The downwash from a hovering helicopter can exceed 100 miles per hour, which could rapidly drive the victim's body temperature below the critical point. If the victim is going to be evacuated by helicopter, it's especially important to protect the head and neck from the rotor wash with plastic or some other nonporous fabric. Ideally, the victim's entire body should be wrapped in windproof garments or material before the rescue helicopter positions itself overhead, and especially if the victim is going to be lifted directly from the water.

Rewarming

Contrary to popular belief, giving the victim warm liquids will not speed up the rewarming process. In fact, it will do just the opposite, because the act of drinking sets up a reflex which moves blood to the extremities and skin. There, the blood will be cooled, and when it returns to the heart, the core temperature will drop more. Do not give the victim alcoholic beverages. Alcohol makes people feel warmer because it causes an increase in the flow of warm blood to the skin, but this heat is easily lost through evaporation or convection, and the overall effect is to lower the temperature of the body's core.

The same three areas of the body which are so important to protect from the cold in the first place are also the areas where heat should be applied to begin rewarming a hypothermia victim. They are: the head and neck; the sides of the chest, and the groin. There is little insulation on these parts of the body, and blood from these areas is quickly transferred back to the heart. Apply heat to these areas using hot water bottles, heating pads, stones warmed by a fire, or anything else you can think of. The warmed blood will quickly pass back to the heart, and the temperature of the body core will begin to rise.

Cover the entire body with blankets during the rewarming process. If no other heat source is available, place the victim in a sleeping bag with one or two other people. In this case, all clothing should be removed to facilitate the heat transfer from the rescuers to the victim; the contact must be skin to skin. If a fire is used to warm the victim, remove the victim's insulating clothing because it will prevent the heat from reaching the body. Finally, the victim should be taken to a medical facility as soon as possible for further treatment and observation because further complications, such as pneumonia or heart trouble, could arise.

Hypothermia is a quiet killer. Most victims do not realize how serious their condition may be. All they know is that they are cold. It does not take long for the condition to progress to the danger point, but by then, the victims will be unable to help themselves. By keeping your head after an accident, and following the basic guidelines just outlined, the chances are excellent that a real tragedy can be averted.

FLOATPLANE RECOVERY

Your first responsibility after an accident is for the health and safety of your passengers and yourself. Only after everyone has been safely returned to civilization should you turn your attention to your airplane. Unless it has been damaged beyond repair, you, or your insurance company, will probably want to get it back. If you managed to land on a flat piece of ground without damaging the plane, recovery will be a matter of fixing the problem that forced you down in the first place and transporting the plane to the nearest body of water large enough to permit a takeoff. This process will probably involve a partial disassembly of the airplane so it can be moved by truck.

It may be possible to fly the plane out once it has been fixed if you were lucky enough to land on a very long, very flat, grassy field, but the chances of being able to do so are pretty slim since you'll need at least as much space as you would for a normal water takeoff. If you're in the vicinity of an airport, your floatplane can be taken there for repair, and then by using a special dolly, it can

be flown off the runway (Fig. 18-1). The dolly will probably have to be constructed on the spot, or you may be able to locate an operator who will ship one to you.

If you went down in sparsely settled country, your plane will probably have to be recovered by helicopter. Here again, the plane will have to be partially disassembled so the helicopter can sling it out. This is an extremely expensive process, but if your plane is relatively undamaged, it will probably be worth it. In some parts of the world, Alaska and northern Canada for example, airplane parts are so valuable that salvage companies will often purchase and recover a plane that is wrecked beyond repair just so they can strip off and sell all the undamaged parts.

When a floatplane capsizes in the water, its floats will generally continue to support it even though the plane is upside down. If the plane went over onto its back because a wing tip or a float dug into the water while it was moving at high speed, it may have sustained some damage, but if the plane was simply blown over by a strong wind while at a mooring or taxiing slowly, it will

Fig. 18-1. A Cessna 180 lifting using a specially constructed dolly to take off from a paved runway. When the plane lifts off, brakes are activated which bring the dolly to a stop so it can be retrieved. (Courtesy of the EDO Corporation)

probably be completely intact. The problem is to return the plane to an upright position without causing any more damage to the airframe, which is not an easy thing to do. Too many undamaged, capsized floatplanes have been totally destroyed by inept salvage crews. If your plane should ever become inverted in the water for any reason, make sure the people you engage to recover it are experienced in the field of floatplane salvage.

If your plane capsizes, don't allow anyone to tow it into shallow water. Towing the plane to shallow water increases the risk of dragging it upside down across the bottom, which would result in substantial damage. If it's necessary to move the plane, it must be towed extremely slowly. The wing, tail, and control surfaces were designed to fly through air, not water, and they can easily be buckled if they are forced through the water at too great a speed.

Don't begin the recovery operation until you're prepared to deal with the airplane once it's lifted out of the water. Interior components, radios, and instruments will have to be removed immediately and dried out to prevent rust or corrosion from forming, and the engine will have to be flushed out, dried, and protected against further corrosion.

If the plane has been immersed in salt water, the situation is very serious. The water will work its way into every corner and crack of the airframe, and unless the entire plane is thoroughly flushed out with fresh water, corrosion will start to form that could eventually render the plane unairworthy. A method often used to halt the spread of corrosion on a plane that has just been removed from salt water is to quickly remove the wings, tail surfaces, and engine, and immerse all these components, together with the fuselage, in a fresh-water lake. The lack of oxygen will slow the spread of corrosion, and as the fresh water permeates the entire airplane, all the salt will be flushed away.

If your plane has capsized near the end of the day, it would be better to leave it in the water overnight and begin the recovery operation in the morning since it is

Fig. 18-2. Mechanics at Kenmore Air Harbor begin the long process of rebuilding a de Havilland Beaver. This one was acquired from military surplus. The company specializes in taking old, worn out or wrecked Beavers and turning them into airplanes that are better than they were when they first rolled out of the factory.

vital that the flushing and drying operations be carried out as soon as the plane is exposed to the air. Carefully tow the plane to water deep enough to safely float the plane, but shallow enough to enable recovery if it should sink. If the plane is in tidal waters, make sure it won't hit the bottom when the tide goes out. Put out several anchors to keep the plane from drifting into shallow water, and mark the spot with a separately anchored buoy. In the unlikely event that the plane should sink, the buoy will enable you to find it in the morning.

There are many ways to right a capsized floatplane. Jay J. Frey, the EDO Corporation's vice president in charge of float operation, recommends the following technique in his book, *How to Fly Floats*. Position a salvage vessel equipped with a crane off the tail of the airplane and position the end of the boom so it is directly above the propeller. Place a lifting bridle around the propeller and slowly and gently raise the nose of the airplane out of the water. It's important to have plenty of extension on the boom so the plane will not be pulled back into the salvage vessel as it is being raised. Lift the plane in small increments, allowing time for the water to drain from the fuselage and wings between lifts. This step is especially important if the floatplane is fabric-covered, because the weight of the water could easily rip the fabric off the airframe.

When the lifting rings on the upper surfaces of the wings are exposed, secure the plane to the boom with a temporary line and reattach the lifting bridle to the rings. Remove the temporary line and continue lifting the plane until it is in a vertical position. After pumping the water out of the float compartments that are above the surface, attach a line to the tiedown ring on the tail and, using another boat, pull the tail of the floatplane away from the primary salvage vessel. This action will restore the plane to an upright position, and it can be lifted into the air in a level attitude. Before lifting the plane clear of the water, be sure to pump out the remaining float compartments so the weight of the water trapped inside won't stress or break the float struts or their attach points.

If the plane is structurally undamaged, it can be towed to shore on its own floats, but if you suspect it may have sustained damage, particularly to the float system, the plane should be set onto the deck of the salvage vessel or transported to shore while suspended from the crane. As soon as the floatplane is set on shore, begin the process of flushing, cleaning, and drying immediately. Repairing the damage sustained during the accident is secondary to protecting the plane from corrosion.

If you have an accident and are in doubt as to the best method of recovering your airplane, a long-distance call to a seaplane base experienced in the techniques of floatplane recovery and repair will be well worth the cost (Fig. 18-2). If you are unfamiliar with these facilities, a call to one of the float manufacturers or the national headquarters of the Seaplane Pilots Association can get you the names of the repair facilities in your area.

I hope you never have to use any of the information contained in this chapter. The modern floatplane is a strong, reliable machine, and as long as you exercise good judgment while operating it, your flights will always end with both you and your plane on an even keel.

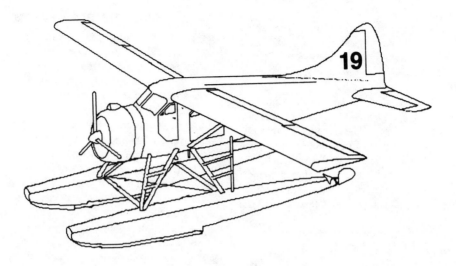

The Cross-Country Floatplane

T HE DAY THE WORDS, *AIRPLANE, SINGLE-ENGINE sea,* are added to your pilot's certificate will be a proud one, indeed. All those hours of learning and practice will have paid off, and you'll join the ranks of pilots who have discovered both beauty and adventure in the world of floatplanes. Whether your preference is for the awesome silence of glacier-draped coastal fjords, the vast serenity of the north woods lake country, or the dazzling blue waters of the Florida Keys, a floatplane provides countless hours of enjoyment as you fish, hunt, camp, or just relax amid some of the most beautiful scenery nature has to offer.

The same capabilities that make a floatplane so unique are also responsible for many of the floatplane's limitations, and taking a cross-country trip requires careful planning. If you're flying a landplane, the large number of airports throughout the United States and Canada makes it easy to plan a fairly direct route. Such is not the case if you're flying a floatplane, because although lakes and rivers offer countless landing sites, there are relatively few places where you can get fuel. Fuel availability is usually the primary concern when planning a cross-country trip in a floatplane, and the location of the seaplane bases in your area may force you to take

a circuitous route to your destination.

For the operators of older floatplanes designed to use 80-octane fuel, the growing number of Supplemental Type Certificates (STCs) allowing aircraft to use automotive fuel turns every boat marina into a potential refueling stop. This situation doesn't help the owners of new or high-performance floatplanes, all of which require high-octane aviation fuel.

Fuel is easier to obtain in some areas than it is in others. The Pacific Northwest, western and coastal British Columbia, the Yukon Territory, and Alaska all depend heavily upon the floatplane; so there are many seaplane facilities where fuel is available. The same is true of the lake country in Maine, Minnesota, Ontario, and Quebec. The central United States and Canada, on the other hand, have very few seaplane facilities, and you will have to do some careful planning if you want to fly through these areas in an airplane equipped with straight floats. In this regard, amphibious floatplanes give you the best of both worlds, for they allow you to use regular airports if seaplane bases are scarce or you want to keep your plane out of salt water. If you're going to be doing a lot of your flying in areas where seaplane facilities are few and far between, the versatility of an amphibious float may well be worth its higher cost.

In some parts of the country where there were no natural sites suitable for the establishment of a seaplane base, the local residents created their own sites. These artificial seaplane "ponds" can be found in Juneau, Alaska, where a large pond is located next to the runway at the International Airport, and in the southern United States, where floatplanes are sometimes used to support the oil fields in the swamps and along the coast (Fig. 19-1). Juneau's pond was created when earth was excavated to build the airport runway, and it eliminated the need for a separate fueling facility for seaplanes. The same trucks that fuel the landplanes on the airport can drive over to the pond and fuel the floatplanes. Other coastal towns in Alaska are considering the construction of similar ponds, especially those where high winds and rough water often make it difficult to land and dock a floatplane in the harbor.

CHOOSING A ROUTE

The most important thing to have when choosing a cross-country route is current information. You need to know how many seaplane facilities are located along, or near, your proposed route; where they are located; and if they have the type of fuel you require. The closure of just one seaplane base can leave a gap in your proposed route too large to cross and force you to pick an alternate route that may take you hundreds of miles out of your way. For this reason, it is vital that you have the most up-to date facilities information available *before* you begin to plan your trip.

The best source of route information is the Seaplane Pilots Association (SPA). The staff has compiled a directory of the best routes along both coasts and across the country for pilots flying airplanes on straight floats. They also have a listing of all the seaplane bases in the United States, with information on the type of fuel they sell and the services each one has to offer (Fig. 19-2). This information is in addition to the directory of seaplane training facilities the SPA publishes in its *Water Flying Annual*. These directories are kept current, and you can call the SPA for the latest information regarding a specific route.

In addition, the SPA has regional field directors located throughout the country. Their names are listed in each copy of the quarterly publication, *Water Flying*, as well as the *Water Flying Annual*. A letter or phone call to the field directors located along your proposed route can net you all sorts of valuable and current information. Of course, the best way to obtain current information about the seaplane facilities along your route is to contact them directly.

KNOW THE REGULATIONS

The regulations governing the operation of seaplanes vary from state to state, and between the United States and Canada, so it's important that you learn the regulations covering the specific areas you plan to visit. Some lakes, rivers, and coastal waters are closed to seaplanes; so you should contact the state aeronautical department in every state along your route to find out if any of the places you plan to visit are closed.

Finding out exactly which waters are open and which are closed to seaplanes can be a time-consuming process because of the number of local, state, and federal agencies involved. Some lakes and rivers are under the jurisdiction of the Army Corps of Engineers; some are governed by state regulations; some by city ordinances; and some are privately controlled. If the body of water lies within the boundaries of a national park or forest, it may be under the jurisdiction of the Parks Department or the Bureau of Land Management. Sometimes a body of water falls under the jurisdiction of several agencies, and one agency's decision concerning seaplane operations may be overruled by another agency. It can get confusing, and the best solution is to contact the appropriate agencies directly. The seaplane bases can also provide you with information about the regulations currently in effect in their area.

It's not within the scope of this book to list all the different seaplane regulations currently in force in the United States and Canada, but by way of illustration, here are some typical examples of the regulations you will encounter. These particular regulations apply only to lakes in the Portland District of Oregon State that are under the jurisdiction of the United States Army Corps of Engineers, so do not assume that the bodies of water along your route or at your destination are covered by a similar set of regulations.

1. Seaplanes may be operated seven days a week between sunrise and sunset at all Portland District Lakes with the exception of Big Cliff and Applegate lakes.

2. Once on the water, seaplanes shall be considered boats and must be operated in accordance with marine rules of the road. Seaplanes in the water may taxi to any area on the lake subject to the restrictions for those lakes described under Specific Provisions.

3. Commercial operation of seaplanes at Corps lakes

Fig. 19-1. A floatplane pond in Louisiana.

is prohibited unless authorized by the District Engineer.

4. Seaplane operators planning to land on Corps lakes should notify the Project Manager's office beforehand. Fluctuating lake levels or heavy recreational activity may necessitate use of alternate landing areas.

5. Seaplanes on project lands and waters in excess of twenty-four hours shall be securely moored at mooring facilities and at locations permitted by the District Engineer. Seaplanes may be temporarily moored on project waters and lands, except in areas prohibited by the District Engineer, for periods less than twenty-four hours provided that (1) the mooring is safe, secure, and accomplished so as not to damage nor endanger the rights of the Government or members of the public and (2) the operator remains in the vicinity of the seaplane and reasonably available to relocate the seaplane if necessary.

6. Seaplanes are prohibited within five hundred feet of dam structures or as otherwise indicated under Specific Provisions.

7. Seaplanes are prohibited within two hundred feet of any marked swimming area.

8. Seaplanes are prohibited within two hundred feet of lake shorelines except when taxiing to and from the shoreline. Taxi speed shall not exceed five knots.

9. Prior to using any designated public boat ramp, the seaplane operator must have permission from either the Corps Project Manager or the specific boat ramp manager if ramps are within areas managed by other entities.

Following these general rules of operation is a list of Specific Provisions, two samples of which read as follows:

1. Lake Bonneville—Seaplanes are prohibited within one thousand feet upstream and two thousand feet downstream of the spillway and five hundred feet upstream and six hundred feet downstream of the powerhouses. Restricted areas are designated by signs placed at conspicuous places. CAUTION: Seaplane operators should be aware that Indian fishing nets throughout the lake could be a hazard during landing and takeoff.

2. Cottage Grove Lake—Seaplanes are prohibited

Fig. 19-2. Kenmore Air Harbor, located at the north end of Seattle's Lake Washington, is the largest floatplane facility in the United States. This picture was taken during the summer. During the winter, the facility is jammed with both private and commercial floatplanes, as well as de Havilland Beavers that are brought down from Alaska for overhaul or refurbishing.

south of a line marked by buoys across the lake from the east shoreline near Wilson Creek Park to the west shoreline near Cedar Creek. WARNING: Seaplane operators should be aware that heavy boat traffic may be encountered on weekends and holidays.

As you can see, you will need more information than you can get off of sectional and WAC charts. Besides a copy of the regulations themselves, you'll need topographical maps or marine charts in order to locate the various points, bays, coves, creeks, islands, and bridges used to designate specific areas of operation.

Regulations vary among states, cities, and even years. A lake or harbor that was open to seaplane operations last year may be closed this year, and vice versa. The regulations address a multitude of issues. Because of local noise ordinances, some bodies of water are open only to

seaplanes with three-bladed propellers, while on others, crowded conditions have resulted in regulations prohibiting high-speed step taxiing. What's legal in one place may be illegal someplace else; so make sure you know all the current regulations in force along your route.

In addition to the regulations governing your floatplane while it's on the water, you'll need to know the regulations governing your airplane while it's in the air. Part 91 of the Federal Aviation Regulations contains the general operating and flight rules for aircraft in United Stated airspace, and I'm certainly not going to attempt to list them all here. If you plan to make a flight into Canada, however, you should be aware of the differences between its VFR regulations and the ones here in the United States.

In Canada, the minimum visibility for VFR flight in

controlled airspace is 3 miles, and you must remain either 500 feet above, 500 feet below, or 1 mile horizontally from, the clouds. The minimums in the United States are 3 miles of visibility while remaining either 500 feet above, 1000 feet below, or 2000 feet horizontally from, the clouds. The Canadian VFR minimums in *uncontrolled* airspace less than 700 feet above ground level (agl) are 1 mile of visibility while remaining clear of the clouds. The minimums in the United States are the same, but they apply to any altitude up to 1200 feet agl.

The VFR minimums in controlled Canadian airspace above 700 feet agl are 1 mile of visibility, and you must remain 500 feet above or below, or 1 mile horizontally from, the clouds. In the United States, the VFR minimums in uncontrolled airspace above 1200 agl are 1 mile of visibility, and you must fly either 500 feet above, 1000 feet below, or 2000 feet horizontally from, the clouds. There is a special area west of the coastal mountains in British Columbia which extends out to, and includes, Vancouver Island and the Queen Charlotte Islands, in which the minimum VFR visibility in uncontrolled airspace is 2 miles instead of 1 mile.

Flying "VFR-on-top" is an accepted practice in the United States (FAR 91.121a), but it is illegal in Canada. Also, VFR flights in Canada are conducted at odd or even thousand foot altitudes only, not the odd thousand plus 500 feet or even thousand plus 500 feet altitudes used in the United States.

If you're planning to fly VFR in Canada, you are required to carry enough fuel for the duration of your flight plus 45 minutes. In the United States, you are only required to have 30 minutes worth of reserve fuel unless you're planning to fly at night, when you must have a 45-minute reserve.

SALTWATER OPERATIONS

If your cross-country trip is going to require you to land and take off in salt water, you'll have to do battle with corrosion. Even if your floatplane has the optional corrosion-proofing package offered by most airframe manufacturers, there are several things you should do before your trip to help ward off the corrosive effects of salt water.

Every time you take off or land, the tail of your airplane is enveloped in spray. The spray will work its way through the seams and gaps in the skin and control surfaces and eventually become trapped in the countless nooks and crannies between the structural components inside the tail. Wherever water comes in contact with bare aluminum or steel, corrosion or rust will eventually be

the result, and if the water is salt water, the deterioration process will be very rapid. You can't prevent the spray from getting inside the after fuselage and tail, but you can prevent it from coming in contact with bare metal.

Crawl back into the rear of the fuselage and coat all metal surfaces with zinc chromate primer, followed by a coating of paralketone or grease. Then go over the entire plane and coat all the bare steel parts you can find— bolts, nuts, fasteners, engine-mount bolts and fittings, turnbuckles, wires, and cables—with paralketone or grease. Be careful not to get any paralketone on any moving parts, or on cables where they run through guides or pulleys. Put a generous coating of grease on all aileron, elevator, rudder, trim tab, door, and window hinges. A lot of spray gets blown up under the wing by the propeller; so lower the flaps and liberally coat the flap tracks, rollers, and pushrods with grease. Finally, grease the water rudder hinges and pivots and the pulleys that guide the steering and retraction cables. All this grease will get a little messy, and at the end of a day's flight you'll have dirty streaks on the sides, wings, and tail of your airplane, but grease is a lot easier to remove than corrosion.

Preparation is, however, only half the battle. Once you've entered a saltwater environment, it's vitally important that you perform preventative maintenance on a daily basis to keep corrosion from gaining a foothold on your plane. When you begin operations in salt water, thoroughly hose off your plane with fresh water at the end of each day's flying to remove all traces of salt that may have accumulated during takeoff and landing. Pay special attention to the aft fuselage and tail, as well as the sides and bottoms of the floats. If your plane is equipped with amphibious floats, flush out the wheel wells and give the main-wheel and nosewheel struts a good rinsing. Regrease any hinges that look like they need it.

It's also a good idea to spray the inside of the engine cowl, and the engine itself, with rust-preventing oil such such as WD-40. This oil will keep moisture and salt spray off the bare metal parts of the engine. The engines on many airplanes are painted, but as the engine heats up and cools off, the paint cracks and flakes away, exposing the bare metal underneath. The oil will prevent these areas from rusting. The best time to spray the engine is while it's still warm after a flight. Don't spray oil on the engine when it's hot.

PLANNING YOUR TRIP

When you are planning your trip's itinerary and schedule, keep in mind the fact that floatplanes have slower cruise speeds and shorter ranges than landplanes. Don't try to cover too much distance in one day, and make sure you can carry sufficient fuel for each leg of your trip. Call ahead to make sure fuel is available at the stops along your route. If you're going to an extremely remote area, you may have to arrange for fuel to be dropped off at specific locations along your route, or delivered to you at your destination, and these arrangements must be made well in advance of your departure. Incidentally, this can be a very expensive undertaking; 4 or 5 years ago, the price of delivered fuel in the Canadian arctic was as high as 25 dollars a gallon, and it is undoubtably more now.

If your trip is going to take you to areas devoid of established seaplane bases, you may have to refuel your plane with gas contained in 5-gallon cans or 55-gallon drums. The fuel in these containers is usually contaminated with water, dirt, and rust, so you will need some way of filtering these contaminants out as you pour the fuel into your tanks. One of the most popular filters is a chamois skin, which not only filters out the dirt and rust particles, but also absorbs water while allowing the fuel to pass through to the tank. It has recently been discovered, however, that the fine hairs from a chamois filter, particularly a new one, can get into the fuel and subsequently plug the injectors of a fuel-injected engine. Although the instances of this actually happening have been few, the FAA considers it a potentially dangerous situation, and has issued warnings about using chamois skins as fuel strainers. The alternative is to use a synthetic or paper filter of some sort.

Check the Weather

Allow time for weather delays. As a floatplane pilot, you're more dependent on weather than a landplane pilot, who at least doesn't have to worry about high winds making a runway surface too rough for takeoffs or landings. If you're flying in a coastal area, the often unpredictable marine weather can keep you tied to the dock for days, and fog is an ever-present problem. Start checking the weather along your route several days in advance of your departure. By watching the weather trends develop, you can get some idea of what to expect during your flight, and you will be better prepared to make the final go or no-go decision.

Get a thorough weather briefing before you leave, and pay particular attention to the surface winds and visibility. These two weather elements are the ones with which you'll be most concerned because most floatplane flights are conducted at relatively low altitudes above the ground. The surface winds will tell you how rough the water is

likely to be along your route, and the visibility will give you advance warning of haze, fog, or rain.

Maps and Charts

Make sure you have all the appropriate maps for the areas you'll be visiting. In addition to sectional and WAC charts, it's a good idea to carry en-route low-altitude charts, too. Even though they are designed to be used by pilots flying IFR, the en-route charts contain a lot of useful information for VFR pilots, as well. Airway and intersection locations, route distances, minimum terrain-clearance altitudes, and the location and frequency of navaids are easy to find on an en-route low-altitude chart.

Don't forget to bring the topographical maps and marine charts that cover your route. They'll give you valuable information about the configuration and depth of lakes, bays, and rivers that you simply can't get from your aviation charts. If you're flying over coastal waters, remember to stick a current tide table in your flight bag. There's nothing more frustrating than sitting in the mud while you wait for the tide to come back in.

Pack the Right Clothes

There are some special items of clothing you should carry with you, regardless of the climate or time of year you're taking your trip. A pair of boating or deck shoes will keep you from slipping on wet docks and float decks, and they're comfortable to wear for long periods of time. If you're going to be beaching your airplane, take along a pair of high-top rubber boots or hip waders. Rarely will you be able to step directly from a float to the shore, and having the proper footgear along will keep you from getting your feet wet and cold. Make sure you have some good raingear with you, too. The combination of heavy waterproof pants and durable waterproof jacket with a hood will keep you dry no matter how hard it rains. It's also a good idea to keep some warm clothes in the plane at all times. The winds off a lake or bay can be chilling, even in summer, and when the weather turns nasty, you'll be glad you brought that old wool sweater or coat along.

Don't forget to take a good pair of sunglasses. Polaroid glasses are best because they cut the glare off the water and also help you see below the surface when you check for underwater obstacles.

FLIGHT PLANS

You should always file a flight plan for anything other than a local flight. The very nature of the floatplane indicates that you will probably be flying over sparsely settled areas, which makes a flight plan even more important. Make sure you give a thorough description of your route so in case of an accident, the search and rescue teams will know exactly where to begin looking. By the same token, once you filed your flight plan, stick to it. It doesn't do any good to file a detailed flight plan and then deviate from it, because if you are forced down, your chances of being found quickly are greatly diminished.

You must file a flight plan when you cross the border between either Canada or Mexico and the United States (FAR 91.84). Flight plans are not required for flights within the United States, but they are in Canada. You have your choice of two types of flight plans when you're in Canada: a flight plan, or a flight notification. A *flight plan* is good for only one flight, and if it has not been closed within 30 minutes after your estimated time of arrival (ETA), search efforts are begun. A *flight notification*, on the other hand, can cover several flights, and search efforts are not begun until 24 hours after the ETA given for the last flight listed on the notification. You are required to file a flight *plan* when crossing one of Canada's international borders.

CLEARING CUSTOMS

If your trip is going to take you across an international border, you must file a flight plan to a designated airport of entry so you can clear customs before continuing on to your ultimate destination. As a floatplane pilot, you can also clear customs at any designated port or harbor of entry, providing you can land and dock there. The customs officials in the country you are entering must be advised of your flight in advance so they can meet and inspect your airplane. The easiest way to advise them is to include a notification to customs when you file your flight plan with a Flight Service Station (FSS) before you take off. Generally, the phrase, "Advise customs," is all that is needed, and should be included in the "Remarks" box on your flight plan form. The Flight Service Station will pass this information to the station at your destination, and they will notify the local customs officials of your flight, and when you intend to arrive. Normally, customs requires at least 1 hour advance notice of your arrival, although some airports of entry such as Ketchikan, Alaska, require 2 hours advance notice. There is no charge for reporting to customs unless the official has to travel some distance to reach you, or if you arrive before or after normal working hours.

After you land at your specified airport or port of entry, you, as the pilot-in-command, are responsible for keeping your passengers and cargo with the airplane until the customs official arrives. Don't let anyone wander off; it's a serious offense.

If you're entering Canada, the customs officer meeting your plane may want to conduct an inspection of both the plane and its contents and ask you questions pertaining to your trip until he is satisfied that you will be using the plane only for pleasure or health reasons, and not for profit. You will then be issued a cruising permit, which will be valid for a specified period of time up to 12 months. Once you have this permit, you won't have to report to Canadian customs for the remainder of your trip.

Normally, you will not have to check in with Canadian customs prior to the start of your return flight to the United States. If, however, you entered Canada with articles requiring a temporary permit, you will have to report to Canadian customs for completion of the permit documentation before you take off for the United States.

In the unlikely event of a forced landing after crossing an international border, but prior to clearing customs, first secure your airplane and then contact the authorities as soon as possible. Remain with your plane until the customs officials arrive.

If high winds or rough-water conditions prohibit you from landing at the port of entry specified on your flight plan, you'll have to find an alternate landing site. If you're in contact with a Flight Service Station, keep the staff there advised of your intentions, and when you've located a safe landing site, have them notify customs of your new destination. After you land and secure your plane, remain with it until a customs officer can reach you, and be prepared to pay a fee to cover the expense of sending the officer to your location.

CROSS-COUNTRY TECHNIQUES

Flying cross-country in a floatplane is a unique experience. The fact that you fly lower and slower than most landplanes gives you the opportunity to observe and enjoy your surroundings while staying out of the often-congested airspace above you. The basic cross-country techniques for floatplanes and landplanes are similar, but there are some specific differences and techniques worth noting.

Navigation

The biggest difference between flying a floatplane on a long, cross-country flight and flying a landplane on a similar flight lies in the type of navigation each pilot will use. Where the landplane pilot tends to rely on electronics (VOR, DME, ADF, RNAV, etc.), the floatplane pilot generally relies on dead reckoning and pilotage. A compass, a hand-held flight computer, and a finger on a chart are the primary tools of floatplane navigation. Make it a practice to draw your course on the appropriate chart or charts, and then follow what you've drawn. It is especially important to do so in areas dotted with islands and crisscrossed with channels. If you don't carefully compare what you see out the window with what you see on the chart, you can easily become lost.

After you receive your weather briefing and have a good idea of the winds you will encounter en route, spend a few minutes with your flight computer making sure that you will be able to carry enough fuel for each leg of your trip. There are several hand-held, electronic flight computers on the market, and they make short work of the basic time-speed-distance-fuel consumption calculations. Personally, I prefer my old, round, manually operated Jeppesen CR-3 Computer because the batteries won't ever wear out and there aren't any metal or electronic components to corrode, but regardless of the type of computer you use, make sure a strong headwind won't run your tanks dry short of your destination.

As long as you've got your flight computer out, calculate the magnetic heading for each leg of your route. As you know, a VOR (VHF Omnirange) depends on line-of-sight signals for position information, and if you're flying low, the signals may be blocked by the surrounding terrain. The only navigation instruments you can really depend on are the compass and the clock; so even if you plan to navigate using the VOR stations along your route, take the time to calculate and jot down the magnetic heading and flight time for each leg of your flight. Then, if weather or beautiful scenery causes you to fly at a lower altitude, you'll have something to fall back on when the VOR quits working.

Actually, a VOR would be last on my list when selecting radio navigation equipment for a floatplane. I've found an Automatic Direction Finder (ADF) to be a much more useful instrument, because it is not as dependent on altitude as a VOR and it can home in on commercial radio stations as well as low-frequency, nondirectional beacons. In my opinion, however, the best form of radio navigation for a floatplane is Loran-C, or computerized long-range navigation. Loran is one of the oldest forms of radio navigation around, but with the advent of the computerized version, it's been given a new lease on life.

Unlike a VOR, Loran-C does not fly you to or from a fixed ground station. Instead, it uses a group of low-frequency transmitters, called a *chain*, to fix your current position. The chains are under the jurisdiction of the United States Coast Guard, and there are several of them located along the east and west coasts and in Alaska. Canada is also establishing a network of Loran chains. Each chain, or group of stations, is located hundreds of miles from the next chain, and the modern Loran-C units will automatically switch from one chain to the next as your flight progresses, and will automatically select signals from the strongest stations within each chain.

Once the on-board computer has tuned in the closest chain and determined your plane's location, it can guide you to any destination or waypoint you choose. All you have to do is enter the latitude and longitude of the waypoint, and the computer does the rest. Besides the course-deviation display, Loran-C receivers can also display your current position (in terms of latitude and longitude), your time and distance to the waypoint you have defined, your current heading, and your current ground speed. Also, because it depends upon low-frequency signals for its position information, Loran-C can guide you along a course that is hundreds of miles long, regardless of your altitude. In fact, the set will display its information just as accurately when you're on the water as it will when you're 10,000 feet agl.

Loran-C accomplishes all this by comparing the time differences between a signal from a master station and the signals from at least two secondary stations within each chain. Where the older Loran sets displayed the time difference as a numerical code that corresponded to lines of position on a Loran plotting chart, the new Loran-C units automatically convert the time difference to latitude and longitude. When you enter the latitude and longitude of a waypoint, the computer compares this position with your current position, and determines the great-circle (shortest) route to the waypoint. The steering display then shows you whether you are to the right or left of this route. If you have entered the exact coordinates of a waypoint, Loran-C can often bring you well within 100 feet of the point.

Loran-C is used commercially to guide helicopters to isolated off-shore oil wells, and by aerial fish-spotters to give accurate school locations to vessels on the surface. As a floatplane pilot, you can use Loran-C to locate a specific lake or a seaplane base tucked away in a tiny coastal cove. By entering multiple waypoints, you can use Loran-C to precisely guide you through a complex maze of islands, even if low weather forces you to fly right down on the deck.

Even more amazing is the fact that airborne Loran-

C receivers are not that expensive. A Loran set suitable for VFR flying can be obtained for under $3,000, while the receivers certified for IFR use cost upwards of $7,000. The only drawback to Loran-C is that currently only the eastern and western edges of the United States and Canada are covered by Loran chains. There is a midcontinental gap which has no Loran coverage; so your receiver wouldn't be reliable for part of an east-west trip across the country. For flights in the island- and lake-dotted areas of the Pacific Northwest, western Canada, and Alaska, as well as the northeastern states and the Caribbean, Loran-C can make life a lot easier, and it's well worth the cost. (See TAB Book No. 2370, *Flying with Loran C*, by Bill Givens.)

If most of your float flying is going to be over coastal waters, a marine-band transceiver is a handy thing to have on board. When flying up the Inside Passage along the coasts of British Columbia and Alaska, for example, you will often be out of range of a Flight Service Station or anyone else with a VHF radio. The waters of the Passage do, however, carry a steady stream of fishing boats, tugboats, ferries, and cruise ships between Seattle and Alaska, and a marine radio will put you in contact with all of them. The ability to contact surface vessels can be a valuable asset in case of an emergency, as well as providing you with another source of weather information. By using the marine operator, you can even make a long-distance telephone call.

Flying Floats in Low Weather

Low-weather flying, or *scud running*, is as potentially dangerous in a floatplane as it is in a landplane. Continued flight into marginal or IFR weather conditions is the single greatest cause of general aviation accidents, and you should never allow yourself to be pressured into flying in weather you're not sure you can handle. There are, however, times when low-weather flying can be accomplished in relative safety if you're flying a floatplane and you follow a few basic rules. The first requirement is that you should always be flying within reach of a body of water large enough to land on. The protected waters of Washington's Puget Sound, the Inside Passage to Alaska, and the lake country of northern Minnesota, Manitoba, Ontario, and Quebec are examples of areas where your flight will probably carry you over more water than it will land. The advantage of being over, or near, water is that should the ceiling really start coming down, you'll be able to land and wait until the situation improves. The water you're flying over must, however, be smooth enough to land on. Water covered with swells or the open ocean is

as inhospitable to your floatplane as dry land, and you should think twice before attempting to fly over these areas in marginal weather.

Don't fly over unfamiliar territory in low-weather conditions. Patches of fog or mist can hide sections of the terrain around you, and if you don't have a good mental picture of the area, you can easily become disoriented. When flying over water, always keep the shoreline in sight, but leave yourself enough room to make a 180-degree turn toward it if the visibility ahead of you drops below minimums. By turning toward the shore, you will always have a visual reference to help you maintain altitude. The horizon is usually indistinct or completely obscured in low weather, and if you execute your 180-degree turn away from the shoreline, the loss of a visual reference could cause you to become disoriented and inadvertently stall or enter a spiral dive.

If the visibility drops to a little over a mile, slow down, especially if you are following a shoreline. Give yourself an additional margin above a stall by lowering the flaps to their normal takeoff position, and slow-fly along the beach. By reducing your speed, you'll have time to react if a rocky bluff suddenly looms out of the mist ahead of you, or if you see that you're going to fly into a fog bank. Low weather tends to concentrate air traffic; so turn your landing lights on, and keep a sharp eye out for other aircraft. You never know when someone may come barreling out of the mist toward you; so be prepared to take some quick evasive action if another airplane should suddenly appear.

Keep track of your compass headings so you can accurately make a 180-degree turn if you should suddenly fly into an area of poor visibility. Fog has a mind of its own, so keep an eye on what's going on behind you. You don't want to get into a situation where there is impenetrable fog all around you. If you do find yourself in this situation, the best solution is to pull the power off and land, assuming the water beneath you will permit it. Once you're safely on the water, you can beach the plane and wait for the weather to improve, you can shut the engine down and drift, but be careful that you don't drift right along with the bad weather.

If your problem is a local fog bank that's between you and what you know is better weather up ahead, you can land and taxi your plane until the visibility improves to the point where you can take to the air once again. Keep an eye on your engine temperature gauges when you take this solution, however. Some planes will overheat if they are taxied for a long time; so you may have to shut down occasionally to let the engine cool down. Also keep in mind that taxiing for long distances on the water will throw a monkey wrench into your fuel consumption calculations, and you'll probably need to refuel sooner than you had planned. If the water conditions allow you to taxi on the step, do so, but be very careful. It's bad enough to wreck a floatplane, but it's downright embarrassing to wreck it by running into a boat.

If the water is too rough for a safe landing, your second alternative is to climb. As long as there is fuel in its tanks, your floatplane is safest in the air, and if you have received sufficient training to allow you to climb, cruise, turn, and descend on instruments, you may be able to climb above the fog or low clouds to better visibility. Once you're there, try to establish contact with a Flight Service Station or an Air Route Traffic Control Center for assistance in establishing your position and setting a course for an area with better visibility.

This is an emergency situation, and emphasizes the importance of sticking to familiar territory when flying in low weather. For example, Kenmore Air Harbor's charter pilots are kept out of the air an average of only 6 days a year, a remarkable record, considering the unpredictable weather in Puget Sound and southwestern British Columbia, but the pilots are all on a first-name basis with every beach, bluff, bay, cove, and island in the area. Unless you have the same familiarity with the area in which you fly, stay out of the air when the ceiling begins to shroud the tops of nearby hills in mist, and patches of fog start piling up in the valleys. It can be a beautiful sight, but the beauty conceals a beast, and you can quickly get into trouble if you take on something you aren't equipped to handle.

Float Flying in Cold Weather

If you fly your floatplane off the water when the air temperature is at or below freezing, the spray thrown onto the plane during takeoff can freeze, immobilizing some of the moving surfaces and components. Although ice may form on the aileron, elevator, and trim tab hinges, you can exert enough leverage with the stick or yoke and the trim mechanism to break the ice away. The air and water rudders are, however, another story. The water can freeze on the guides and pulleys that carry the steering cables for the water rudders, and if these cables become locked in the ice, the air rudder will be immobilized as well. The same thing applies to the water rudder retraction cables. If they are frozen to their guides and pulleys, you may be unable to lower them after you land.

The solution is to seesaw the rudder back and forth after you take off until you can visually determine that

all the water on the floats has frozen. By moving the rudder back and forth, the water rudder cables will not stay still long enough to freeze, and while a tunnel of ice may form around the moving cables where they pass through their guides, the cables themselves will not be immobilized. Do the same thing with the water rudder retraction system. After you lift off the surface, keep lowering and retracting the water rudders until all the water on the floats has frozen.

If you take an amphibious floatplane off the water in freezing conditions, you'll really be busy. In addition to your gynmastics on the rudder pedals and the retraction handle, you'll also need to cycle the gear several times to keep ice from locking it in the retracted position. There will be a lot of water up in the main wheel wells and on the nosewheel retraction system; so continue to cycle the gear until there's no doubt that all the water has either drained away or frozen. If you're planning to land on the water, the situation is not as critical, but if you intend to land on a runway, you could get a rude surprise when you go to lower the gear and nothing happens. Don't forget, if the gear is frozen inside the floats, the manual system won't bring it down either. Start cycling the gear as soon as you're safely off the water and have established a positive rate of climb, and don't stop cycling it until you're sure it will come down when you need it. If, by some chance, it does become frozen in the retracted position, land in the water again and taxi slowly around until the ice weakens enough to break off when you operate the gear. Then take off and start the cycling procedure again.

Measuring a Lake From the Air

It's fairly easy to determine the length of a runway. It's either printed on your charts or listed in an airport directory. Even if you can't find its exact length, it's a safe assumption that it's long enough for something or it wouldn't have been built in the first place. It's a little harder to determine the length of an unfamiliar lake (Fig. 19-3). If the lake is small, it may not appear on your aviation charts, and even if it does, the scale of the chart is such that it's impossible to get a very accurate measurement of the lake's length. Topographical maps are more useful in this respect since their smaller scales make it possible to include greater, and more accurate, geographic detail.

What if you don't have a topographical map with you? What if you're beginning to run into bad weather, and you decide to land and wait it out, but you're not sure if the lake you've come across is long enough to take off

Fig. 19-3. A small mountain lake in the Cascade Range. One way of determining the length of this lake is by using the method described in this chapter. This particular lake can only be entered from the far end, where a stream spills out into the valley below.

from again? Is there any way to accurately determine the length of the lake from the air? Fortunately, there is, and it's a relatively simple procedure, based on noting the time it takes you to overfly the lake and comparing this time to a chart which relates ground speed and time to distance (Fig. 19-4). When determining if the lake is long enough for your floatplane, don't forget to take into account the effect the altitude will have on your plane's takeoff performance, and make sure you'll have enough room to take off and safely clear any nearby obstacles.

First, pick one of the ground speeds listed in the left column that best suits your floatplane. For instance, if you're flying a Super Cub, 80 knots would probably be your choice. If you're in a Cessna 185, you might rather use a ground speed of 90 or 100 knots. The ground speeds, times, and distances on the chart are based on true airspeeds at sea level on a standard day. True

airspeed varies with temperature and pressure, and increases approximately 2 percent per 1000 feet of altitude gain. To maintain your chosen ground speed, then, you must subtract the additional airspeed you've "gained" by virtue of your altitude.

Let's say, for example, that you want to determine the length of a lake that is at an elevation of 4000 feet, and you want to use a ground speed of 90 knots. To obtain an accurate time, you should fly over the lake as low as possible while remaining clear of any obstacles, so I will assume that your timing flight will be made at an altitude of approximately 4000 feet. First, adjust your floatplane's power and trim to maintain an indicated airspeed of 90 knots. Then use your flight computer to determine your current true airspeed based on your indicated altitude, the outside air temperature, and your indicated airspeed. (You should really use the *pressure*

LANDING DISTANCE CHART

GROUND SPEED (KNOTS)	DISTANCE IN FEET							
	2000	3000	4000	5000	6000	8000	10,000	12,000
70	17	26	34	43	52	69	86	103
80	15	23	30	38	45	60	75	90
90	13	20	27	33	40	53	67	80
100	12	18	24	30	36	48	60	72

Fig. 19-4. This chart can be used to determine the approximate length of a lake or other landing area prior to the landing itself, so you can be sure that you'll be able to take off again.

altitude, which is the pressure recorded when your altimeter is set on 29.92 inches of mercury, and your *calibrated airspeed*, which is your indicated airspeed corrected for position and instrument error. For this particular purpose, however, your indicated altitude and airspeed will be accurate enough.) If your true airspeed calculates out to be 96 knots, subtract 6 knots from your indicated airspeed of 90 knots to find the airspeed you must maintain to yield true air and ground speeds of 90 knots. In this case, an airspeed of 84 knots will produce a ground speed of 90 knots, assuming there is no wind.

Another way to determine the airspeed needed to maintain a given ground speed is to make use of the fact that true airspeed increases approximately 2 percent per 1000 feet of altitude gained. Using the same lake, an altitude of 4000 feet translates into an airspeed increase of approximately 8 percent. Eight percent of 90 knots is 7.2 knots ($0.08 \times 90 = 7.2$), which you can round off to 7 knots. Seven knots subtracted from your indicated airspeed of 90 knots equals 83 knots, which is the speed you'll have to hold to maintain a true air and ground speed of approximately 90 knots. This method is not as accurate

as actually computing your true airspeed, because it's based on a standard day and does not allow for temperature changes, but it will at least get you into the ball park.

Once you have determined the indicated airspeed that will yield your chosen ground speed of 90 knots, overfly the lake at that airspeed and note the elapsed time in seconds. Find this time on the chart in the row labeled "90 Knots." The number directly above it in the "Distance" row is the length of the lake. If your measured time falls between two of the times on the chart, you'll have to interpolate the actual length of the lake. For example, if it takes you 24 seconds to overfly a lake at a ground speed of 90 knots, the lake is 3500 feet long. If there is a wind blowing, make a timed run at the same true airspeed in both directions and average the two resulting distances to get the correct length of the lake.

USING A PADDLE

Like a plumber's helper, your paddle will be your salvation in all sorts of situations. You can fend yourself off

238

from a dock, pole yourself off of a sandbar, extend it to steady a boarding passenger, and bury it in the sand for a tiedown. You can even use it to paddle your plane.

Paddling a floatplane is not as easy as you'd think it is. If there's a wind blowing, you won't be able to do much except slow your backwards drift, but in light or no-wind conditions, your paddle can be quite useful, especially if you're trying to slowly approach a rocky beach or ease into a tight spot at a dock. The advantages of using a paddle are that it is slow, and the chances of doing any serious damage to your plane are slim.

I've found that the best place to kneel when paddling a floatplane is up by the forward float strut. In this position, you can paddle on the inside of the float as well as the outside without interference from the spreader bars and brace wires, and the float strut will give you something to brace against.

The only way you'll be able to paddle your plane in a straight line is to first lower the water rudders. If you leave them up, you'll only succeed in turning yourself in a circle because your paddling force will be applied some distance out from the centerline of the plane, causing it to pivot around the float opposite the one on which you're kneeling. By lowering the water rudders, the pivoting tendency will be reduced. It won't disappear completely, however, so if you're paddling on the outside of the float, you'll have to pull your paddle in towards you at a slight angle to keep the plane tracking straight. If you're paddling on the inside of the float, you'll have to push the paddle away from you slightly as you stroke. To move the nose to the left or right, reach out beside you with the paddle and draw it straight in towards the float. The plane will turn in the direction you're reaching. Backpaddling will slow your plane to a stop or begin to back it up. Of course, the job of paddling will be made much easier if there's someone in the cockpit to work the water rudders in response to your commands from outside.

Maneuvering a floatplane with a paddle is not an exact science, and you'll have to experiment to find out just how responsive your plane is to your efforts. The time to learn how your floatplane handles under paddle power is not when you suddenly find yourself in a tight situation. Instead, find a dock or a beach where you can practice paddling without the risk of running a wing into a piling or grinding a float onto a rock. Then, on a nice day, spend an hour or two maneuvering your floatplane around with the paddle, and find out just how responsive your plane is. You'll be that much better prepared in the event a real docking or beaching problem requires you to paddle the plane correctly the first time.

NOISE ABATEMENT

As we saw in Chapter 10, aircraft noise has become a major issue today. Every sector of the aviation world is affected, from international and municipal airports to heliports. Floatplanes are not exempt from the growing pressure to eliminate noise by eliminating aircraft operations altogether, and in fact, they often seem to draw more fire from residential communities and environmental groups than any other segment of aviation. Many lakes across the country that have been used by seaplanes for years have recently been closed to them as a result of pressure brought to bear on government agencies by various environmental groups. The sole issue is noise. Ironically, many of the lakes that have been closed to seaplanes are still open to boaters; so while it's illegal to make noise for a few moments when you take off in a seaplane, it's perfectly legal to run around the lake all day in a boat with an unmuffled engine.

On the positive side, many lakes are being opened, or, in some cases reopened, to seaplanes, thanks largely to the efforts of the Seaplane Pilots Association. The final steps toward opening a body of water to seaplane operations sometimes takes place in a courtroom, but the first and most important steps always take place in the cockpits of our airplanes. The image the public has of seaplanes and seaplane pilots is based upon our individual actions, and it takes only one incident on the part of one inconsiderate pilot to taint a community's image of water flying in general. This is why it's so important that all of us practice noise abatement techniques and procedures whenever possible, even when taking off from a remote wilderness lake. Some of the most vocal groups opposing the operation of seaplanes are wilderness preservation societies, and although there may be no one in sight when you take off, there could be backpackers or campers in the vicinity who don't like the sound of a seaplane prop at flat pitch echoing off the hills.

I can understand how they feel. I personally don't care for the sound of unmuffled trail bikes and snowmobiles, and their endless snarling off in the distance can become very irritating as it reverberates around the mountains. At least seaplanes only make noise for a few minutes during takeoff, and then they're gone. The trail bike and snowmobile drivers have just as much right to be there as I do, however, and I know they are getting just as much pleasure from being in the back country as I am. And that's really the bottom line. It doesn't much matter how we choose to enjoy the things that nature has created. What's important is that we respect the environment around us, and take care to leave it the way we found it.

I take issue with the more militant environmental groups and individuals who try to portray the seaplane community as a sort of aerial motorcycle gang which loves to roar around the wilderness with no regard for their surroundings and making as much noise as possible with their machines. On the contrary, I think the reason most seaplane pilots get interested in water flying in the first place is because of their love and appreciation for the wilderness. All the seaplane pilots I know are just as concerned about the preservation of the wilderness as the groups that are trying to ban them from visiting it.

As we've seen, there are several things you, as a floatplane pilot, can do to lessen the noise impact of your plane. First, reduce your engine rpm as soon as possible after takeoff. A reduction of a mere 200 rpm can make a dramatic difference in the noise output of your propeller. Of course, the safety of you and your passengers should be your first concern. If obstacles in your path dic-

tate climbing with maximum power until they are cleared, then do so, but whenever possible, reduce your climb rpm. If you're taking off from a lake or harbor that's surrounded by residential areas, remain over the water until you have climbed to at least 1000 feet agl before crossing the shoreline, and avoid takeoffs in the early morning or late evening.

The airplane manufacturers are as aware of the noise problem as anybody else; so most of the high-performance floatplanes available today come with quieter, three-bladed propellers as standard equipment. The floatplanes that really have noise problems are the Cessna 180s and older 185s and 206s that are equipped with two-bladed propellers. The de Havilland Beaver was also originally equipped with a two-bladed propeller, which made for a fairly noisy airplane on takeoff. All these planes can be equipped with three-bladed props, and while this is an expensive conversion, it's worth it in terms of better rela-

Fig. 19-5. This Cessna 180 has been equipped with a more powerful engine (270 horsepower) and a three-bladed propeller. Increased performance is not the only benefit. The new propeller is not as noisy during takeoff as the original, two-bladed propeller. The engine and propeller modifications were developed by Kenmore Air Harbor.

tions with your neighbors (Fig. 19-5). If you're renting a floatplane equipped with a two-bladed propeller, or if the cost of converting your own floatplane to a three-bladed propeller is currently out of reach, you can still go a long way toward improving the public image of seaplanes by keeping your rpm as low as possible during takeoff and climbout.

Of course, the best way to improve relations with the community is to introduce as many people to the joys of float flying as possible. After you have your seaplane rating, take people for rides whenever you can. If you can get them into the plane, even the staunchest environmentalists will enjoy the panoramic view as you soar over snow-capped peaks plunging into crystal clear waters, the solemn beauty of countless forested lakes in the north woods country, the rugged splendor of a Pacific coastline, or the tropical sparkle of a Caribbean lagoon.

The floatplane's world is indeed a beautiful one. In an age when most of man's machines are designed to change the world, the floatplane is a welcome exception. I have a bumper sticker which reads, "Only seaplanes and canoes can visit a wilderness and leave no trace behind," but the truth in this statement rests with you and me. If we exercise good judgment in the operation of our floatplanes, and show consideration for the other people who share and enjoy our world with us, that bumper sticker will continue to be true for a long time to come.

I hope you get your seaplane rating. You'll find it a challenging and enjoyable experience, and one which will give a whole new meaning to the word, *flying*. The first time I saw a floatplane winging its lonely way through the silver skies of the Pacific Northwest, I was hooked, and I hope you will be, too. Have fun, and remember, keep your float tips up.

A de Havilland Beaver waits for its next assignment on a windy winter day on Lake Washington.

Appendix

Seaplane Pilots Association
421 Aviation Way
Frederick, MD 21701

Publishes a quarterly magazine, *Water Flying,* as well as the *Water Flying Annual.* Constantly monitors legislation that may affect seaplane operations, and actively works to keep open waters that are in danger of being closed, and reopen waters that have already been closed.

FLOAT MANUFACTURERS

Canadian Aircraft Products, Ltd.
2611 Viscount Way
Richmond, B.C., V6V 1M9
Canada

Manufactures floats for the Bellanca Scout and Citabria, Cessna models 170, 172, 175, 180 and 185, Maule models M-4 and M-5, the Piper PA-18 Super Cub; and the de Havilland DHC-6 Twin Otter.

Capre, Inc.
805 Geiger Rd.
Zephyrhills, FL 33599

Manufactures floats for Taylorcraft models F-19 and F-21; the Piper J-3 Cub and the PA-18 Super Cub; Cessna models 172, 175, 180, 185, ;and 206; Maule models M-5 and M-6; and the Stinson 108.

DeVore Aviation Corporation (PK Floats)
6104B Kircher Blvd., N.E.
Albuquerque, NM 87109

Manufactures floats for the Bellanca Citabria and Scout; Piper PA-18 Super Cub; Cessna models 170, 172, Hawk XP, 180, 185, and 206; and the Maule M-5.

EDO Corporation
Float Operation
14-04 111 St.
College Point, NY 11356

Manufactures floats for the Bellanca Champion 7ECA, the Bellanca Citabria and Scout; Piper PA-12 Super Cruiser, PA-18 Super Cub, PA-22 Tri-Pacer, PA-23 Aztec, PA-28 Cherokee 160, PA-28 Cherokee 180, PA-32 Cherokee Six; Cessna models 170, 172, Hawk XP, 180, 185, and 206; Maule models M-4, M-5, M-6, and M-7; Actic Tern model S1B2; Helio Courier H-250 and Helio Super Courier H-295; de Havilland DHC-2 Beaver; and Pilatus Porter. Makes amphibious floats for Cessna models 180, 185, and 206; Maule models M-5 and M-6; the Helio Super Courier H-295 and Helio models 700 and 800.

Fiberfloat Corporation
895 Gay St.
Bartow, FL 33830

Manufactures floats for the Piper PA-18 Super Cub; Maule models M-4 and M-5; Cessna models 172 and Hawk XP; and the Bellanca Scout.

Wipaire, Incorporated (Wipline Floats)
South Doane Trail
Inver Grove Heights, MN 55075

Manufactures floats for Cessna models 185 and 206; the de Havilland DHC-2 Beaver; and the GAF N22B Nomad (Australia). The company also manufactures amphibious floats for Cessna models 185 and 206; the de Havilland DHC-2 Turbo-Beaver; the Pilatus Porter; and the GAF N22B.

Bibliography

Casey, Louis, and Batchelor, John. *The Illustrated History of Seaplanes and Flying Boats*. London: Phoebus Publishing Company/BPC Publishing Limited,1980. History, 128 pgs.

Fisk, William D. *Fundamentals of Float Flying, Seaplanes in the Mountain Lakes, and Glacier Flying*. Kenmore, Washington: William D. Fisk, 1964. Technique, 45 pgs.

Frey, Jay J. *How to Fly Floats*. College Point, NY: EDO Corporation, 1972. Technique, 37 pgs.

Hoffsommer, Alan. *Flying with Floats*. North Hollywood, CA: Pan American Navigation Service, Inc. 1966. Technique, 146 pgs.

Kurt, Franklin T. *Water Flying*. New York: Macmillan Publishing Company, Inc., 1974. History and Technique, 272 pgs.

Newstrom, Gordon K. *Fly a Seaplane*. Grand Rapids: Gordon K. Newstrom, 1983. Technique, 53 pgs.

Palmer, Henry R. *The Seaplanes*. Fallbrook, Calif: Aero Publishers, Inc. 1965. History, 52 pgs.

Vorderman, Don. *The Great Air Races*. Garden City, NY: Doubleday and Company, 1969. History, 288 pgs.

Index

OTHER POPULAR TAB BOOKS OF INTEREST

Unconventional Aircraft (No. 2384—$17.50 paper)

Celluloid Wings (No. 2374—$25.50 paper)

Guide to Homebuilts—9th Edition (No. 2364—$11.50 paper; $17.95 hard)

Flying Hawaii—A Pilot's Guide to the Islands (No. 2361—$10.25 paper)

Flying in Congested Airspace (No. 2358—$10.25 paper)

How to Master Precision Flight (No. 2354—$9.95 paper)

Fun Flying!—A Total Guide to Ultralights (No. 2350—$10.25 paper)

Engines for Homebuilt Aircraft & Ultralights (No. 2347—$8.25 paper)

Student Pilot's Solo Practice Guide (No. 2339—$12.95 paper)

The Complete Guide to Homebuilt Rotorcraft (No. 2335—$7.95 paper)

Pilot's Guide to Weather Forecasting (No. 2331—$9.25 paper)

Flying The Helicopter (No. 2326—$10.95 paper)

The Beginner's Guide to Flight Instruction (No. 2324—$13.50 paper)

How To Become A Flight Engineer (No. 2318—$6.95 paper)

Aircraft Dope and Fabric—2nd Edition (No. 2313—$9.25 paper)

How To Become An Airline Pilot (No. 2308—$8.95 paper)

Building & Flying the Mitchell Wing (No. 2302—$7.95 paper)

Instrument Flying (No. 2293—$8.95 paper)

The ABC's of Safe Flying (No. 2290—$8.25 paper; $12.95 hard)

Cross-Country Flying (No. 2284—$8.95 paper; $9.95 hard)

The Complete Guide to Single-Engine Cessnas—3rd Edition (No. 2268—$7.95 paper; $10.95 hard)

Aircraft Construction, Repair and Inspection (No. 2377—$13.50 paper)

Your Pilot's License—3rd Edition (No. 2367—$9.95 paper)

Welcome to Flying: A Primer for Pilots (No. 2362—$13.50 paper)

The Complete Guide to Rutan Aircraft—2nd Edition (No. 2360—$13.50 paper)

Build Your Own Low-Cost Hangar (No. 2357—$9.25 paper)

Sabre Jets Over Korea: A Firsthand Account (No. 2352—$15.50 paper)

All About Stalls and Spins (No. 2349—$9.95 paper)

The Pilot's Health (No. 2346—$15.50 paper)

Your Mexican Flight Plan (No. 2337—$12.95 paper)

The Complete Book of Cockpits (No. 2332—$39.95 hard)

American Air Power: The First 75 Years (No. 2327—$21.95 hard)

The Private Pilot's Handy Reference Manual (No. 2325—$11.50 paper; $14.95 hard)

The Joy of Flying (No. 2321—$10.25 paper)

The Complete Guide to Aeroncas, Citabrias and Decathlons (No. 2317—$15.50 paper)

Lift, Thrust & Drag—a primer of modern flying (No. 2309—$8.95 paper)

Aerial Banner Towing (No. 2303—$7.95 paper)

31 Practical Ultralight Aircraft You Can Build (No. 2294—$8.25 paper)

Your Alaskan Flight Plan (No. 2292—$8.95 paper)

Pilot's Weather Guide—2nd Edition (No. 2288—$7.95 paper)

Flying VFR in Marginal Weather (No. 2282—$9.25 paper)

How to Fly Helicopters (No. 2264—$10.25 paper)

How to Take Great Photos from Airplanes (No. 2251—$5.95 paper; $8.95 hard)

TAB TAB BOOKS Inc.

Blue Ridge Summit, Pa. 17214

Send for FREE TAB Catalog describing over 750 current titles in print.